Where to Watch Birds in NEW ZEALAND

More than 30 of the country's best birding locations

KATHY OMBLER

Revised and updated 2010

First published in 2007 by New Holland Publishers (NZ) Ltd
Auckland • Sydney • London • Cape Town

www.newhollandpublishers.co.nz

218 Lake Road, Northcote, Auckland 0627, New Zealand
Unit 1, 66 Gibbes Street, Chatswood, NSW 2067, Australia
86–88 Edgware Road, London W2 2EA, United Kingdom
80 McKenzie Street, Cape Town 8001, South Africa

ISBN: 978 1 86966 154 0

Publishing manager: Christine Thomson
Editor: Mike Bradstock
Design: IslandBridge
Cover design: Nick Turzynski

A catalogue record for this book is available from the National Library of New Zealand

3 5 7 9 10 8 6 4 2

Colour reproduction by Pica Digital Pte Ltd, Singapore
Printed by Times Offset (M) Sdn Bhd, Malaysia

Front cover photograph by Dennis Buurman: Chatham Islands albatross
Back cover photographs by Brent Stephenson/EcoVista: top: wrybill; below: kokako

Brent Stephenson/EcoVista: C2(top), C4(top), C5(top), C6(top), C8(bottom), C11(both)
Dave Hansford/Origin Natural History Media: C1(top), C2(bottom), C4(bottom), C9(top), C10(top), C13(top), C14(top), C16(both)
Helen Gummer/Black Robin Photography: C15
Jason Elsworth Photography: C5(bottom), C6(bottom), C9(bottom), C12,
Shaun Barnett/Black Robin Photography: C1(bottom), C3, C7, C8(top), C13(bottom), C14(bottom)
Steve Baker/Black Robin Photography: C10(bottom)

Acknowledgements

Many people have provided me with helpful comment and advice. Thanks to Nick Allen, Karen Baird, John Barrett, Tony Bouzaid, Dennis Buurman, Meg and Mike Collins, Wynston Cooper, Andrew Crossland, Detlef Davies, Rachael Dippie, Barry Dunnett, Raewyn Empson, Amy Engelhaupt, Lloyd Esler, Colin Galbraith, Jenny Gamble, Chris Gaskin, Phil Gillooly, John Groome, Shireen Helps, Warren Jowett, Joan Leckie, John Marsh, Gerry McSweeney, Chris Petyt, Suzi Phillips, CJR Robertson, Rodney Russ, Stuart Slade, Bruce Stuart-Menteath, Fergus Sutherland, Claire Travers, Tamsin Ward-Smith, Keith Woodley and Supporters of Tiritiri Matangi.

Thanks also to Department of Conservation staff throughout New Zealand for support, advice, and checking copious drafts. Special thanks to Peter Anderson, for his massive effort in Northland, also to John Adams, Tony Beauchamp, Brent Beaven, Wayne Boness, Jim Campbell, Phred Dobbins, Beau Fraser, Paul Gasson, Peter Gaze, Tony Green, Richard Griffiths, Roy Grose, Halema Jamieson, George Hadler, Kathy Houkamau, Ken Hunt, Kennedy Lange, John Mason, Ian McClure, Bruce McKinlay, Pete McLelland, Mike Morrissey, Emma Neill, Colin O'Donnell, Keith Owen, Nic Peet, Ralph Powlesland, Brian Rance, Hugh Robertson, Emily Sancha, Ray Scrimgeour, Tim Shaw, Russell Squire, Graeme Taylor, Doug Veint, David Wilson, Thelma Wilson and John Wotherspoon. Of course, none of these people is responsible for any errors or omissions in this book.

For support during my research travels, sincere thanks to Maui Rentals Ltd, also to Aurora Charters, Ruggedy Range Wilderness Experience, Stewart Island Flights, Venture Southland Tourism, Ulva Goodwillie, Greenvale B&B and Bay View Motel (Stewart Island/Rakiura), Elm Wildlife Tours, Monarch Wildlife Cruises, Penguin Place, Royal Albatross Centre, Tourism Dunedin (Dunedin), Albatross Encounter, Hapuku Lodge and Treehouses, Sounds Air (Kaikōura), Ōkārito Nature Tours (South Westland), Rae Garland and Sue Newlands (Auckland).

Thanks to editor Mike Bradstock for tidying a huge and convoluted manuscript. For their backing and belief in this project, sincere thanks to New Holland publisher Belinda Cooke and publishing manager at the time Matt Turner.

For round-the-clock encouragement and advice, thanks to Marieke Hilhorst, Dave Hansford, Naomi O'Connor, Dave Chowdhury, Tania Stanton and Shaun Barnett (The Guild).

And very special thanks to John, Jenny and Sally for all your support, and for the bird clock.

Contents

Introduction

New Zealand is well known for its land birds, unique species that have evolved in isolation over millions of years and are seen today in magnificent natural settings. In the absence of native land mammals (except two small species of bat), birds occupied a wider range of ecological niches than in most other countries. Some became as large as mammals. Safe from predation our most ancient birds, kiwi and kākāpō, evolved as flightless browsers, while kōkako evolved as poor fliers and learned instead to simply run through the trees.

Perhaps less well known is the fact that New Zealand has the world's greatest diversity of seabirds. Eighty-four species, of which nearly half are endemic, breed on the mainland and offshore and subantarctic islands. Millions of other seabirds visit our coastal and oceanic waters, including shearwaters, petrels, prions and around three-quarters of the world's albatrosses – more species than are seen anywhere else. Wading birds are abundant too. Each spring, over 200,000 Arctic-breeding waders fly halfway around the globe to our harbours and wetlands.

The country is young in terms of human settlement yet forest clearance, wetland drainage and introduction of animal pests have seriously affected habitats and wildlife. It is not a proud history. Species have become extinct, others teeter on the brink, and today many are rare or critically endangered.

On a brighter note, from early times conservationists have acted to halt further destruction and the legacy of their vision is an impressive network of national parks, reserves and sanctuaries. Over one-third of all New Zealand is now protected as conservation land.

Today, conservation scientists are at the leading edge of species-recovery work. Government agencies, conservation organisations and local communities all play their part. Habitat restoration, predator control, relocation of vulnerable species and captive-breeding programmes are helping turn the tide, to make a brighter future for New Zealand's special birdlife.

This book is not a definitive guide to every birdwatching site in New Zealand. Rather, it explores a selection of the best birding opportunities in a diversity of natural areas, throughout World Heritage Sites, internationally significant wetlands, national parks, island reserves and outstanding seabird habitats. The book has been written in the hope that everyone, be they avid birders with a list to tick or simply lovers of nature and beautiful places, will find pleasure in exploring these places.

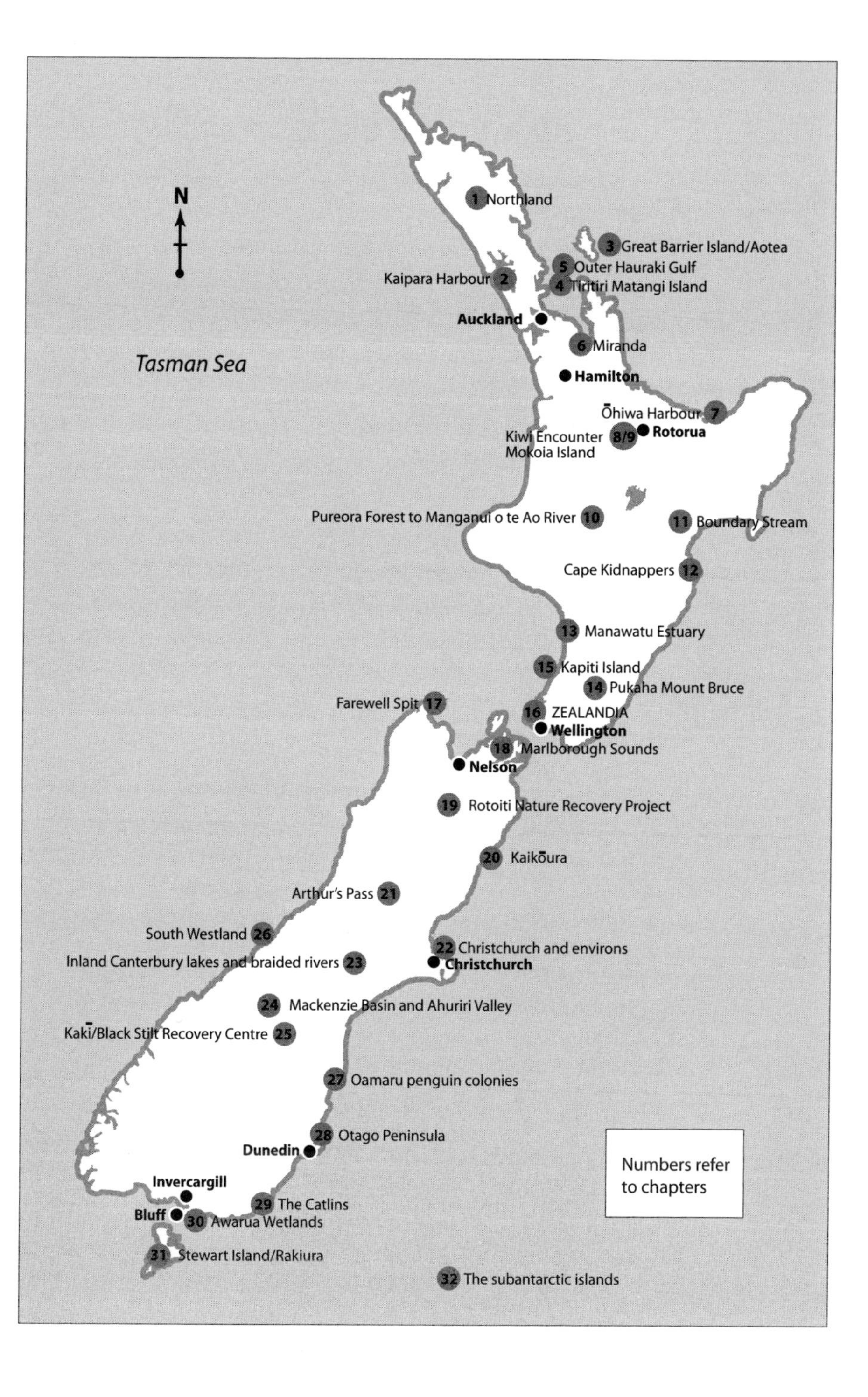
N
Tasman Sea
1 Northland
3 Great Barrier Island/Aotea
5 Outer Hauraki Gulf
Kaipara Harbour 2
4 Tiritiri Matangi Island
Auckland
6 Miranda
Hamilton
Ōhiwa Harbour 7
Kiwi Encounter
Mokoia Island
8/9
Rotorua
Pureora Forest to Manganui o te Ao River 10
11 Boundary Stream
Cape Kidnappers 12
13 Manawatu Estuary
15 Kapiti Island
14 Pukaha Mount Bruce
Farewell Spit 17
16 ZEALANDIA
Wellington
18 Marlborough Sounds
Nelson
19 Rotoiti Nature Recovery Project
20 Kaikōura
Arthur's Pass 21
South Westland 26
22 Christchurch and environs
Inland Canterbury lakes and braided rivers 23
Christchurch
24 Mackenzie Basin and Ahuriri Valley
Kakī/Black Stilt Recovery Centre 25
27 Oamaru penguin colonies
28 Otago Peninsula
Dunedin
Numbers refer to chapters
Invercargill
29 The Catlins
Bluff
30 Awarua Wetlands
31 Stewart Island/Rakiura
32 The subantarctic islands

About this book

The chapters in this guide cover a selection of the 'best' birding areas of New Zealand, meaning the emphasis is on a wide geographical distribution and a representative range of habitats and species. The areas covered differ significantly in size – from small but significant islands, to extensive mainland regions – with guidance provided for planning a birding-focused itinerary.

Some chapters describe places that are open for the public to see species-recovery work and habitat restoration. These offer an insight into some of New Zealand's most successful conservation stories.

Many introduced birds are particularly conspicuous around New Zealand. Some of these are mentioned in some chapters, but the focus of this book is primarily and unashamedly on the native species.

Iconic birds

New Zealand has some endemic species that stand out for their uniqueness and rarity. The list below is somewhat arbitrary but includes many of the birds that people travel worldwide to see. Also listed, where relevant, are the locations in this guide where these birds might be seen.

Kiwi

With modern DNA testing techniques, scientists have established that there are five species of New Zealand's most iconic bird. (More testing could yet differentiate these even further.) All are threatened or critically endangered.

Brown kiwi (*Apteryx mantelli)* live throughout the central and northern North Island: *see* Northland (Trounson Kauri Park), Kiwi Encounter.

Little spotted kiwi/pukupuku (*Apteryx owenii*) survive only on a few islands and within Karori Wildlife Sanctuary: *see* Tiritiri Matangi Island, Kapiti Island, ZEALANDIA: The Karori Sanctuary Experience.

Great spotted kiwi/roroa (*Apteryx haastii*) live in the northern forests and mountains of the South Island. *See* Rotoiti, Arthur's Pass (possibly heard, unlikely to be seen).

Ōkārito brown kiwi/rowi (*Apteryx rowi*) is confined to Ōkārito forest in Westland/Tai Poutini National Park. *See* South Westland (probably heard, possibly seen).

Tokoeka are divided into three distinct populations. Haast tokoeka (*Apteryx australis* 'Haast') live around the remote Haast Range, in Mt Aspiring National Park, and Fiordland tokoeka (*Apteryx australis* 'Fiordland') live in Fiordland National Park, while Stewart Island tokoeka (*Apteryx australis* 'Rakiura-Stewart Island') live throughout Stewart Island and are unusual in that they feed during the day as well as the night. *See* Stewart Island/Rakiura.

Kōkako (*Callaeas cinerea wilsoni*)

A member of the endemic wattlebird family, an ancient family of birds that includes saddleback and the now extinct huia. Known for its haunting, chime-like song, the kōkako is a poor flier yet moves with agility by running and hopping through the trees. *See* Tiritiri Matangi Island, Pureora Forest Park, Mapara Wildlife Reserve, Boundary Stream, Pukaha Mt Bruce.

Saddleback/tīeke (*Philesturnus carunculatus*)

Another wattlebird, and conspicuous by the saddle-like brown stripe across its back. Both the North and South Island subspecies have been the focus of pioneering island translocations made to save their populations, and subsequently other species. *See* Stewart Island/Rakiura, ZEALANDIA: The Karori Sanctuary Experience, Kapiti Island, Mokoia Island, Tiritiri Matangi Island.

Takahē (*Porphyrio hochstetteri*)

Thought to be extinct until its rediscovery in the Fiordland mountains in 1948 and initially recorded in its own genus, *Notornis*, the bird is now placed with pūkeko in the genus *Porphyrio*. Its population is increasing thanks to a DoC captive-breeding programme. *See* Kapiti Island, Tiritiri Matangi Island.

Stitchbird/hihi (*Notiomystis cincta*)

One of New Zealand's rarest birds, thought to be of the honeyeater family until recent DNA analysis confirmed they are the only member of a bird family that's possibly related to the wattlebirds. Original populations survive only on Little Barrier Island and self-sustaining populations are becoming established through translocations to islands and sanctuaries. *See* Tiritiri Matangi Island, Kapiti Island, ZEALANDIA: The Karori Sanctuary Experience, Pukaha Mt Bruce.

Mōhua/yellowhead (*Mohoua ochrocephala*)

Once widespread in South Island forests, the mōhua now survives only in a few isolated pockets of beech forest in Fiordland, mountains around the Landsborough valley, and Southland. Closely related to whitehead and brown creeper, mōhua feed and nest high in trees and are particularly vulnerable to tree-climbing rats and stoats. *See* The Catlins.

Kea (*Nestor notabilis*)

New Zealand's mountain parrot is considered rare, despite the fact it can be so noticeable around South Island mountain car parks and other public areas, with its screeching, boisterous and often destructive behaviour. *See* Arthur's Pass, South Westland.

Kākā (*Nestor meridionalis*)

This bush parrot is closely related to the kea. Large and vociferous populations in localised areas can be misleading, because in many cases the birds are old and either close to their limit of or beyond breeding age. Kākā can commute over long distances, between islands and mainland forests, often over cities. *See* Stewart Island/Rakiura, South Westland, Arthur's Pass, ZEALANDIA: The Karori Sanctuary Experience, Kapiti Island, Pukaha Mt Bruce, Pureora Forest Park, Great Barrier Island/Aotea, Northland.

Blue duck/whio/kōwhiowhio (*Hymenolaimus malacorhynchos*)

The only member of its genus, the blue duck evolved early in New Zealand's isolated history. It is one of four ducks worldwide that lives permanently in fast-flowing rivers, and populations are now confined to relatively remote mountain and forest rivers and streams. *See* Manganui o te Ao River.

Black stilt/kakī (*Himantopus novaezelandiae*)

One of the world's rarest waders, now essentially confined to braided rivers and wetlands in the Mackenzie Basin. DoC's captive breeding programme at Twizel has reversed its decline, from a low of just 23 birds to more than one hundred adults. *See* Mackenzie Basin and Ahuriri Valley, Kakī/Black Stilt Recovery Centre.

Wrybill/ngutuparore (*Anarhynchus frontalis*)

The only bird in the world with a sideways-bent bill, wrybill is a vulnerable species that breeds in Canterbury's braided rivers then migrates to northern tidal harbours from late summer to winter. *See* Miranda, Kaipara, Ōhiwa, Northland, Manawatu Estuary, Christchurch and environs, Inland Canterbury, Mackenzie Basin.

Yellow-eyed penguin/hoiho (*Megadyptes antipodes*)

One of the world's rarest penguins, with a distinctive yellow 'headband' and iris. Since serious declines during the mid- to late 20th century the bird's mainland population has stabilised, due in part to conservation efforts by the Yellow-eyed Penguin Trust, conservation staff and private landowners with colonies on their land. *See* Otago Peninsula, The Catlins, Stewart Island/Rakiura, subantarctic islands.

Northern royal albatross/toroa (*Diomedea sanfordi*)

One of the world's largest albatrosses, the northern royal breeds on the Otago Peninsula, just an hour's drive from downtown Dunedin. The northern royals also breed on the Chatham Islands, while the even larger southern royal species breeds on the subantarctic Auckland and

Campbell Islands. *See* Otago Peninsula, Kaikōura, Stewart Island/Rakiura, subantarctic islands.

Tūī (*Prosthemadera novaeseelandiae*)

Prolific in native forests, on offshore islands and in private gardens, even in the middle of some cities. Distinctive for the white tuft under its throat, and obvious for its varied and melodious songs and mimicry, tūī is one of the two New Zealand members of the honeyeater family, the other being bellbird/korimako. It is found throughout mainland New Zealand, and two subspecies live on the Chatham Islands. Likely to be seen in most places mentioned in this book.

Kākāpō (*Strigops habroptilus*)

Flightless, nocturnal, the heaviest parrot in the world and saved from the brink of extinction in the late 20th century, the kākāpō has no parrot relatives and a combination of features not shared by any other species. The remaining population is managed by DoC's Kākāpō Recovery Team on remote island reserves that are closed to the public.

Black robin (*Petroica traversi*)

This is another species saved from the brink of extinction, from five birds including one female in 1980, to 237 birds in 2010. The now well-established population lives on two small, closed island reserves in the Chathams group, remote and inaccessible to the general public.

Seabirds

New Zealand has the greatest diversity of seabirds in the world, with 84 species, of which nearly half are endemic, and many more international species visiting New Zealand waters. More species of albatross can be seen here than anywhere else. *See* Hauraki Gulf, Kaikōura, Otago Peninsula, Stewart Island/Rakiura, subantarctic Islands.

Bird names

Some New Zealand birds have only Māori names, some only English, and many have both Māori and English names. With some species there are also dialectic and regional variations in the Māori name, and these are given where appropriate to the region being described.

Where birds have dual names, both are given at the first mention in each chapter. Thereafter, for the sake of simplicity the name given is the one more commonly used in Heather and Robertson's *Field Guide to the Birds of New Zealand* (see Bibliography). An exception is mōhua or yellowhead (*Mohoua ochrocephala*). The name mōhua, though less commonly used, is preferred to avoid confusion with the introduced yellowhammer (*Emberiza citronella)*. Many New Zealanders also call the smaller species of albatross 'mollymawks' but the term 'albatross' is exclusively used in this book.

With species that have North, South and Stewart Island/Rakiura subspecies, these are not generally distinguished, except in the case of the New Zealand robin (*Petroica australis*) to avoid confusion with Chatham Islands black robin (*Petroica traversi*).

All species and their scientific names are listed in the index.

Species names are deliberately uncapitalised. This follows the style of the Ornithological Society of New Zealand's scientific journal *Notornis* and other respected national bird and conservation publications.

Times

The times given in 'Hot spots' are a very general indication, allowing for travel and birdwatching. The times given in 'Best birding areas' are more detailed, describing travel, guided tour or walking times, as applicable.

Phone numbers

Unless otherwise stated, all free-calling (0800) numbers listed apply only within New Zealand.

Conservation status

World Heritage Sites. The World Heritage Convention, established by UNESCO, recognises areas with such special natural and/or cultural values that their protection is of global importance. New Zealand has three World Heritage Sites: Tongariro National Park, Te Wāhipounamu-South West New Zealand and the subantarctic islands.

Ramsar sites. The 1971 Convention on Wetlands, signed in Ramsar, Iran, has listed over 1200 sites worldwide recognised as Wetlands of International Importance. New Zealand has six such sites: Firth of Thames, Whangamarino Wetlands, Kopuati Peat Dome, Manawatu Estuary, Farewell Spit and Awarua Wetlands.

Nature Reserves and Scientific Reserves. The highest conservation status and protection is accorded to these areas, which are set aside because of the rarity, scientific interest or uniqueness of their natural features. Entry is generally restricted, with exceptions known as Open Sanctuaries where access is conditional upon taking care to avoid introducing unwanted plants or animals or disturbing the natural features. Open Sanctuaries listed in this book include Ulva Island, Tiritiri Matangi Island and Kapiti Island, which all offer opportunities to see some of New Zealand's most endangered birdlife.

Wildlife Refuge. An area of land, generally encompassing some waterway set aside to protect the wildlife and 'game birds' therein. Restrictions are often put in place, for example motorised craft and dogs are not permitted.

Water Conservation Orders. These recognise the outstanding amenity or intrinsic values of some water bodies, and can be used to preserve waters in their natural state or protect their wild and scenic nature.

A conservation order can restrict or prohibit water extraction, discharges and other uses.

Organisations

Ornithological Society of New Zealand (OSNZ). Membership includes professional ornithologists, government agencies, students and amateur observers. OSNZ publishes the *Atlas of Bird Distribution in New Zealand* (latest edition 2007), the New Zealand Recognised Bird Names (NZRBN) database (due for revision 2009), the quarterly scientific journal *Notornis* and the quarterly news magazine *Southern Bird.* (www.osnz.org.nz)

Department of Conservation (DoC). This is the central government organisation charged with managing and conserving the natural and historic heritage of New Zealand. More than a third of New Zealand is legally protected and administered by DoC as conservation land – including national parks, forest (or conservation) parks, reserves, wetlands and island sanctuaries. Many of these are important bird habitats covered in this book. DoC also licenses tourism operators on conservation land, runs visitor information centres, provides brochures and guidebooks and maintains interpretation signs, walking tracks and camping sites in parks and conservation areas. (www.doc.govt.nz)

National Bird Banding Scheme. DoC also manages this scheme. The use of bands is widespread in international bird research, and New Zealand has been at the forefront of adapting new technology for banding studies. DoC asks that anyone who finds a banded bird should report the sighting to the Banding Office, P.O. Box 10420, Wellington, or send an email to bandingoffice@doc.govt.nz. If the bird is dead, remove the band, flatten it and post it to the above address, stating your name and when and where the bird was found. If the banded bird is alive and the band number and colour combination can be seen clearly, please report it to the banding office. Don't guess what cannot be clearly seen.

New Zealand Birding Network. This is a group of operators offering specialist bird-watching oriented tours, excursions and accommodation throughout New Zealand. It includes national tour operators, local operators and expedition cruise companies, many of them mentioned in this guide. (www.birdingnz.co.nz)

Royal Forest and Bird Protection Society. New Zealand's largest conservation organisation, its objectives are to preserve and protect indigenous flora and fauna and natural features and landscapes. A member of the World Conservation Union and the New Zealand partner designate of Birdlife International, 'Forest and Bird', as it is usually called, has branches throughout New Zealand, undertakes conservation advocacy and projects, and publishes the quarterly journal *Forest and Bird.* (www.forestandbird.org.nz)

Information for international birders

What New Zealand might lack in numbers of endemics, it surely makes up for not only in the uniqueness of its bird species, but in simply being a magnificent place to visit. The natural landscapes – mountains, glaciers, forests, lakes and coastline – the ease of getting around, the standard and choice of accommodation and the fine wining-and-dining opportunities combine to make New Zealand a recognised top tourism destination. For birders, this is an added bonus.

Prices. Prices listed for guided tours and cruises are provided as a guide only, and are liable to change.

Seasonality. The seasons referred to in this book are *austral* seasons; for example, 'winter' corresponds to the northern hemisphere summer.

Game bird hunting season. May sees the opening of the annual season for hunting certain wildfowl in New Zealand, with the season continuing into July in some regions. The birds seem to have some sixth sense of the looming danger, and the start of each season sees them flocking in great numbers to the protection of wetland sanctuaries and reserves. Some native as well as introduced species are 'fair game' for this annual Kiwi tradition, and are hunted from camouflaged hides, locally known as maimai, in wetlands and estuaries throughout New Zealand. Included in this legal harvest, albeit with daily bag limits, is the native grey duck, which has seriously declined in numbers owing to competition and hybridisation with introduced mallard.

Travelling by road. New Zealand traffic travels on the left-hand side of the road. Seat belts are compulsory. Most New Zealand roads are sealed, two-way and well signposted. Motorways or freeways serve the largest cities and North Island roads are generally busier than those of the South Island. Many roads leading to some of the birding areas in this guide are 'off the beaten track', and as such may be unsealed, often winding and a little bumpy – but usually lead to a rewarding destination. If not used to driving on unsealed ('metal') roads, be extremely careful, keep your speed down and don't brake suddenly. Exercise common sense about where you stop: pull right off the road and don't stop where the view for drivers overtaking you is obstructed.

Rented campervans are a popular way of travelling, and well catered for at holiday parks and camping grounds throughout the country. For birders they offer independence – the ability to be at prime birding spots at dawn or dusk or when the tide is right. Maui Rentals is one of the major campervan operators: see www.maui-rentals.com. There are also numerous car-rental companies but during the tourist season, especially December–February, demand is heavy and bookings need to be made well ahead. For longer tours, another option is to buy a vehicle through one of the 'backpacker vehicle' companies, many of which will undertake to buy the vehicle back from you at the end of your trip.

The New Zealand Automobile Association (AA) offers members of affiliated clubs in other countries a 6-month 'overseas club' membership. This entitles overseas members to six free road-service callouts, free maps and guides, domestic travel booking service, information on current road conditions and other benefits. For other drivers, AA also offers a 6-month visitor membership for $99. (www.aa.co.nz)

Travelling by sea. Two ferry companies, Interislander and Bluebridge, operate a number of passenger and vehicle services daily between the North and South Islands (Wellington/Picton). The journey takes around 3 hours, and as a bonus generally offers good seabird watching (albatrosses, shearwaters, petrels, penguins, terns, gulls). Some rental companies offer options to leave a car on one island and pick up another after the crossing, thus saving the car passage fare. Booking is advisable, especially during December and January. These services can be booked online at www.interislander.co.nz or www.bluebridge.co.nz.

Travelling by train. New Zealand's rail services are sadly lacking, though the three long-distance journeys available are particularly scenic. These are the Overlander (Auckland–Wellington, with stops at some towns along the way), TranzCoastal (Picton–Christchurch, via Kaikōura) and TranzAlpine (Christchurch–Greymouth, via Arthur's Pass). Each service runs in both directions and can be booked on www.tranzscenic.co.nz. There are also some commuter trains servicing Auckland and Wellington.

Travelling by air. Air New Zealand (www.airnewzealand.co.nz) serves all major cities and most provincial towns daily. Pacific Blue (www.flypacificblue.co.nz) and Jetstar (www.jetstar.com) fly between the main cities. Several small regional airlines offer daily and chartered services throughout New Zealand.

Accommodation. New Zealand has options for all requirements and budgets, from backpacker dormitory-style accommodation to the luxury end of the market, with lodges located in magnificent natural settings, sometimes with excellent bird habitats. Hostels or backpackers throughout the country offer excellent value for independent travellers, ranging from dormitories to ensuite rooms. Motels offer similar independence for birders wishing to travel at particular times of the day to birding sites. These are self-contained with kitchen and bathroom facilities. All bedding and linen is provided and they are serviced daily.

For those wanting to engage with the locals, there are bed-and-breakfast and farmstay operators, including some hosted by other birding enthusiasts. Many are identified in relevant chapters of this book.

There are camping grounds throughout New Zealand. Some have cabins and motels as well as tent sites and powered sites for caravans and campervans, and call themselves 'holiday parks'. The Department of Conservation (DoC) has over 240 vehicle-accessible campsites on conservation land that range from informal 'self-registration' sites with basic facilities such as toilets and cold water, to serviced sites that can be pre-booked, with hot showers and regular rubbish collection. For a full list visit www.doc.govt.nz.

Those travelling independently in campervans should note and abide by local by-laws regarding 'freedom camping'. The growing popularity of this practice has had detrimental effects on the natural environment in many popular areas. See www.camping.org.nz for guidance.

Qualmark. This is New Zealand's official quality standard for tourism operations, including accommodation, transport and visitor activities (www.qualmark.co.nz). All tourism operators that carry a Qualmark rating, including birding guides, have been independently assessed. All businesses carrying the Qualmark logo are also assessed on their environmental performance. Enviro Awards are given to top performers.

Tourism New Zealand. This official international tourism marketing agency offers travel information, maps, itineraries, activities and accommodation information. (www.newzealand.com)

Climate and seasonality. New Zealand's climate ranges from subtropical in the north to temperate in the south. In winter, snowfalls are common in the mid- to southern regions of the South Island, particularly in mountain areas, and in the central North Island. Away from the mountains, winter temperatures are mild (compared with those of the UK, northern Europe and USA) and generally do not fall below freezing. Winter weather is frequently quite settled, with cool but clear, calm and sunny days.

Summer is New Zealand's busiest season for international visitors, in particular from January to March. However, there is no need for birders (or any visitors for that matter) to restrict themselves to this busy time. The weather can remain mild throughout the shoulder seasons, birding sites remain accessible, and popular tourism regions are less crowded. If it fits with the seasonality of the birds you want to see, it's definitely worth considering travelling at off-peak times.

Biosecurity. This is taken very seriously in New Zealand, where recent incursions have included some serious insect pests and a river-fouling species of alga called didymo. A quarantine service polices all ports of entry and you will have to fill in a declaration on arrival. Instant fines may be charged against transgressors.

All outdoor equipment must be cleaned, sterilised and dried before you travel – and, of course, again when you return home. See www.biosecurity.govt.nz for more details.

Dangerous animals and pests. New Zealand is one of the few countries where there are no dangerous animals in the outdoors. There are a few poisonous spiders, but incidents involving these are extremely rare. Wasps, mosquitoes and sandflies in some regions are the main pests. Sandflies (similar to northern hemisphere blackflies) can be very bothersome, particularly in many South Island areas, and insect repellent is essential, though not always totally effective. The secret to minimising the bother of sandfly bites is to cover up, apply repellent frequently and, if bitten, to apply antihistamine cream *immediately* to the spot.

Safety. While New Zealand is generally a very safe country to travel in, a few people have had unfortunate experiences, in particular break-ins to vehicles left at some walking-track car parks. Seek local advice from information centres, and don't leave valuables in your vehicle.

Visitor Information Centres. DoC Visitor Centres are located in national parks, other conservation areas and some city centres. i-SITE Visitor Information Centres are part of New Zealand's official information network and located in all cities and most towns. They are open 7 days a week and offer free information and a New Zealand travel booking service. www.i-SITE.org.

Access and etiquette. Public accessways through private land are generally clearly signposted; however, laws of trespass are more strict in New Zealand than in some other countries, so it pays to ask permission if in any doubt. Never climb over fences by standing on the wires, or over gates by standing on the bars. Leave farm gates as you found them, whether open or closed.

Weather and tides. See www.metservice.co.nz for the New Zealand weather service. Land Information New Zealand produces official tide tables. For trip planning, tidal predictions twelve months ahead can be found on the website www.hydro.linz.govt.nz/tides/majports/index.asp. NIWA Science offers a similar service on www.niwascience.co.nz/services/tides. Local weather and tides information is also available from daily newspapers.

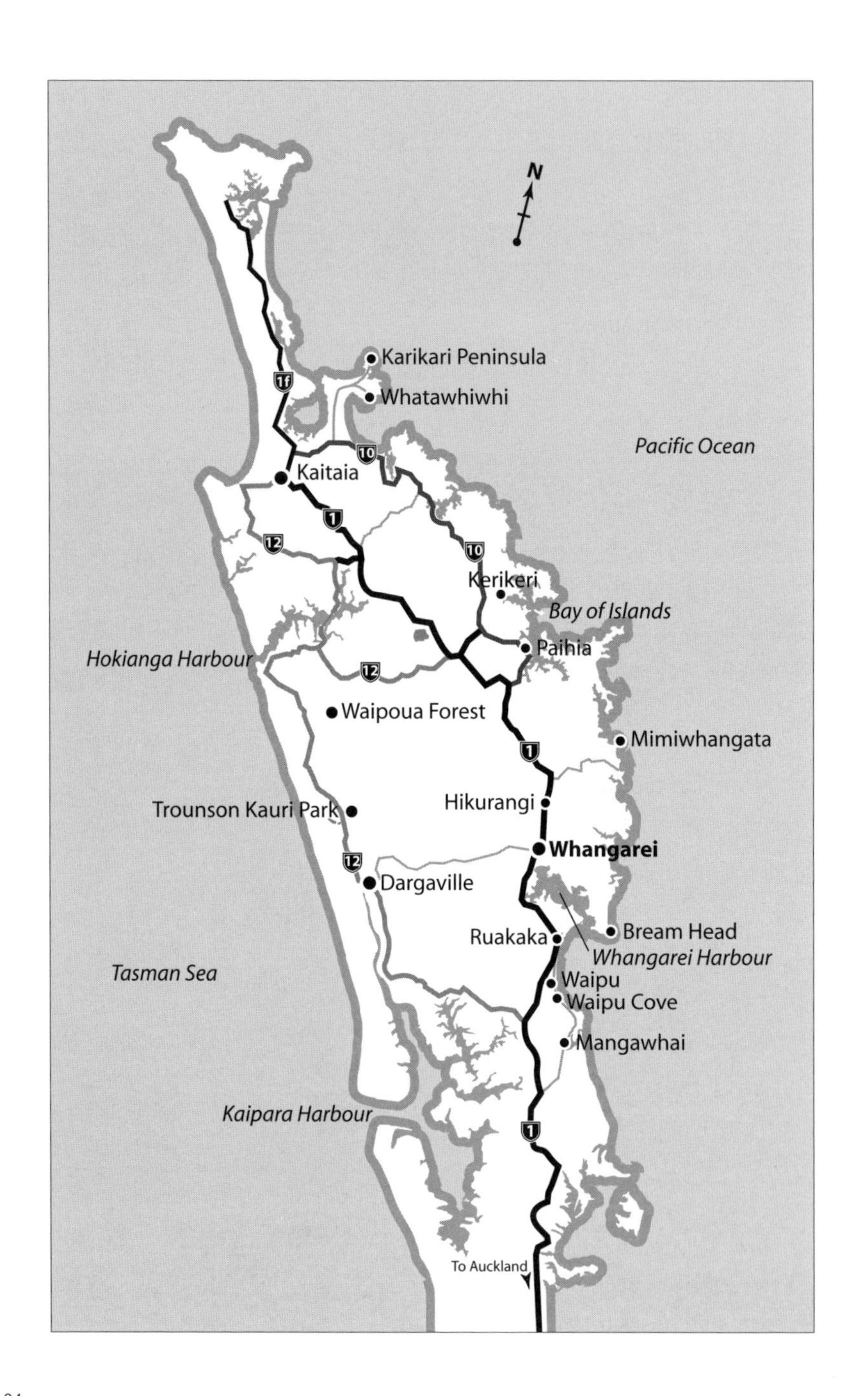
N
Karikari Peninsula
Whatawhiwhi
1f
10
Pacific Ocean
Kaitaia
1
12
10
Kerikeri
Bay of Islands
Paihia
Hokianga Harbour
12
Waipoua Forest
Mimiwhangata
1
Hikurangi
Trounson Kauri Park
Whangarei
12
Dargaville
Ruakaka
Bream Head
Whangarei Harbour
Tasman Sea
Waipu
Waipu Cove
Mangawhai
Kaipara Harbour
1
To Auckland

I

Northland

Where North of Auckland.

What's special Harbours, beaches, estuaries, dune lakes and wetlands favoured by migrant waders, seabirds and coastal birds. Subtropical kauri rainforests, home to original brown kiwi populations.

Birds to look for New Zealand fairy tern/tara-iti (mainly in spring and summer), bar-tailed godwit/kūaka, lesser knot/huahou and other international waders (in spring and summer), South Island pied oystercatcher/tōrea, banded dotterel/tuturiwhatu and wrybill/ngutuparore (winter), pied stilt/poaka, variable oystercatcher/tōrea, brown kiwi, New Zealand dotterel/tuturiwhatu, royal spoonbill/kōtuku-ngutupapa, banded rail/ moho-pererū, fernbird/ mātātā, Buller's shearwater and other shearwaters and petrels, various shags, gulls, herons, terns and waterfowl, including brown teal/pāteke (year-round).

Birdwatching options Self-guided walks, guided evening walks (for brown kiwi), roadside spots, nature cruises, seabird cruises.

Top spots

- Whangārei Harbour (over high tide)
- Ruakaka Estuary (over high tide)
- Waipū Estuary (half-day, over high tide)
- Mangawhai Estuary (half-day)
- Karikari Peninsula (half- to one day)
- Mimiwhangata Coastal Park (half-day)
- Trounson Kauri Park (overnight)
- Bream Head Scenic Reserve (half-day)
- Seabird cruises (half-day to multi-day).

When to go Any season. Spring and summer are best for internationally migrating waders and New Zealand fairy tern and autumn/winter for New Zealand migrants. Note that Northland is a popular holiday region, especially from Christmas to mid-January, and camping grounds in particular are likely to be crowded.

Background

Northland's landscape is a mosaic of hilly farmland and several pockets of rainforest reserve, fringed along the west coast by long, isolated beaches and indented harbours, and along the east by inlets, bays, estuaries, sand spits and islands. The east coast is more heavily populated and tourism is major business.

While there is a noticeable paucity of forest birdlife in Northland, the region is a stronghold for brown kiwi, a threatened species subject to concentrated recovery programmes in six kiwi sanctuaries throughout the North Island, including one at Bream Head near Whangārei.

What Northland might lack in forest species, it certainly makes up for in its coastal and wetland habitats. Several thousand international and New Zealand waders make annual migrations to the same beaches, inlets and estuaries that support resident wader species. This includes two special endemics: the endangered New Zealand fairy tern and threatened New Zealand dotterel.

Of the seabirds seen regularly along the Northland coast, shearwaters and petrels are especially prolific, particularly during spring and summer. Many of these breed on the Poor Knights Islands, a small group of islands and rock stacks (best known as an outstanding diving destination), which are the sole breeding ground of more than 2 million Buller's shearwaters.

Best birding spots

⊳ Mangawhai Estuary

Mangawhai Wildlife Refuge encompasses a large sand spit, sandy estuary, mangroves, small mudflats and salt marsh areas.

Mangawhai is the main breeding site for fairy tern: 3–4 pairs generally nest here. It is also an important breeding area for New Zealand dotterel, with around 25 resident pairs. Other breeding species include variable oystercatcher, Caspian tern and sometimes white-fronted tern.

International waders, in particular bar-tailed godwit and lesser knot, visit during summer. South Island pied oystercatcher can be seen during autumn and winter. Pied stilt, white-faced heron, reef heron/matuku moana and a diversity of other waders are found here year-round. Banded rail can sometimes be seen in the upstream mangrove area, and fernbird are present in some of the larger, upstream salt-marsh sites.

To reach Mangawhai, from Waipū township drive either along the coastal 'Discovery Highway' for 25 km, or south on SH1 and turn east just north of Te Hana and drive 12 km to the small beach settlement. The estuary is accessible by vehicle right to the water's edge; however, a boat is necessary to cross from here to the spit. Alternatively, the base of the spit is accessible from the end of Raymond Bull Road off Black Swamp Road. This can be reached via Insley Street, south of Mangawhai township. From Mangawhai it is about 2 km to the end of Raymond Bull Road, and from there it is a 4-km walk to the end of the spit.

⊳ Whangārei Harbour

The harbour supports high numbers of international and New Zealand migratory waders. The most conspicuous are bar-tailed godwit (around 5000–7000 birds) and lesser knot (2500–4000). Other international visitors include Pacific golden plover and Asiatic whimbrel, along with occasional rarities such as terek sandpiper and red-necked stint.

New Zealand migrants include some 3000 South Island pied oyster-catcher, 400 banded dotterel and smaller numbers of wrybill and royal spoonbill. Caspian tern breed on islands in the harbour. Other terns, plus shags, gulls, herons, pied stilt, Arctic skua (summer) and ducks can also be seen. Kingfisher/kōtare and Australasian harrier/kāhu are often seen, while banded rail have been observed in mangrove areas.

One accessible high-tide roost is at Skull Creek. This is located off the end of Hewletts Road, about 16 km south of Whangārei off SH1 (seek access permission from Hewletts' farm). Another roost is located off Takahiwai Road, just past Petuharakeke Marae, before the climb to the top of the hill (seek permission from the nearby farmhouse). To reach Takahiwai Road, turn onto Tree Point Road off SH1 24 km south of Whangārei (or 2 km north of Ruakaka).

▷ Ruakaka Estuary

This wildlife refuge is a sandy estuary with mangroves and other salt-marsh vegetation. International and New Zealand waders visit here in smaller numbers than on Whangārei harbour, except during high spring tides, when the favoured harbour roosts are inundated and bird numbers at Ruakaka can swell to thousands.

Good numbers of variable oystercatcher and white-fronted tern are also present, as well as a few pairs of New Zealand dotterel, which breed here. There are also likely to be Caspian tern, Australasian gannet/tākapu, spur-winged plover, gulls and several species of shag.

To view the birds, travel to Ruakaka township, 26 km south of Whangārei on SH1. The Ruakaka Reserve Motor Camp is located on the south side of the estuary.

▷ Waipū Estuary

Waipū and Ruakaka estuaries are similar in terms of size and species present; however, Waipū is also one of only four breeding sites for New Zealand fairy tern, with up to three nesting pairs. A wildlife refuge here encompasses a sand spit, lagoon, sandy estuary and salt marsh with mangroves.

To reach the estuary, turn off SH1 at Waipū township (38 km south of Whangārei) onto Waipū Cove Road, and drive about 3 km. Turn left onto Johnson Point Rd, a short no-exit road leading to the estuary, lagoon and spit. Getting to the spit itself requires wading across at low tide, or taking a boat or kayak across at high tide. Alternatively, drive a further 4 km to Waipū Cove beach settlement and from the camping ground walk northwards along the spit.

▷ Bream Head Scenic Reserve

Some of the finest coastal forest in the North Island, including old pōhutukawa trees growing right to the water's edge, attracts kākā, New Zealand pigeon/kukupa, tūī, bellbird/korimako (mainly in summer) and the occasional red-crowned parakeet/kākāriki and tomtit/miromiro. Coastal birds can include reef heron, Caspian and white-fronted tern, pied shag/kāruhiruhi, little shag/kawau-paka, red-billed gull/tarāpunga and black-backed gull/karoro.

Bream Head, located at Whangārei Heads 30 km from the city, is one of the six kiwi sanctuaries in the North Island, and intensive control work is carried out here on cats, possums and mustelids. Access is by a steep 1-hour walk to Peach Cove, where the kākā population is usually most active. The Peach Cove Track is signposted from the reserve car park off Ocean Beach Road, 1 km before Ocean Beach. Access to the DoC hut at Peach Cove must be pre-booked.

▷ Mimiwhangata Coastal Park

The park is about 50 km north of Whangārei. Turn off SH1 5.5 km north of Hikurangi township onto Russell Road, which will lead to Helena Bay. From here, turn south to Teal Bay and follow the signs to the park.

The endangered brown teal is present in several of the park's wetlands. Other species here include various ducks, shags, New Zealand pipit, pied stilt, spotless crake, pūkeko and Australasian harrier. On the adjacent beaches New Zealand dotterel, variable oystercatcher, gulls, terns and sometime blue penguin can be seen.

Bookings for accommodation at the park lodge or shearers' quarter should be made well in advance, especially in summer; there is also a camping area. For bookings and advice on where to see the birds in the park contact the resident ranger, 09 433 6554. Bookings can also be made with DoC in Whangārei, 09 430 2133.

⊳ Karikari Peninsula

An interesting mixture of wetlands, gumlands, an ephemeral lake, high-tide roosts and sandy beaches provides habitats for wetland birds and waders.

Lake Ohia was drained by kauri-gum diggers over a hundred years ago; today fernbird frequent the dense surrounding sedge, fern and manuka gumland vegetation. Waders from nearby Rangaunu Harbour sometimes roost and feed on the temporary pans. These can include turnstone, Pacific golden plover, sharp-tailed sandpiper, New Zealand dotterel and banded dotterel. Australasian bittern/matuku are present in the swampy sites, while spotless crake can sometimes be heard calling from wet sedge areas.

Lake Ohia is located beside Whatawhiwhi Road – look for a signposted access on Lake Ohia Road, 500 m north of the Inland Road/SH10 junction.

Waimangu Lagoon, between Karikari Bay and Whatawhiwhi township, is a recently created wetland supporting a large number of waterbirds. These include paradise shelduck/pūtangitangi and other ducks, shags and possibly Australasian little grebe, Australasian bittern and fernbird. Close by, on Karikari Beach and its spit, New Zealand dotterel, variable oystercatcher, Caspian tern, white-fronted tern, white-faced and reef heron can be found. The easiest access to the lagoon and beach is through Carrington Resort (permission must be sought), on the left about 2 km past Whatawhiwhi township. The resort has also restored a 364 ha wetland on its own property. Alternative access is from Whatawhiwhi Holiday Park on Whatawhiwhi Road, 3 km past the lodge.

Lake Waiporohita is a small dune lake on Puwheke Road on the north-western tip of Karikari Peninsula. Here several duck species, shags, kingfisher and occasional Australasian bittern and Caspian tern can be seen. Puwheke

Beach, 2.5 km past the lake, is worth a look for New Zealand dotterel, variable oystercatcher, pied stilt, white-fronted tern and Caspian tern.

⊳ Trounson Kauri Park

Brown kiwi are the major birding feature in this small predominantly kauri forest, and guided evening walks offer a reasonable chance of a sighting. Since 1995, Trounson has been managed as one of New Zealand's 'mainland island' conservation projects, in particular for research on species such as brown kiwi, New Zealand pigeon/kukupa and the threatened carnivorous kauri snail. Paths and boardwalks built to protect sensitive kauri tree roots from constant footfalls provide easy walking and some tracks are accessible by wheelchair. The park's campground manager is also the licensed guide for the evening walks. As well as brown kiwi, morepork/ruru can sometimes be seen and heard. Other native creatures encountered include kauri snails, cave wētā and eels.

Trounson is located just off SH12, the main road along the western side of Northland, 30 km north of Dargaville and 17 km south of Waipoua Forest. From SH12, turn onto Trounson Park Road at Kaihu township and drive 3 km to the park.

⊳ Seabird cruises

A few birding companies operate guided cruises off the eastern coast of Northland. Possible sightings include tropical and subtropical breeders, including Kermadec petrel (from the Kermadec Islands) white-naped petrel (Macauley Island) and providence petrel (Lord Howe and Norfolk Islands). There are also occasional sightings of albatross moving north from their subantarctic breeding grounds. In the Bay of Islands, marine mammals are the main drawcard of nature cruises operated by several companies; however, these cruises are also good seabird watching opportunities as many seabirds are often associated with dolphins and the fish schools they pursue. Buller's, fluttering and flesh-footed shearwaters, Australasian gannet, white-fronted tern and Arctic skua are all likely to be seen. Trips to the outer bay, including the regular 'Hole in the Rock' cruises, are best.

Getting there Roads head into Northland from Auckland (SH1), and from Helensville and Kaipara Harbour in the west (SH12). Several coach companies offer regular coach services travelling north from Auckland and around Northland. Air New Zealand has daily flights from Auckland to Whangārei, Kerikeri and Kaitāia.

Getting around Birding opportunities covered in this chapter are spread throughout Northland, some a good day's driving from others. Several bus companies provide regular town-to-town services, although a private car is probably the best option. Two main roads travel much of the length of Northland (the tourism industry markets this as the Twin Coast Discovery Highway) – SH1 generally follows the eastern side, while SH12 in the west includes a magnificent 20-km stretch through kauri forest.

Accommodation Northland offers the excellent range of accommodation one would expect of such a popular holiday and tourist region – from luxury lodges to backpackers and camping spots. For travel during the busy summer season, bookings should be made well ahead.

Several places are worth noting, as they are located at the places covered in this chapter or hosted by keen birders and locally knowledgeable folk. These are:

Ruakaka Reserve Motor Camp: tent sites, powered sites and cabins, directly across-river from high-tide wader roosts. 09 432 7590, or www.motorcamp.co.nz.

Camp Waipū: tent sites, powered sites and cabins, at the base of Waipū sandspit. 09 432 0410, or www.campwaipucove.com.

Mimiwhangata Coastal Park: self-contained lodge, backpacker-style shearing quarters and camping. 09 433 6554.

Carrington Resort: Qualmark 5-star accommodation and golf course on Karikari Peninsula, restored wetland onsite and access on request to adjoining birding spots. 09 408 7222, or www.carrington.co.nz.

Trounson Kauri Park: tent sites and powered sites adjacent to the park. 09 439 0621.

Peach Cove Hut: DoC hut at Bream Head, bookings essential. 09 470 3304.

Kerikeri Birders' Rest: self-contained units, hosts Detlef and Carol Davies offer local birding tours, including brown kiwi. 09 407 3874 or detlefdavies@yahoo.com.

Facilities Whangārei city and major Northland towns Dargaville, Kaikohe, Paihia, Kerikeri, Kaikohe and Kaitāia, have all facilities. Smaller towns have shops and fuel, while good restaurants, cafes and takeaway outlets are found in towns and small settlements throughout Northland. Museums, craft galleries, golf courses, wineries and several high-quality short walks through impressive kauri forest are all worthy distractions from birding.

Information

Waipoua Forest Visitor Centre, 09 439 6445 or paihia@visitnorthland.co.nz.

Bay of Islands i-SITE Visitor Centre, Paihia, 09 402 7345 or visitorinfo@fndc.govt.nz.

Whangārei i-SITE Visitor Centre, 09 438 1079 or whangarei@i-SITE.org.

Licensed guiding operators

Trounson Kauri Park: evening guided tours to see and hear kiwi and other nocturnal animals. 09 439 0621.

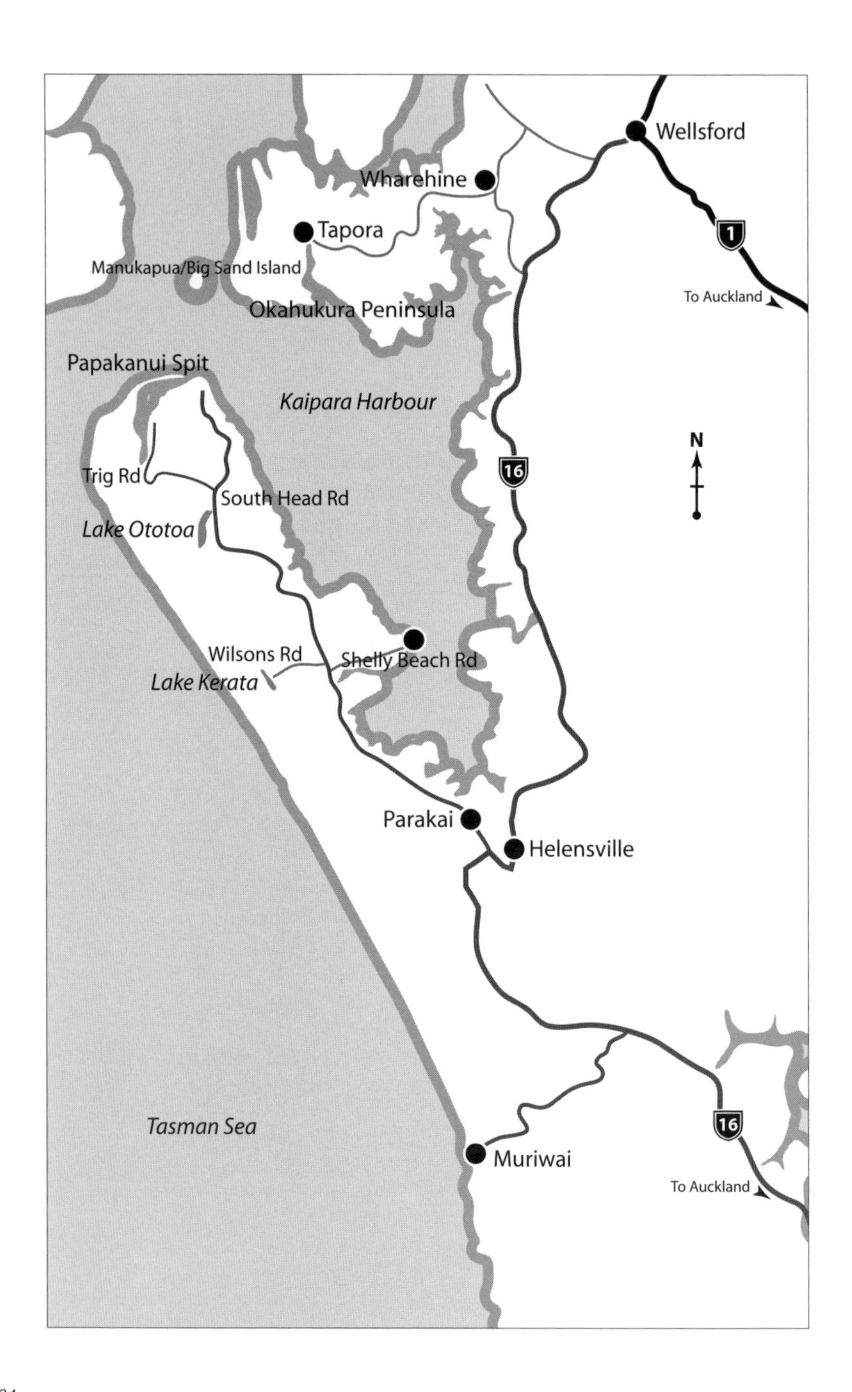
Wellsford
Wharehine
Tapora
1
Manukapua/Big Sand Island
To Auckland
Okahukura Peninsula
Papakanui Spit
Kaipara Harbour
N
Trig Rd
16
South Head Rd
Lake Ototoa
Wilsons Rd
Shelly Beach Rd
Lake Kerata
Parakai
Helensville
16
Tasman Sea
Muriwai
To Auckland

2
Kaipara Harbour

Where North-west of Auckland, 1–2 hours' drive from downtown.

What's special A vast harbour, sand islands and spits – important habitats for migrant waders and rare and endangered shorebirds, plus freshwater lakes with other waterfowl species.

Birds to look for Bar-tailed godwit/kūaka, lesser knot/huahou, turnstone, little tern and other international waders, New Zealand migrants: South Island pied oystercatcher/tōrea, wrybill/ngutuparore, banded dotterel/tuturiwhatu and black-billed gull/tarāpunga, fairy tern/tara-iti, New Zealand dotterel/tuturiwhatu, variable oystercatcher/tōrea, white-fronted tern/tara, Caspian tern/taranui, fern bird/mātātā, Australasian bittern/matuku, Australasian little grebe, spotless crake/pūweto, New Zealand dabchick/weiweia, royal spoonbill/kōtuku-ngatupapa, paradise shelduck/pūtangitangi and black swan.

Birdwatching options Self-guided walks, roadside watching.

Top spots

- Manukapua/Big Sand Island and Birds Beach/Journeys End (Okahukura Peninsula)
- Papakanui Spit Wildlife Refuge and Waionui Inlet (South Kaipara Head)
- South Kaipara Peninsula lakes
- Shelly Beach.

When to go Year-round – spring/summer for Arctic migrants, summer/autumn/winter for New Zealand migrants.

Background

Kaipara Harbour is the largest harbour in New Zealand. It is a particularly significant habitat for shorebirds and for thousands of migrant waders. The broad, shallow harbour extends some 60 km north–south, and its coastline winds around bays, inlets and peninsulas for over 3000 km.

Habitats include sandspits, dunes, shell banks, salt marshes, estuaries with mangroves, freshwater lakes and a mixture of native forest, plantation pine forest and farmland. Because of treacherous sandbars at the harbour mouth, the Kaipara is rarely used by shipping. Land use around the harbour is dominated by farms, forests, orchards, vineyards, lifestyle blocks and small towns. Favoured birding spots are in remote, sometimes inaccessible coastal locations, no doubt a factor for the survival here of New Zealand fairy tern.

Papakanui Spit, on South Kaipara Head, is one of only four remaining breeding sites for the tiny tern, which was once widespread around the North Island and eastern South Island coastline. The terns nest from October to February, and the other three breeding sites are found close by on east coast beaches. When not breeding, most of the entire population (35–40 birds) live around the Kaipara Harbour.

Since plummeting to only three breeding pairs in 1984 the population has recovered slightly, thanks to measures such as fencing and predator control in nesting areas, and warden patrols during breeding seasons to safeguard the vulnerable, beach-site nests from 4WD vehicles, dogs and other dangers. More recently, transferring eggs and chicks between nests to increase productivity has also helped.

Papakanui Spit and Manukapua/Big Sand Island in the north of the harbour are also breeding sites for New Zealand dotterel. Both locations are major Asia/Pacific Flyway sites for international waders. New Zealand migrants, in particular South Island pied oystercatcher and wrybill, are also present from late summer to winter. In recent seasons, the black-billed gull has expanded its range and started to nest around the Kaipara Harbour.

Best birding areas

⊳ Manukapua/Big Sand Island and Birds Beach/Journeys End

Manukapua, meaning 'cloud of birds', is a fitting name for what is considered one of New Zealand's most important sites for migratory waders. (Best visiting time is October to March.) The low-lying island features dunes colonised by pingao and other dune grasses, coastal shrub lands, salt marsh and pans with *Sarcocornia* (glasswort) vegetation.

The island sits just off the tip of Okahukura Peninsula, about 40 minutes' drive from Wellsford. Drive 3 km south-west from Wellsford on SH16 and turn right onto Port Albert Road. After 6 km, turn left onto Wharehine Road, then after another 6 km turn right onto Run Road and continue for 15 km to the small settlement of Tapora. This road passes Stables Landing on the Tauhoa River, a good spot to see royal spoonbills.

At Tapora, continue past the community hall onto Okahukura Road for 5 km and turn left at the DoC Okahukura Reserve sign onto a sandy farm track. Vehicle access here is at the landowner's discretion; the gate is generally left open, otherwise park at the farm gate. Leave all gates as you found them. Travel across the farm for 1 km and park under the pine trees. (Do not drive onto the sand.) It is an easy 15-minute walk to the coast and across to Manukapua/Big Sand Island. The causeway to the island has a solid base underfoot and is dry except for around two hours either side of high tide when the water may be up to knee-deep.

Arctic waders, in particular bar-tailed godwit and turnstone, are likely to be roosting at high tide on the coastal pan just across the causeway and at the island's northern and southern ends. Some rarities can be spotted in these places. Wrybill, banded dotterel, New Zealand dotterel and fairy tern are all likely to be present further around the north-west corner.

It's best to go on a rising tide and stay through a full tide, which pushes the waders off their vast mudflat feeding grounds and up onto the island, so plan a stay of 4 to 5 hours (take food and water). A track that crosses the middle of the island passes through coastal shrubs, habitat for fernbird, bittern, banded rail and spotless crake.

Birds Beach is a good spot for observing waders from the comfort of your car. From Tapora, look for Journeys End Road, which turns off Okahukura Road and leads to a picnic area beside Birds Beach. You may also see fairy tern and Caspian tern.

▷ Papakanui Spit Wildlife Refuge and Waionui Lagoon

Papakanui Spit, which shelters Waionui Lagoon from the open sea at the northern tip of the South Kaipara Peninsula, is one of four breeding sites for fairy tern. New Zealand dotterel, variable oystercatcher, Caspian tern and white-fronted tern are also known to breed on this spit. It is also an important high-tide roost for waders, with up to 10,000 birds roosting here at any one time, in particular bar-tailed godwit, lesser knot, South Island pied oystercatcher and wrybill. Waionui Lagoon is regarded as one of the Kaipara Harbour's main pre-migratory meeting sites for Arctic waders.

Muriwai gannet colony

The most easily accessible of the three mainland gannet colonies in New Zealand is located just south of Kaipara Harbour on the west coast beach, Muriwai. The colony is in Muriwai Regional Park, a windswept stretch of surf beach, rolling black sand dunes and native coastal forest, with walking tracks and picnic spots. It is about 45 minutes' drive from central Auckland, and easily reached by 12-km detour from SH16, en route to South Kaipara Peninsula.

Australasian gannet/tākapu first became established on the rock stacks and islets just offshore of a headland called Ōtakamiro in the early 1900s. As the colony grew, the birds started nesting on the headland cliffs. Today around 1200 pairs nest here each summer. A few birds stay throughout the year, although most are present from August to March, with chicks from late November.

Papakanui Spit can be viewed from Waionui Lagoon. Access is through Woodhill Forest, though public entry is sometimes prohibited owing to commercial forestry operations, fire danger or air force activity on a weapons range at the head of the peninsula. Birders are advised to phone ahead to Woodhill Forest (0800 732 738) to check whether access is open. To reach Waionui Lagoon, drive straight through Parakai township and on to South Head Road. Just out of Parakai, a sign on the left states whether forest access is open. Continue for 31 km and turn left onto Trig Road, then after 100 metres turn right through a gate onto Tasman Road. This is the access road through Woodhill Forest to the lagoon. This gate is locked when forest access is closed.

Drive through the forest for about 3 km to the lagoon. From the car park at the road's end, walk for 15 minutes to a raised area known as Ti Tree Island, where there is a good view of Papakanui Spit. Although birds

The best place for seeing the gannets is Tākapu Refuge Walk, a gently graded walk over the headland to platforms that overlook the colony (about 25 minutes return). The steep lava cliffs and rock stacks, surf, and constant action from the colony itself create a spectacular setting. White-fronted tern/tara and blue penguin/kororā may also be seen.

Follow SH16 towards Helensville past the townships of Kumeu and Huapai. Turn left at Waimauku and follow the signs for 12 km to Muriwai, turning left up a steep hill to reach the gannet colony. Tākapu Refuge Walk is clearly signposted from the car park at the southern end of Muriwai Beach.

will be numerous, a telescope is handy for viewing birds on the Spit itself. It is possible to walk along the shore to the lagoon entrance, or wade across the lagoon (knee-deep at low tide; a swim at high tide) to the island at the end of the Spit.

▷ South Kaipara Peninsula lakes

Freshwater dune lakes on South Kaipara Peninsula provide habitats for water fowl, including New Zealand dabchick, Australasian little grebe, Australasian bittern, spotless crake, pūkeko, paradise shelduck/pūtangitangi, mallard and black swan. The lakes are nestled in a mix of farmland, pine, kānuka and coastal broadleaf forest. Forest birds such as grey warbler/riroriro, fantail/pīwakawaka, New Zealand pigeon/kererū, plus Australasian harrier/kāhu, welcome swallow and kingfisher/kōtare are all likely to be seen.

The best lake for easy access and bird-viewing is Lake Kereta, reached by driving from Parakai along South Head Road for 15 km, then turning left onto Wilsons Road and driving 5 km to the lake edge. This road is partly unsealed, steep and winding in parts, but passes over a ridge crest with a great view of the ocean and harbour. Alternatively, 200 metres back up the road from the lake, a DoC sign indicates a public walking track. This follows a grassy path for 5 minutes through kānuka forest (look and listen for fantail and grey warbler) beside a small wetland, to a pleasant grassy clearing with good views across the northern end of the lake.

Lake Ototoa is the largest of the dune lakes and partly surrounded by some of the last coastal broadleaf forest remaining on the peninsula. However, depending on the water level, access around the lake edge can be restricted and bird viewing is not always as good as at Lake Kereta. Turn off South Head Road onto Donaghue Road, 25 km from Parakai, and drive about 300 m past the community hall to an 'angler's access' signpost on the right. A 5-minute track follows a grassy strip, then descends through kānuka forest to the lake's edge.

⊳ Shelly Beach

This settlement offers good views of the inner Kaipara Harbour, particularly off the long wharf. Look for reef heron, pied and black shags, oystercatchers and Caspian terns. In winter royal spoonbill roost on a large rock 30 m offshore. Turn right off South Head Road 14 km from Parakai and drive 5 km to the settlement. For a view of the rock drive south to the end of Omana Avenue and walk the short beach access track.

Getting there Auckland, the closest city to Kaipara Harbour, is the main gateway to New Zealand. The city is served by international and national airlines, and inter-city bus services.

Because of the long, narrow shape of Kaipara Harbour, there is a significant distance by road between the main birding locations. Unless travelling with a national birding-tour operator, self-driving is the only option to get to these spots.

Wellsford, at the northern end of the harbour, is the nearest major town to Manukapua/Big Sand Island. It sits at the junction of SH1 and SH16, 1.5 hours' drive north of central Auckland and 45 minutes' drive north of Helensville.

The South Kaipara Peninsula is most easily reached by heading out of Auckland on the north-western motorway and following the signs to Helensville. At a T-junction 1 km before Helensville, turn left and drive through the mineral springs town of Parakai, then continue down South Head Road. All birding spots on the peninsula are accessed from this road, which follows the backbone of the peninsula.

Getting around Private transport is a necessity. Remember that some of the sites included in this chapter require phoning ahead to ensure access is open. There are no specialist birding operators in the Kaipara area, although some national operators bring clients to Manukapua/Big Sand Island. Kaipara Cruises operate group charters on the harbour from Helensville, ranging from 4-hour trips to 2- and 3-day cruises. These are not focused on birds, although many birds will inevitably be seen. 09 420 8466 or kaiparacruises@xtra.co.nz.

Accommodation The Kaipara region has a delightful range of accommodation: bed-and-breakfasts located on organic orchards and macadamia nut farms, motels and holiday parks by mineral pools, beachside camping areas, self-contained cottages, backpackers and homestays. Auckland, with everything from international hotel chains to boutique lodges and backpackers, is also close by.

Facilities Wellsford and Helensville offer a full range of services – shops, supermarkets, fuel, banks, ATMs and information centres. Parakai has a small store, tavern, restaurant and an excellent mineral pool complex. There is a cafe on South Kaipara Peninsula at the Macadamia Nut Farm, and a store at the Shelly Beach Motor Camp. There is a public toilet at Lake Ototoa, but no facilities at Lake Kerata or Waionui Lagoon.

The closest public toilet to Manukapua/Big Sand Island is at the Tapora public hall, or at a small picnic area by Waikiri Creek Estuary, at the end of Journeys End Road near Tapora. Otherwise, the closest facilities of any kind are in Wellsford.

Information

Helensville Information Centre: 27 Commercial Road, 09 420 8060, hvlinfo@xtra.co.nz, www.helensville.co.nz.

Kumeu Information Centre: 299 SH16, 09 412 9886.

Auckland Regional Council (Muriwai Regional Park): 09 366 2000.

3

Great Barrier Island/Aotea

Where Outer Hauraki Gulf, 30 minutes' flight from Auckland.

What's special New Zealand's fourth largest and one of the least modified inhabited islands, with few introduced predators. Birdlife thrives in coastal dunes, estuaries, inlets and extensive forests. It is home to threatened species including brown teal/pāteke and black petrel/tāiko.

Birds to look for Black petrel, Cook's petrel, brown teal, New Zealand dotterel/tuturiwhatu, variable oystercatcher/tōrea, kākā, North Island robin/toutouwai, fernbird/mātātā, red-crowned parakeet/kākāriki, tūī, bellbird/korimako, New Zealand pigeon/kererū, Australasian bittern/matuku, spotless crake/pūweto, banded rail/moho-pererū, New Zealand and Arctic migrant waders (spring and summer), shining cuckoo/pīpīwharauroa and long-tailed cuckoo/koekoeā (spring and summer).

Birdwatching options Guided walks, self-guided walks.

Top spots

- Whangapoua Estuary (2–3 hours)
- Windy Canyon Track–Hirakimata/Mt Hobson (3–5 hours, evenings)
- Glenfern Sanctuary (2 hours)
- Kaitoke Swamp (1–2 hours)
- Okiwi Reserve (30 minutes).

When to go Year-round. October–May for black petrel, spring and summer for Arctic waders.

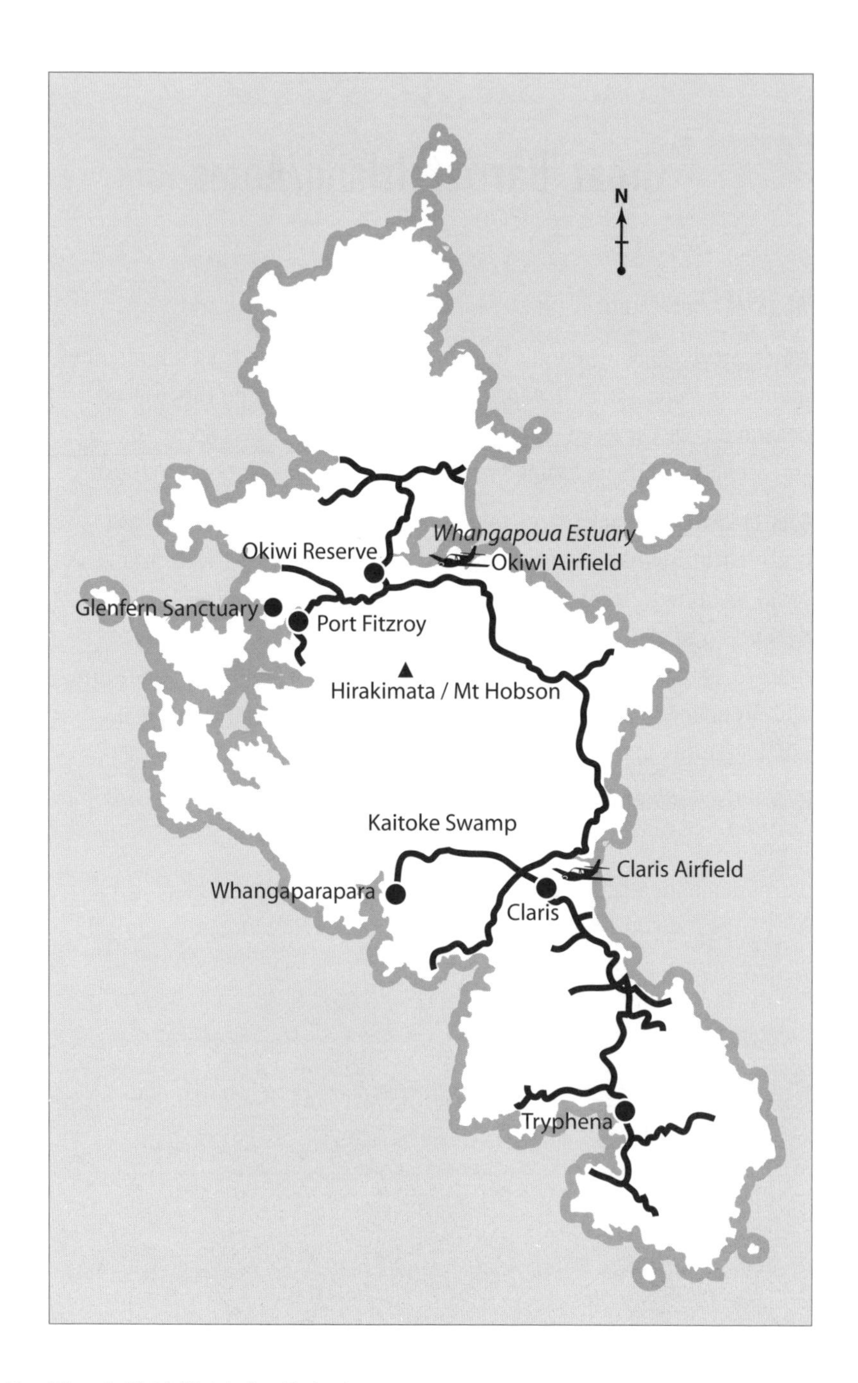
N
Whangapoua Estuary
Okiwi Reserve
Okiwi Airfield
Glenfern Sanctuary
Port Fitzroy
Hirakimata / Mt Hobson
Kaitoke Swamp
Claris Airfield
Whangaparapara
Claris
Tryphena

Background

Named for its position as a 'barrier' between the Hauraki Gulf and Pacific Ocean, Great Barrier Island's relative isolation has saved it from large-scale settlement and development. More than 60 per cent of its 27,000 ha is managed for conservation.

Most mammalian pests that have wreaked so much havoc elsewhere have never been introduced to Great Barrier, so the island has an impressive flora and fauna including rare and endemic plants, diverse forest, wetland and shorebirds, and 13 species of lizard.

The rugged, mostly volcanic island is dominated by forest-covered hills, pierced along its centre spine by rocky buttresses that rise to the highest point at Mt Hobson/Hirakimata. Although much of the island's original kauri forest was logged, significant areas remain. The coastline consists of sandy beaches, coastal dunes, tidal creeks, estuaries, rocky headlands, offshore islands and indented harbours.

Great Barrier is a stronghold of brown teal, one of the rarest duck species in the world. The Whangapoua basin and estuary is one of their favoured areas, with patches of swampy former farmland fenced off to enhance nesting habitat. These dabbling ducks forage mainly at night on grassland, shallow estuaries and freshwater wetlands.

Another threatened bird with its main breeding population on Great Barrier is the black petrel. The largest colony is on Mt Hobson/Hirakimata.

Of the forest birds, kākā, tūī, New Zealand pigeon, fantail/pīwakawaka and grey warbler/riroriro are probably the most visible. Banded rail/ moho-pererū are likely to be seen on the bush edges, in fern patches and along roadsides. New Zealand dotterel and variable oystercatcher frequent the eastern beaches and estuaries, along with South Island and Arctic migrant waders. Seabirds such as blue penguin/kororā, Australasian gannet/tākapu, petrels and shearwaters are often seen off the coast.

Great Barrier is a popular holiday destination with tramping tracks and mountain-bike trails, short walks, surfing, sea kayaking, diving, boating and fishing.

Best birding spots

⊳ Whangapoua Estuary

During summer hundreds of brown teal flock here. Best views are just down from the DoC camping area before the high tide turns, when large numbers of brown teal and waders follow the water as the tide goes out. New Zealand dotterel and variable oystercatcher also feed here, while banded dotterel/tuturiwhatu and wrybill/ngutuparore are likely to visit in summer through to early winter. Bar-tailed godwit/kūaka and other Arctic migrants are present in summer.

⊳ Windy Canyon–Hirakimata/Mt Hobson

Black petrel nest in burrows on the upper slopes of Mt Hobson. Any time from October to April (adults arrive in October to court and nest, chicks fledge in April/May), by walking up Windy Canyon Track just on dusk you can see the shadows and hear the flurry of these petrels returning home after a day at sea. Close to the summit the birds can be seen around the boardwalk track en route to their nests. The track is well maintained and can be negotiated at night, but there are steep drop-offs. Take a torch.

⊳ Glenfern Sanctuary

A major restoration programme including predator-proof fencing on 150 ha of private land and adjacent reserve land, near Port Fitzroy, has been undertaken by the landowners with help from government and council funding. A 2-hour guided tour is available, and species most likely seen include kākā, New Zealand pigeon, fantail, grey warbler, North Island robin (reintroduced after a 100-year absence), kingfisher/kōtare, banded rail, tūī, brown teal and, from February to May, a possible glimpse into a black petrel nest.

The guided tour involves driving by Unimog vehicle to a lookout point, then a walk along forest and boardwalk trails including a suspension-bridge walk into the crown of a 600-year-old kauri tree.

Kaitoke Wetlands

The track to the Kaitoke hot springs follows the edge of an area known as Kaitoke Swamp. With patience, Australasian bittern, spotless crake and fernbird can sometimes be seen from boardwalk sections of this track. While here, it's worth continuing to the hot springs, a series of small sulphurous pools sculpted into the stream bed. The track starts from Whangaparapara Road, which crosses the island linking Claris with Whangaparapara Harbour. The return walk to the springs takes about 1.5 hours, not including birding and hot springs bathing time.

Okiwi Reserve

This reserve is a top spot to view the island's prolific forest birds, with magnificent, mature pūriri trees and regenerating nīkau. The most obvious birds are kākā, tūī, New Zealand pigeon, red-crowned parakeet and banded rail. Okiwi School pupils have 'adopted' the reserve and carry out pest control with help from DoC staff.

The reserve is located on Mabey Road, adjacent to the school. It takes no more than 20 minutes to wander the small reserve, but is a lovely place to sit and observe the birds.

Getting there Several flights operate daily to Great Barrier Island from Auckland Airport, as well as less frequent flights from North Shore Airfield, Whangarei, Coromandel and Tauranga. Flights from Auckland take about 30 minutes and cost around $150–200 return, with specials available. There are two airfields on the island, Claris and Okiwi (which is closed during winter). Three airlines operate flights:

Fly My Sky, 09 256 7026 or 0800 222 123, greatbarrier@flymysky.co.nz, www.flymysky.co.nz.

Great Barrier Airlines, 0800 900 600, gba@gbair.co.nz, www.greatbarrierairlines.co.nz.

Sunair Aviation, from Whitianga, 0800 786 247. Note that weather can affect flight schedules.

Sealink operates a vehicle and passenger ferry several days each week from downtown Auckland to Tryphena, and once a week to Port Fitzroy, further north. The voyage to Tryphena takes around 4 hours and offers excellent seabird-spotting opportunities. Fares are around $105 return, with various concessions available.
09 300 5900, 0800 732 546, info@sealink.co.nz, www.sealink.co.nz.

Getting around Some 56 km of roads traverse Great Barrier and self-driving is probably the most convenient way to tour the island, with rental vehicles available from several companies. However, most roads are narrow, unsealed, steep, winding and prone to wash-outs during heavy rain. There are also shuttle bus and taxi services. Great Barrier Buses offer multi-day passes so passengers can be dropped off and picked up from walking tracks. Many accommodation providers offer complimentary airport or ferry transfers.

Keep a careful eye out for wildlife, for example banded rail and the large endemic chevron skink by day and black petrel and brown teal, which have a habit of waddling slowly along the roads at night, in particular around Okiwi.

Accommodation This caters to a range of budgets, including luxury lodge, private self-contained cottage, motels, homestays, backpackers and DoC camping grounds. A few properties require 4WD access. Booking is essential year-round (especially for DoC camping sites in summer), and some places are closed in winter.

Facilities General stores and fuel are available at the main settlements of Port Fitzroy, Whangaparapara, Claris and Tryphena. As with accommodation, there is a good range of restaurants and cafes available, albeit at scattered locations. During winter it is advisable to book ahead and confirm opening hours.

Eftpos and credit cards are accepted at most outlets but there is no ATM on the island. Cellphone coverage is unreliable, though there are card-and-coin phones at several locations. There is no main power and water supply or sewerage system on the island; electricity comes by private generator or solar power, and there is no street lighting, so pack a torch.

Information

Department of Conservation Visitor Centre, Ferry Building, Quay Street, Auckland, 09 379 6476, aucklandvc@doc.govt.nz, Great Barrier Island Area office (office hours) 09 429 0044.

Auckland i-SITE Visitor Centre, 09 367 6009 or 0800 282 552, or www.greatbarriernz.com.

Great Barrier Island New Zealand Visitor Information Tourism Guide, www.thebarrier.co.nz.

Guiding companies

Glenfern Sanctuary: guided tour through private forest sanctuary, costs operate on a sliding scale from $75 each for two people to $35 each for 7–10 people. Tours are limited to 10 and require at least 1 day's notice. 09 429 0091, info@glenfern.co.nz, www.glenfern.org.nz.

Discover Great Barrier: offers a 3-day walk with accommodation options to suit different budgets; the high-end around $950. Also offers shorter walks by request. info@discovergreatbarrier.co.nz, www.discovergreatbarrier.co.nz.

Recommended reading *Great Barrier Island,* edited by Don Armitage. Christchurch: Canterbury University Press, revised edition 2004.

4

Tiritiri Matangi Island

Where Hauraki Gulf, near Auckland.

What's special One of New Zealand's major conservation stories, this 220-ha island is now one of the most easily accessible places to see an excellent range of endemic birds. It is one of the few scientific reserves open to the public.

Birds to look for Saddleback/tīeke, North Island robin/toutouwai, takahē, fernbird/ mātātā, stitchbird/hihi, red-crowned parakeet/kākāriki, kōkako, kākā, tūī, bellbird/korimako, whitehead/pōpokatea, rifleman/tītīpounamu, brown teal/pāteke, spotless crake/pūweto, little spotted kiwi/kiwi-pukupuku, blue penguin/kororā plus other seabirds and shorebirds.

Birdwatching options Guided walks, self-guided walks.

When to go Year-round. Winter is less crowded, though the weather can be unsettled.

Background

Over 50 islands are scattered throughout the Hauraki Gulf. These are part of Hauraki Gulf Marine Park, established in 2000 to ensure the protection and integrated management of all the various reserves, sanctuaries, waterways and marine reserves within the Gulf.

Some islands are a mixture of conservation land and holiday or residential settlements; others are free of animal pests and support significant flora and fauna, thus access to many is restricted but Tiritiri Matangi (often called 'Tiri' for short) has been declared an open sanctuary.

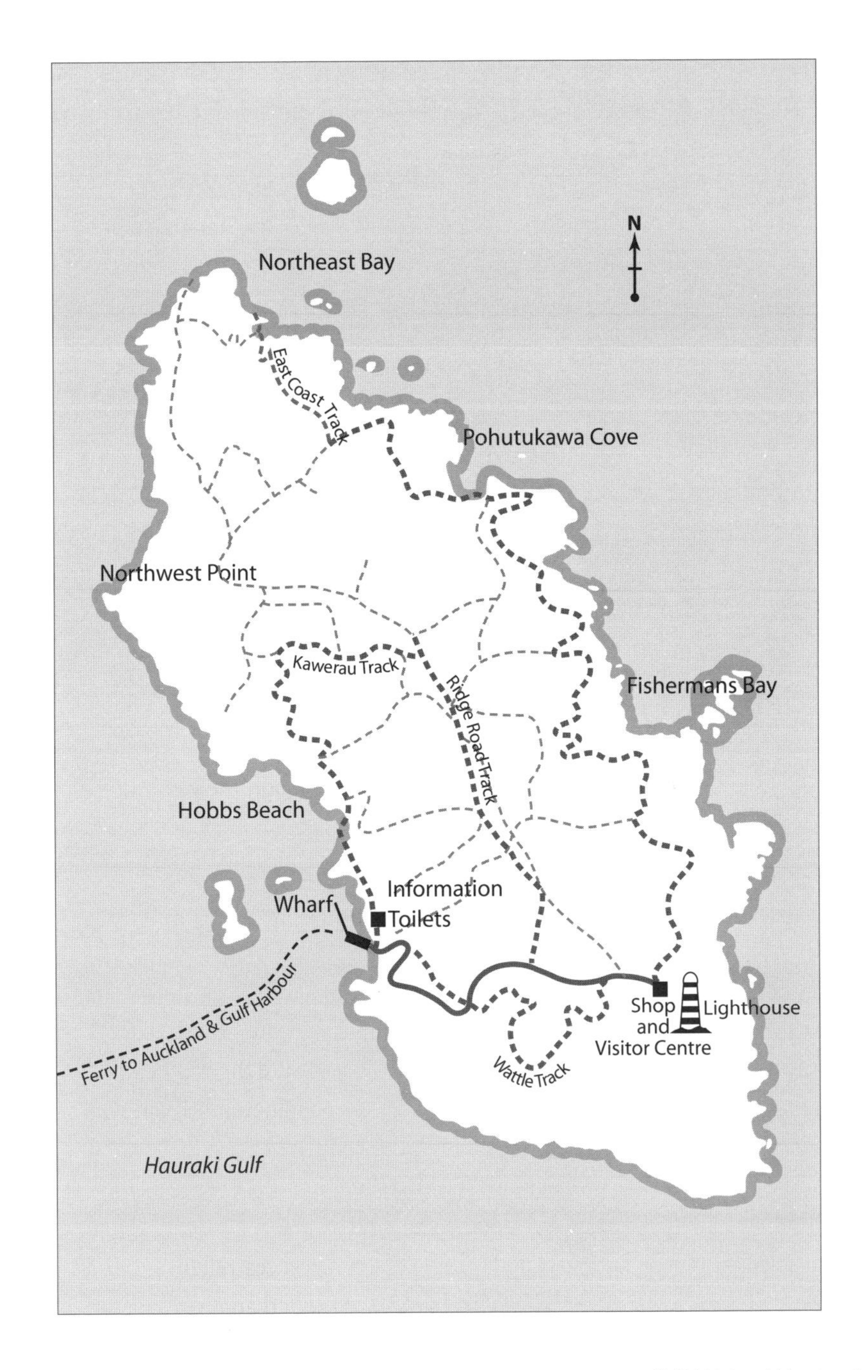
N
Northeast Bay
East Coast Track
Pohutukawa Cove
Northwest Point
Kawerau Track
Ridge Road Track
Fishermans Bay
Hobbs Beach
Information
Wharf
Toilets
Ferry to Auckland & Gulf Harbour
Shop
and
Visitor Centre
Lighthouse
Wattle Track
Hauraki Gulf

The island was farmed for over a hundred years and largely stripped of its original vegetation, so just a few native birds remained in remnants of original forest. After farming activity finished in the 1970s an ambitious community-driven island restoration programme swung into action.

Around 300,000 trees have been planted and natural regeneration has accelerated. Resident species have recovered and saddleback, takahē, stitchbird, red-crowned parakeet, rifleman and kōkako have been successfully introduced. Other species released include robin, whitehead, fernbird, tomtit, brown teal and little spotted kiwi. Seabirds and shorebirds include several species of shag, gull, petrel, shearwater, plus Caspian tern/taranui, white-fronted tern/tara, and variable oystercatcher/tōrea. Generally by day blue penguin are at sea fishing but when breeding and moulting (from July to March), they may be seen in nesting boxes near the island wharf. Tuatara have also been introduced to the island, and are sometimes seen by visitors.

While some purists suggest the restored status and introduction of so many species makes Tiritiri Matangi contrived, other visitors are thrilled by the abundance and easy visibility of birds in the young forest. The island is managed by DoC in close liaison with the Supporters of Tiritiri Matangi, a volunteer organisation which spearheaded the restoration effort.

Getting there Day trips run from downtown Auckland and Gulf Harbour on Whangaparaoa Peninsula. Ferries run from Wednesday to Sunday and on public holidays (except Christmas Day), and daily from 26 December to the third Sunday in January. Travelling times are 75 minutes from Auckland and 25 minutes from Gulf Harbour, and the sailing schedule allows a good 5 hours on the island. Up to 150 people can visit by ferry per day; during summer bookings are strongly advised.

Ferry services are provided by 360 Discovery Cruises. Costs are $66/adult and $29/child from Auckland, or $39/adult and $19.50/child from Gulf Harbour. Family, senior and group concessions are available.
0800 360 3472, 09 307 8005, www.360discovery.co.nz.

People can also land from private craft (best access is Hobbs Beach). All visitors are asked to take precautions to prevent the accidental introduction of pests and weeds, such as packing food in rodent-proof containers, checking bags for rodents and ensuring packs and shoes are free of dirt and seeds.

Getting around On arrival all ferry passengers are given an introductory talk by the ranger. Guided walks (about 1.5 hours) are run by the Supporters of Tiritiri Matangi, costing $5/person, and can be booked and paid for at the same time as the ferry trip.

Well-maintained walking tracks range from the gently graded, 1-hour Wattle Track to a 3-hour coastal circuit that is steep in parts. Packs and bags can be transported to the shelter area if required.

Best birding spots Where the birds are depends on the weather and fruiting and flowering seasons. However, Wattle Track, which leads from the wharf to the lighthouse and public shelter area, passes through young regenerating forest and is generally good for seeing a variety of species.

Supplementary feeders along the way are particularly good spots to see tūī, bellbird and stitchbird. Elsewhere on the island open grassland areas, deliberately left unplanted, are favoured habitats and thus likely viewing spots for takahē. These include the wide grassy Ridge Road Track that runs along the central ridge of the island, with great views of the Hauraki Gulf.

Accommodation Basic bunk accommodation is available, but needs to be booked well ahead as there is huge demand. Staying overnight obviously presents an opportunity to hear and possibly see the nocturnal kiwi, penguins coming ashore and to experience one of the most resounding dawn choruses anywhere in New Zealand, including the haunting chimes of the kōkako. Demand for accommodation is so high there is normally more than a year's waiting list for weekends. All long weekends are booked out by Supporters' working groups. The best opportunity is to book from Sunday through to Wednesday, catching the days when the ferry isn't running. This necessitates a longer stay, but a more peaceful one with few people around.

Costs are $20/night (adults) and $15/night for children. Supporters receive a discount. Book online at www.doc.govt.nz/tiritiribunkhouse.

Facilities There are toilets and a public shelter by the wharf, and at the lighthouse area on the top of the island. By the lighthouse there is a shop and visitor centre with complimentary tea and coffee. Cold drinks can be purchased but there is no food for sale on the island.

Information

Supporters of Tiritiri Matangi Inc, www.tiritirimatangi.org.nz.

Department of Conservation, www.doc.govt.nz.

Recommended reading

Tiritiri Island: A model of conservation. Anne Rimmer. Auckland: Tandem Press, 2003.

The Hauraki Gulf: From Bream Head to Cape Colville, Linda Bercusson. Christchurh: Shoal Bay Press, 1999.

5

Outer Hauraki Gulf

Where Hauraki Gulf, immediately north-east of Auckland city.

What's special A vast coastal waterway with endemics and visiting subtropical and subantarctic birds, huge shearwater and petrel colonies; also whales and dolphins. Many island nature reserves, most notably Little Barrier Island.

Birds to look for New Zealand storm petrel (considered extinct for over 150 years) white-faced storm petrel/takahikare-moana, Cook's petrel/tītī, black petrel/tāiko, Buller's shearwater, flesh-footed shearwater/toanui, and numerous other petrels and shearwaters, white-fronted tern, blue penguin/kororā, Australasian gannet/tākapu and occasional albatross species. On Little Barrier Island, kōkako, stitchbird/hihi, saddleback/tīeke, North Island robin/toutouwai, red-crowned parakeet/kākāriki, kākā, New Zealand pigeon/kererū, whitehead/pōpokatea, brown teal/pāteke.

Birdwatching options Seabird cruises (day and overnight), guided and self-guided island walks.

Top spots

- Northern, outer gulf between Little Barrier Island and Mokohinau Islands
- Little Barrier Island (day trips by permit).

When to go Year-round. Seabird species vary throughout the year. Little Barrier is weather dependent, most accessible November–April.

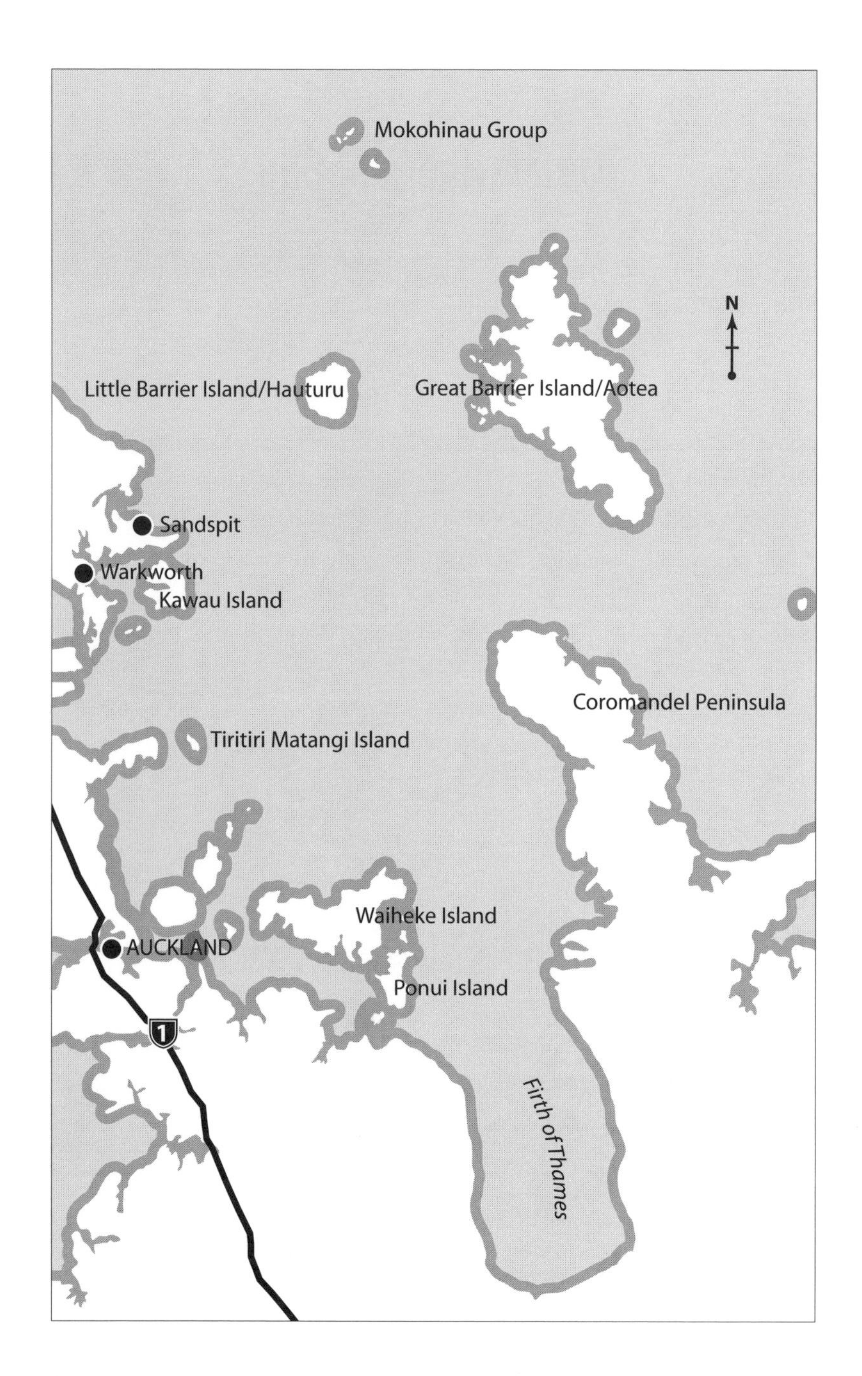
Mokohinau Group
N
Little Barrier Island/Hauturu
Great Barrier Island/Aotea
Sandspit
Warkworth
Kawau Island
Coromandel Peninsula
Tiritiri Matangi Island
Waiheke Island
AUCKLAND
Ponui Island
1
Firth of Thames

Background

The rediscovery in 2003 of the New Zealand storm petrel, thought to be extinct for over 150 years, and subsequent, regular sightings of this bird on gulf birding cruises epitomise the enigma that is the Hauraki Gulf. For here are some of New Zealand's biggest seabird populations, rarest species and most valuable island sanctuaries – right beside the country's largest city.

At least 20 endemic seabirds breed and feed in the Gulf. Other birds visit from northern tropical and subtropical waters, and from the subantarctic. International waders come from the northern hemisphere.

Oceanic waters, in particular the warm subtropical East Auckland Current, influence the outer Gulf and contrast with tidal, reef-strewn inner regions, creating a diversity of nutrient-rich habitats. It's a habitat shared by international shipping and Aucklanders with pleasure boats.

Little Barrier Island or Hauturu, a steep-sided volcanic island covered with relatively unmodified rainforest, has near-original bird populations, as well as reptiles, skinks, bats and the endemic wētāpunga or giant wētā. The last exotic pest, kiore, a species of rat, was finally eliminated in 2004. Essentially, the island today is as close as it comes to a time when humans first arrived in New Zealand; a biodiversity liferaft for birds, plants and invertebrates.

Best birding spots

▷ Seabird cruises

Specialist birding cruises generally range over the northern oceanic waters of the Gulf, beyond Little Barrier Island to the Mokohinau Islands. Trips can be of up to 12 hours' duration (shorter in winter), and feature huge rafts of shearwaters, petrels and terns, often in feeding frenzies as the birds work among school fish or krill.

From September to March huge colonies of white-faced storm petrels breed in the Gulf and are often cited as the highlight of a cruise. Other endemics here are black petrel and Cook's petrel, plus Pycroft's petrel and grey-faced petrel/oi, flesh-footed, Buller's and fluttering shearwaters, fairy prion, blue penguin and the recently rediscovered New Zealand storm petrel. Occasional visitors include short-tailed and Hutton's shearwaters, cape, giant, Wilson's storm and grey-backed storm petrels, and several albatross species.

⊳ Mokohinau Islands

A small, steep and rugged group of islands about 100 km north-east of Auckland, off the northern tip of Great Barrier Island. They support petrel, tern and gannet colonies, plus red-crowned parakeet, bellbird/korimako, tūī and kākā. The black-winged petrel is expanding its breeding range from the subtropics and in recent years has been prospecting nest sites here. Grey ternlet roost on Cathedral Rocks.

Most of these islands are closed nature reserves but cruise operators may land on Burgess Island, which is a scenic reserve. At the least they will find a lee spot close to shore where you can see the birds and rest before the long return to the mainland. Some operators can also organise landings on Little Barrier, but generally they prefer to do this as a separate excursion.

⊳ Little Barrier Island

Some 50 bird species breed here, most descended from the island's original populations but also several relocated from vulnerable mainland sites. Species encountered vary seasonally: in winter kōkako frequently visit the area around the ranger's house; long-tailed cuckoo and shining cuckoo are obvious in spring and summer; stitchbird, saddleback, tūī and kākā are reliably prolific and noisy. New Zealand pigeon gather in massive flocks. Also likely to be evident are whitehead, red-crowned parakeet, tomtit, North Island robin, grey warbler and rifleman/tītīpounamu.

This is one of only two breeding sites for black petrel and one of three for Cook's petrel. Breeding success for Cook's petrel (late winter through summer) has been significantly higher since kiore were eradicated.

Visitor numbers and movements on the island are limited. Landing is only allowed by obtaining a DoC permit at least 20 days in advance, then chartering a licensed boat operator, plus supervisor/guide, and complying with strict biosecurity conditions. Trips are very weather dependent, and landings can involve negotiating chest-high surf on slippery boulders. On arrival, there is a compulsory introductory talk by the DoC ranger.

On the island, walking tracks open to the public explore stream beds, dry ridge lines with kānuka, and dense kauri forest. The two main circuits can each be walked in about 3 hours, but anyone serious about seeing the birds in this mature forest will want to take much longer. Most groups generally spend around 6 hours on the island.

Getting there Auckland is served by international and national airlines and inter-city bus services. Coaches, shuttles and taxis serve all flights.

Seabird cruises generally depart from Sandspit, Ti Point or Leigh, each slightly over an hour's drive from Auckland. A few cruises leave from Gulf Harbour, on the Whangaparaoa Peninsula (40 minutes' drive from Auckland). Public transport can be arranged from Auckland to Gulf Harbour and Warkworth.

Accommodation The beaches, bays and harbours near Warkworth, around Leigh, Mahurangi Harbour, Kawau Bay and Snells Beach are popular holiday areas and offer a full range of accommodation, from luxury lodge, to bed-and-breakfasts, self-contained holiday homes, motels, backpackers, holiday parks and regional park camping areas. Auckland city has a full complement of accommodation including international chain hotels.

Facilities Birders on seabird cruises are expected to be self-sufficient, with food, drink and adequate clothing. If you are susceptible to motion sickness, pre-cruise medication is advised.

Visitors to Little Barrier Island must also be self-sufficient. There are toilets available for visitors.

Information

Warkworth i-SITE Visitor Centre, 09 425 9081, warkworth@i-SITE.org, www.warkworthnz.co.nz.

DoC, P.O. Box 474, Warkworth, 09 425 7812, www.doc.govt.nz.

Little Barrier Island (Hauturu) Supporters' Trust, lenoel@paradise.net.nz.

Licensed operators

Pterodroma Pelagics: a subsidiary of Kiwi Wildlife Tours, offering regular day cruises (up to 12 hours) and occasional overnight tours out of Warkworth, $250/day cruise, 09 422 6868, info@nzseabirds.com, www.nzseabirds.com.

NZ Wrybill Tours: day cruises, about one per month out of Warkworth, $195/person. 06 877 6388, info@wrybill-tours.com, www.wrybill-tours.com.

Dolphin and Whale Safari: inner Gulf cruises from downtown Auckland, focusing on whales and dolphins though birds are an integral part of the experience. Day and evening cruises, 5 hours, $140/adult and $100/child; meal included. 09 359 5987 or 0800 395 673, info@explorenz.co.nz, www.explorenz.co.nz.

Little Barrier Island: a full list of DoC accredited supervisors or guides is supplied by DoC once a permit to visit Little Barrier has been approved. Permits for Little Barrier Island cost $25, contact DoC, P.O. Box 474, Warkworth, 09 425 7812. Allow 2–3 weeks for processing. Given the high costs of water-taxi charter to the island (at least $400), travel in a group is more cost-effective. The maximum number of visitors allowed is 20 per day, and you must clean boots and clothing and check packs. Gear is inspected by a DoC officer at the point of departure.

Recommended reading

Little Barrier Island, Ronald Cometti. Auckland: Reed, 1986.

6

Miranda

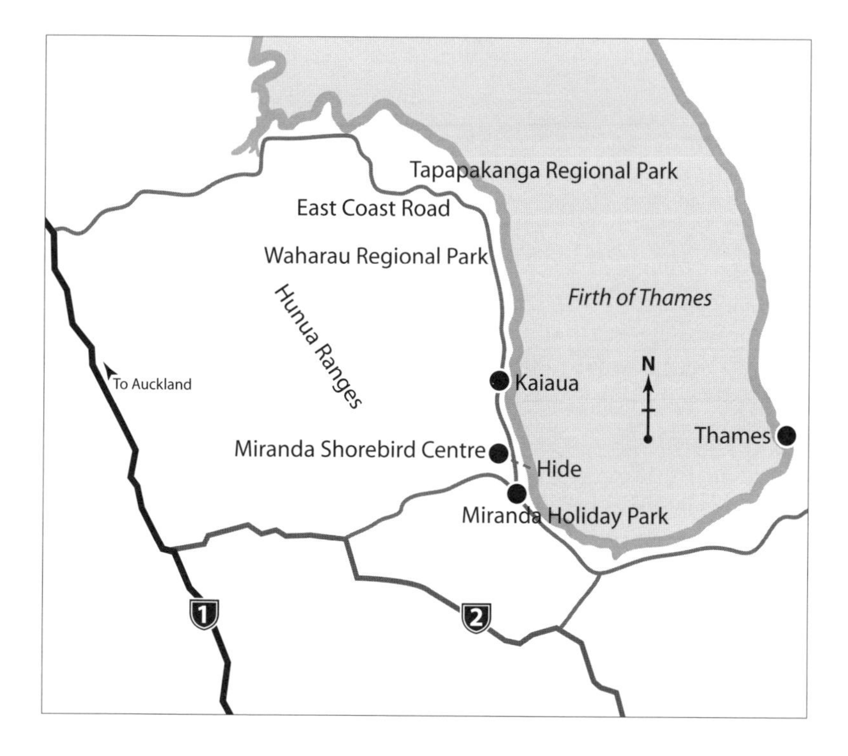

Where Firth of Thames, just over 1 hour's drive south-east of Auckland.

What's special Ramsar-gazetted wetland and a major site on the network of routes flown by several million birds twice every year as they migrate across the world. Intertidal mudflats and shell-bank roosts attract tens of thousands of migratory waders. Easily accessible.

Birds to look for Wrybill/ngutuparore (year-round, mostly late December–July) and other New Zealand migrants: South Island pied oystercatcher/tōrea, banded dotterel/tuturiwhatu and black-billed gull/tarāpunga. Bar-tailed godwit/kūaka, lesser knot/huahou, smaller numbers of turnstone, sharp-tailed sandpiper and red-necked stint plus other Arctic migrants, including potential rarities (summer). Pied stilt/poaka and New Zealand dotterel/tuturiwhatu (year-round).

Birdwatching options Self-guided walks, watching from roadside sites and a hide. Up-to-date information on recent sightings is available at Miranda Shorebird Centre.

Top spots

- Hide Trail
- Taramaire Wildlife Refuge.

When Year-round. September to late March for Arctic migrants; late December to July for South Island migrants. Some migrants stay over.

Background

Some 132 species, 43 of them waders, have been recorded here, including several thousand bar-tailed godwit, lesser knot and other migrants from Siberia and Alaska.

Miranda has 8500 ha of intertidal mudflats where the birds feed on the abundant shellfish, worms, crabs and shrimps, and adjacent shell banks where they can safely roost at high tide. Successive shell banks are laid on mud and fine sediment that has built up over the last 4500 years – and is still building rapidly. During mid- to low tides the most recent ridge can be seen out in the bay, already occupied by roosting birds.

Miranda is one of the most accessible sites in New Zealand for observing waders, in particular wrybill. Each year over 2000 wrybill, about 40 per cent of the population, fly here from their breeding grounds in the braided river beds of Canterbury. Some stay throughout the year. The only bird in the world with a bill that curves to the side, the wrybill is classified by the IUCN as a vulnerable species, and is probably the star attraction at Miranda.

Other New Zealand migrants seen here are South Island pied oystercatcher, banded dotterel and black-billed gull.

Around 6000 bar-tailed godwit and 5000 lesser knot arrive each spring after their 8– to 10-day flight (direct for the godwits) of 10,000–15,000 km. Smaller numbers of turnstone, sharp-tailed sandpiper, red-necked stint and other Arctic waders travel south. Rarities that have turned up at Miranda include ruff and red-necked phalarope. Each year up to 400 Arctic waders, believed to be mostly immature non-breeders, stay through winter.

Miranda and the Firth of Thames is one of the end points of the East Asian–Australasian flyway, the network of routes flown by migrating birds between the northern and southern hemispheres. The Miranda Naturalists' Trust, which operates the Miranda Shorebird Centre, is part of a co-operative international programme to conserve migratory birds by recognising and managing a network of internationally important sites.

Birders visiting Miranda are advised to call at the Centre for migration news, daily tide times, recent sightings, interesting visual displays and advice on the best watching spots. At busy times, volunteers from the Trust are likely to be out at the popular viewing sites, helping birders and safeguarding the birds.

Staff at the Centre encourage people to stay 2–3 hours either side of high tide, as on a rising tide there is a lot of activity and observers can see where the birds are going to go. While low-tide viewing is possible with a telescope, high tide is far better. The Centre also holds special events and open days with guided walks and guest speakers, for example to welcome the birds in September and farewell them at the end of summer.

Many birds breed at Miranda and are present throughout the year. The Firth of Thames is one of the major sites in New Zealand for pied stilt, which number from around 700 during summer to over 4000 in winter. New Zealand dotterel are present in small numbers. Other residents include Caspian tern/taranui, variable oystercatcher/tōrea, white-fronted tern/tara-iti, kingfisher/kōtare, gulls, herons and shags. Mangroves are expanding their range in the Firth of Thames, providing more habitat for banded rail, white-faced heron and pied shag/kāruhiruhi.

Other roosting sites around the Firth of Thames are on the eastern shore at the mouth of the Waihou River and at Tararu, north of Thames.

Best birding areas

> Hide Trail, Ponds and Robert Findlay Wildlife Reserve

A hide overlooks the high-tide roosts on shell banks close to the Miranda Shorebird Centre. There are two options to reach the hide: walk the Hide Trail (50 minutes return), or drive 2 km eastwards from the Centre to the signposted Robert Findlay Wildlife Reserve then walk 150 m across a paddock. The Hide Trail crosses the road from the Centre then passes through open pasture, salt-marsh vegetation and young mangrove forest. Look for banded rail/moho-pererū in the mangroves (year-round) and for skylark, greenfinch and yellowhammer on the farm paddocks. Shortly after the first of two stiles the track meets a roadway and veers left then follows the coast, beside mangroves, to the hide. Be warned: the flimsy-looking fence is likely to be electrified.

Waharau and Tāpapakanga Regional Parks

These two regional parks are worth exploring while in the Miranda region.

Overlooking the western shore of the Firth of Thames are the Hunua Ranges, the largest single area of forest in the Auckland region and home to a small kōkako population. Despite significant logging activity last century the forest contains a rich diversity of mature and regenerating kauri, podocarp and beech forests.

At the north-eastern end of the ranges, Waharau Regional Park climbs from the coast to the Hunua ridge tops, where it meets with Hunua Ranges Regional Park. Waharau protects a diverse altitudinal variety of forests, home to New Zealand pigeon/kererū, tomtit/miromiro, fantail/pīwakawaka, tūī and (increasingly since pest control has been undertaken in the park) bellbird/korimako.

From the road, access crosses the Robert Findlay Wildlife Reserve, open pasture that is QEII National Trust-covenanted land and named for the landowner who has allowed people right of entry to these high-tide roosts since 1869. It's about 5 minutes' walk to the hide, past ponds on the left. Wrybill can usually be seen on these ponds at high tide; other birds here are pied stilt, bar-tailed godwit, lesser knot and occasionally sharp-tailed sandpiper.

▷ Taramaire Wildlife Refuge

This is the other major high-tide roost and can be seen from the roadside 1.5 km north of the Miranda Shorebird Centre. There are several obvious stopping spots north of Taramaire Creek with unimpeded views out to the shell banks.

Just further north is Tāpapakanga Regional Park, a delightful mixture of pōhutukawa-lined beach, open farmland and coastal forest that overlooks the entrance to the Firth of Thames. Resident coastal species here include variable oystercatcher/tōrea, pied shag/kāruhiruhi, black and little shag/kōau, white-faced heron, black-backed gull/karoro and red-billed gull/tarāpunga. Inland, expect to see kingfisher/kōtare, paradise shelduck/pūtangitangi, pūkeko, New Zealand wood pigeon, fantail, grey warbler/riroriro, tūī and introduced pheasant.

Tāpapakanga is located on Deery Road, 500 m from East Coast Road as it approaches the Firth of Thames coast. Waharau is 9 km further south on East Coast Road. Both parks have excellent facilities, including tracks, toilets, picnic and camping areas. 09 366 2000 or www.arc.govt.nz.

Getting there There is no public transport to Miranda. Twice daily Auckland-to-Thames bus services stop at Waitakaruru, 12 km away on SH2, but there is no public transport from there to Miranda.

Self-driving is the best option. Miranda is just over an hour's drive from the centre of Auckland. The simplest route is to drive south from Auckland via SH1 to Pokeno, then turn left off the motorway onto SH2. Look for the Miranda turn-off, signposted on the left, then follow the signs for 20 km to Miranda.

A slower but arguably more scenic route passes through farmland, native forest, regional parks and around the Firth of Thames coast. Follow the motorway south from Auckland, take the Red Hill turn-off and follow the Pacific Coast Highway signs through Clevedon to Kawakawa Bay, then over a small hill to East Coast Road on the Firth of Thames coastline.

Whangamarino Wetlands

Birding access isn't particularly good at these wetlands but they are recognised by Ramsar as internationally important, and as such warrant a mention.

They form part of the extensive freshwater wetlands that were once widespread across the lower Waikato and Hauraki Plains, derived from ash and pumice deposits carried by the Waikato River from the Taupo volcanic zone.

Some 56 bird species have been recorded in the Whangamarino, and up to 50,000 waterfowl live in or visit the 6000 ha of peat bog, swampland, open water, sedgelands and shrub lands of mānuka and cabbage tree.

All this is favoured habitat for fernbird/mātātā, spotless crake/pūwheto and marsh crake, banded rail/moho-pererū and Australasian

(Before turning inland it's worth a look here for New Zealand dotterel in the bay, and for weka along the road beyond the boat launching spot.) Follow the coast through the tiny Kaiaua township to the Shorebird Centre, 11 km from Kaiaua. En route you pass through gravel pits and ponds; check the inland pond for waterbirds and shags.

Getting around Walking, biking or self-driving.

Accommodation The Miranda Shorebird Centre has self-contained units and three bunkroom dormitories with shared kitchen and lounge. Bookings are advisable, especially during summer weekends and public holidays. Costs are $20/adult for a bunk bed and $60–70/night for a self-contained unit (two people, extra for further people).

Miranda Holiday Park, a Qualmark five-star park with camping and campervan sites, motels and mineral springs, is 5 km from the Centre.

bittern/matuku. Other birds present include pied stilt/poaka, kingfisher/kōtare, pūkeko, white-faced heron, black swan and several duck and shag species.

Ecology of the wetlands has suffered considerably from drainage for farm development, introduced weeds and noxious fish. Nevertheless concerted efforts by DoC, Environment Waikato and the National Wetland Trust are making some inroads towards restoration.

While access is difficult, driving 11 km east along Island Block Road (signposted off SH1 motorway just south of Mercer) then 4 km south on Falls Road provides some good views and leads to a high point overlooking the wetland. This is part of a wetlands trail being developed by the National Wetland Trust.

For more information visit www.wetlandtrust.org.nz.

Kaiaua township has a hotel and holiday park, Waharau and Tāpapakanga regional parks have camping areas 10–15 minutes' drive from the Centre and there are several bed-and-breakfasts in the locality.

Facilities The Miranda Shorebird Centre has excellent visual displays, a display of daily tide times and recent sightings, a retail shop (with an excellent selection of New Zealand natural history books) and toilets. Open 9 am to 5 pm (approx).

At Kaiaua, 11 km from the Centre, takeaways and meals are available at the Bay View Hotel, and Kaiaua Fisheries restaurant and takeaways is renowned for fresh, locally caught fish.

The Miranda Hot Springs complex offers a large outdoor hot mineral pool, private spas and sauna, plus shop and cafe.

Information Miranda Shorebird Centre: information, visual displays, shorebird identification, accommodation, education programmes, public talks, training courses and workshops. Owned and operated by the Miranda Naturalists' Trust. Trust members receive a quarterly magazine, accommodation discounts and opportunities to take part in Trust activities.

09 232 2781, shorebird@farmside.co.nz,
www.miranda-shorebird.org.nz.

Recommended reading

Shorebird Migration to and from Miranda, brochure produced by the Miranda Naturalists' Trust.

7

Ōhiwa Harbour

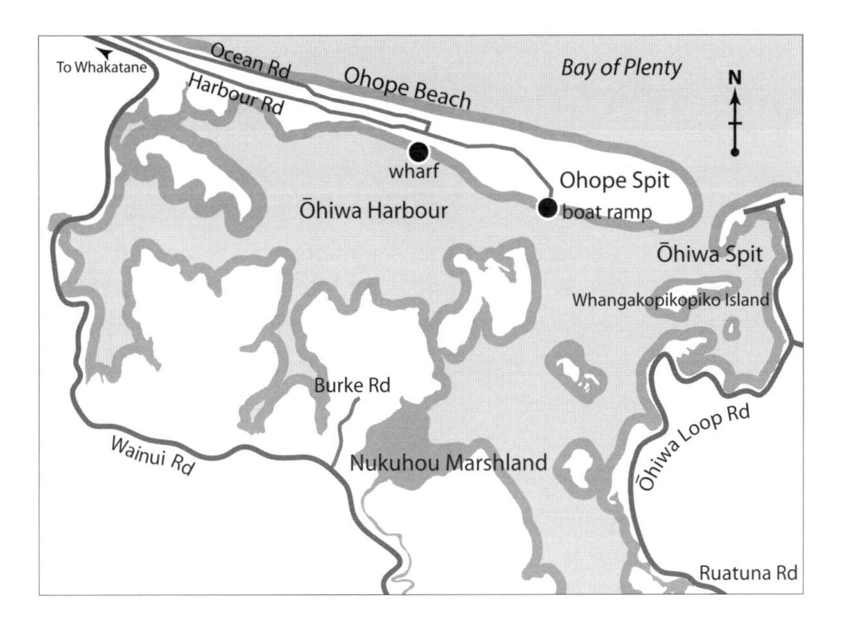

Where Bay of Plenty, eastern coast of the North Island.

What's special Sheltered harbour with sandspits, islands, tidal flats and New Zealand's southernmost mangrove forest, providing habitat for Arctic and New Zealand migratory waders, marsh birds and shorebirds. More than 60 species have been recorded here.

Key species Bar-tailed godwit/kūaka, Pacific golden plover, South Island pied oystercatcher/tōrea, black-billed gull/tarāpunga, New Zealand dotterel/tuturiwhatu, banded dotterel/tuturiwhatu, fernbird/mātātā, pied stilt/poaka, variable oystercatcher/tōrea, white-fronted tern/tara, pūkeko, paradise shelduck/pūtangitangi, Caspian tern/taranui, red-billed gull/tarāpunga, spur-winged plover, white-faced heron.

Birdwatching options Self-guided walks, kayaking, driving around harbour.

Top spots

- Ōhiwa Spit at high tide
- Around harbour margins at low tide
- Nukuhou marshland (dawn or dusk)
- Whangakopikopiko (Tern) Island (viewing from end of Ōhiwa Spit or by kayak – landings by permit only)
- Ohope Spit.

When to go Year-round for resident species, September to late March for Arctic migrants, late December to July for South Island migrants (though some stay over). The annual 'Birds-a-Plenty' Festival welcomes the birds in early October.

Background

Heading to the beaches, harbours and fishing spots is a summer tradition along the Bay of Plenty coast, not just for humans. Each year, three to four thousand Arctic waders make the journey to the 3000-ha Ōhiwa Harbour.

Around 70 per cent of the harbour is exposed at low tide, creating vast sand banks, shellfish beds, mudflats and sea grass (*Zostera*) beds – feeding grounds for both migrant and resident birds. Sandspits and islets provide high-tide roosts and nesting grounds. Marshlands and mangroves around the inland extents of the 86-km shoreline provide habitat for rails, herons, waterfowl and other marshland birds. Bird numbers range from about 1200 in winter to 5200 in summer. About a dozen species are annual visitors, including up to 4000 godwit (of which about 300 overwinter here).

Up to 15 pairs of New Zealand dotterel live on the sandspits and islands. This bird is particularly vulnerable for its habit of nesting in shallow scrapes in the sand, just above the high-tide mark. Here it is at risk from a multitude of dangers including animals, storms and spring tides and humans riding horses or driving off-road vehicles on the beach.

South Island migrants include royal spoonbill/kōtuku-ngutupapa and South Island pied oystercatcher, while black-billed gull occasionally breed on small islands and shell banks in the harbour.

Despite hundreds of years of human occupation and its consequent impact, Ōhiwa is much valued for its natural ecology, with significant areas still covered in natural vegetation.

Getting out onto the water is the best way to view the birds at high tide, though you will need to provide or hire your own boat or kayak as there is no commercial bird-viewing operator. There are also several points where good land-based viewing is possible.

Best birding areas

▷ Ōhiwa Spit

Located on the eastern edge of the harbour, this is a high-tide roost for bar-tailed godwit and other waders, and a nesting site for New Zealand dotterel, white-fronted tern and variable oystercatcher.

The Spit is 40 minutes' drive from Whakatane and 15 minutes' drive from Opotiki. From SH2 turn onto Ruatuna or Ōhiwa Road, or Ōhiwa Beach Road. These lead to Ōhiwa Harbour Road, which ends by the Spit 200 metres beyond the Ōhiwa Family Holiday Park. From the road end follow the obvious track that starts beside an information sign. In summer, take care not to disturb nesting birds. This is also a good spot for scanning the mudflats at low tide for waders.

▷ Nukuhou Marshland

Fernbird live in marsh areas all around the harbour and around 60–80 are concentrated in Nukuhou Marshland, on the harbour's southern coastline. Park at the junction of Wainui and Burke Roads, walk a few metres up to the lookout (enjoy the bird sculptures) and follow a 50-m track down to a small terrace and boardwalk at the edge of the wetland. Listen for the bird's shy chirping, especially in the breeding season from late winter to summer. Dawn and dusk are the best times.

Local resident Stuart Slade, a member of the Nukuhou Saltmarsh Care Group that has been carrying out pest control work in the marsh, is happy to guide and chat about the local birdlife. He can be found just along the road from the lookout, at his historic Cheddar Valley Pottery (also worth a visit). 07 312 4583 or s.m.slade@xtra.co.nz.

▷ Harbour margins

At mid- to low tide, driving around the margins from Ohope Beach along Wainui Road to SH2, and on Ruatuna Road to Ōhiwa Harbour Road along the harbour's eastern shoreline, can reward with sightings of waders and resident birds such as pied stilt, paradise shelduck, variable oystercatcher and kingfisher/kōtare. Several roadside points give good views across the tidal flats or into the salt marshes and mangroves. The inlets closer to Ohope are generally better for mid- to low-tide feeding.

Suggested spots include the inlet on Burma Road (banded rail/moho-pererū are often present, though shy; best times are mornings and evenings) and Waiotane Stream and Tuanui Stream bridges. The inlet beside Ruatuna Road turn-off from SH2, opposite the boat ramp, is worth a look for fernbird, banded rail and possibly spotless crake/pūweto, also pūkeko, Caspian tern/taranui, spur-winged plover and white-faced heron. Continuing along Ruatuna Road into Ōhiwa Loop Road, a wetland cut off from the harbour by the road is also a possible spot for pūkeko and banded rail. The Ohope Oyster Farm is well worth a look for several species.

▷ Whangakopikopiko Island (locally known as Tern Island)

Because of its importance as a breeding site, this small sand island near the eastern edge of the harbour is a DoC Wildlife Refuge with restricted public access. For its size, 11 ha, it supports a significant number of species.

Nesting birds include New Zealand dotterel (during breeding, from mid-October to February, these birds are particularly vulnerable), variable oystercatcher, white-fronted tern and black-billed gull. Viewing with binoculars is worthwhile from the end of Ōhiwa Spit, although the best viewing is by kayak, one hour either side of high tide.

Meg and Mike Collins are the care group coordinators for the Ohiwa Reserves, which include Ohope Spit, Whangakopikopiko Island and Ohiwa Domain. They are happy to guide keen birders visiting these spots. Phone 07 315 4981, email pepito@orcon.net.nz.

The island is also an important high-tide roost. Exactly where the birds roost depends on the tides and wind direction. Depending on the season, birds likely to be visible include bar-tailed godwit, Caspian tern, white-fronted tern, black-billed gull, variable oystercatcher and pied shag.

⊳ Ohope Spit

This spit is 11 km long and largely covered with holiday homes. There is easy access to both the ocean beach and harbour from Ocean and Harbour Roads, which run parallel along the middle of the spit. On the ocean side, Ohope Beach is worth a jaunt for viewing black-backed and red-billed gulls, white-fronted tern and variable oystercatcher. Australasian gannets from a colony on the active volcano of White Island (Whakaari), 50 km offshore, can often be observed diving for fish close to the beach.

At the eastern tip of the Spit a wildlife refuge affords some protection for birds. Some Arctic waders venture to this side of the harbour, and New Zealand dotterel now nest on the Spit.

On the harbour side, walking the shoreline between Ohope Wharf and the spit, there's a good chance of spotting little black, little, black and pied shag/kāruhiruhi and occasionally spotted shag/pārekareka. Introduced pheasant and Californian quail live in the tussocks here.

Getting there Whakatane, the nearest major town, is 90 km from Rotorua and 97 km from Tauranga, and has an airport with daily services on the national air network. From Whakatane it is 7 km by road to Ohope Beach, the township at the western end of Ōhiwa Harbour. Opotiki, 16 km from Ōhiwa Spit, is the nearest town on the eastern side of the harbour. Intercity coaches service Whakatane and Opotiki daily, and local Bayline Coaches runs services between the towns several days a week.

Getting around Travel by private vehicle is best. While Ōhiwa Harbour is a significant birding area, tourism services seem more focused on water sports and fishing. Kayaks can be hired at Ohope Beach and Ōhiwa Bay Family Holiday Park, and are available from some accommodation places.

Accommodation Motels, holiday parks with campervan sites, bed-and-breakfasts and self-contained apartments are available at Ohope Beach, Ōhiwa, Opotiki and Whakatane. If visiting in summer, book well ahead, especially during the peak holiday season from Christmas to the end of January. Fantail Cottage, overlooking Ōhiwa Harbour, is hosted by avid local birders, Meg and Mike Collins, 07 315 4981.

Facilities Whakatane has cafes, restaurants, banks, ATMs, shops, photography specialists, supermarkets, rental vehicle and taxi companies. Ohope Beach has a store and cafes. A restaurant and takeaway bar at Ohope Wharf has a fine outlook across the harbour. Opotiki has cafes, restaurants, banks, ATMs, shops and a supermarket.

Information

Whakatane Visitor Information Centre, cnr Quay Street and Kakahoroa Drive, freephone 0800 942 528, www.whakatane.com.

Ohope Visitor Information Centre, Portside Store, 07 312 4707.

Opotiki Information Centre, cnr St John and Elliot Streets, 07 315 3030, infocentre@odc.govt.nz, www.opotikinz.com.

8

Kiwi Encounter

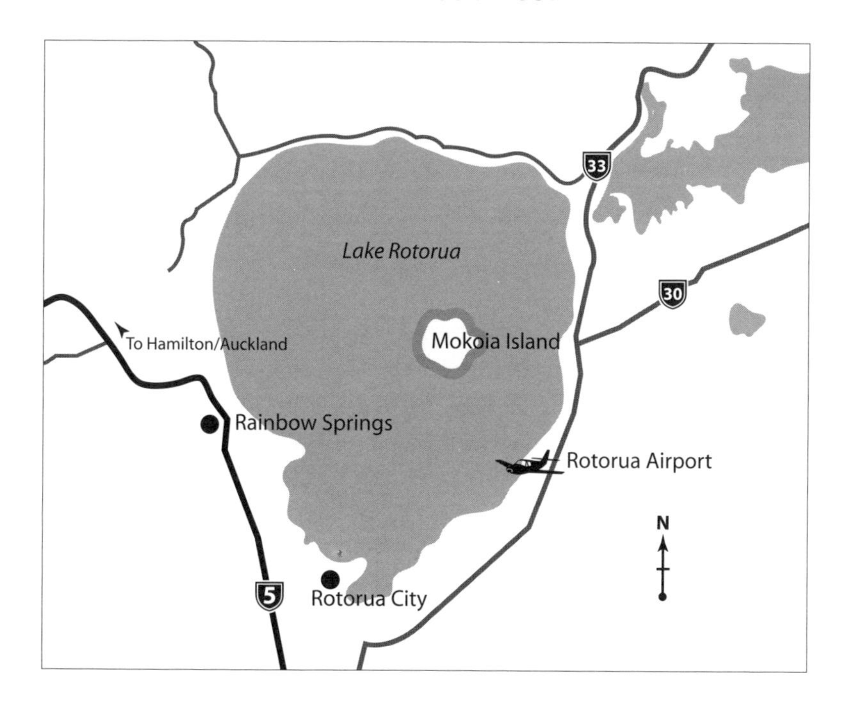

Where Rainbow Springs Kiwi Wildlife Park, Rotorua.

What's special Opportunity to visit a working kiwi hatchery and nursery.

Birds to look for Brown kiwi.

Birdwatching options Daily guided tours looking at and learning about all aspects of kiwi egg incubation, hatching and chick raising.

How long to go Tours last 45 minutes.

When to go Year-round, but best September–April, when chicks are hatching.

Background

Kiwi Encounter has been applauded for its groundbreaking work in hatching and raising kiwi chicks for release back into the wild.

More than 90 per cent of kiwi hatched in the wild do not survive. Most are killed by stoats or other mustelids, despite the intensive predator control work being undertaken in conservation areas throughout New Zealand. These are depressing figures for a species that is not only a national icon, but a bird of extraordinary character, distinction and biological peculiarity.

Enter BNZ Save the Kiwi Trust, a project whereby kiwi eggs are taken from nests in the wild, incubated, hatched and the chicks raised in captivity for around four months, then released once they are big and strong enough to defend themselves. Some chicks are released earlier into fenced reserves such as at Cape Kidnappers (in Hawke's Bay) and Bushy Park (near Wanganui), or onto island reserves, where they are safe from predators.

Operation Nest Egg is just one aspect of the nationwide Kiwi Recovery Programme currently undertaken jointly by the Department of Conservation, Bank of New Zealand Save the Kiwi Trust, community groups and private organisations.

Handling eggs and raising chicks is tricky, and the work carried out by the dedicated staff at Kiwi Encounter has resulted in significant improvement in both the number of chicks hatched and their survival rates.

It started in 1995, when DoC staff brought a cracked egg found in a central North Island forest to Rainbow Springs Kiwi Wildlife Park, which had long been known for its expertise in handling injured wildlife. When that rescue mission was successful, DoC delivered more eggs for incubation. Each year, as techniques improved, Rainbow Springs became more crowded with kiwi chicks for release back into the wild.

Then, in 2004 management at Rainbow Springs elected to build a new dedicated Kiwi Encounter facility and continue funding and developing the hatchery and nursery programme. In the 2009 season, 14 years after successfully hatching its first kiwi egg, the team at Kiwi Encounter hatched, raised and returned 138 chicks to their home forests, and the numbers keep on improving. All entry fees are donated to the National Kiwi Trust that operates Kiwi Encounter.

Getting there Rotorua is a busy tourist destination served by several daily Air New Zealand flights within New Zealand and twice weekly from Sydney, and daily bus services from all major North Island cities.

Rainbow Springs Kiwi Wildlife Park is 6 km north of downtown Rotorua, on SH5. A shuttle bus to the park departs the Rotorua i-SITE Visitor Centre every hour, on the hour.

Getting around Kiwi Encounter tours run every day of the year, every hour from 10 am to 4 pm. Reservations are essential.

Visitors are guided behind dark and sound-proofed windows through the husbandry areas, the incubation room, and the nursery. Some visitors have been lucky enough to witness a chick hatching.

Rainbow Springs Kiwi Wildlife Park also has aviaries with kea, kākā and Antipodes Island parakeet, plus tuatara, skinks and geckos – and the park is involved in national breeding and protection programmes.

Accommodation and facilities Rotorua is one of New Zealand's major tourist centres and has a full range of accommodation, shops, restaurants and other facilities. At Rainbow Springs there is a cafe and shop.

Information

Rotorua i-SITE Visitor Centre, 1167 Fenton Street, 07 348 5179, rotorua@i-SITE.org, www.rotoruanz.co.nz.

Licensed guiding company

Kiwi Encounter, Rainbow Springs, Fairy Springs Road, Rotorua. Tours cost $27.50/adult, $17.50/child, family tickets available.
07 350 0440, freephone 0800 724 626, info@kiwiencounter.co.nz, www.kiwiencounter.co.nz.

9
Mokoia Island

Where Rotorua (*see* map page 75)

What's special A rodent-free, forest-covered island on Lake Rotorua, supporting several endangered species. A particularly good spot to observe saddleback/tīeke.

Birds to look for Saddleback/tīeke, robin/toutouwai, weka, tūī, kōkako. Brown kiwi are also present, though unlikely to be seen or heard during daytime tours.

Birdwatching options Guided walk, self-guided walk.

Top spots All parts of the island are good for viewing birds, even just sitting at the landing.

When to go Year-round.

Background

Mokoia Island is highly regarded today for its conservation values. The island also has great historical significance to the tribe Te Arawa, and is central to the Māori legend of Hinemoa and Tutanekai.

Te Arawa hapū (sub-tribes) lived on Mokoia for hundreds of years, and much of the island was cleared and terraced for crops. European settlers later introduced goats, sheep, cattle, pigs, horses, cats and rats – though fortunately neither possums nor stoats found their way to Mokoia.

Today, the island is privately owned and managed as a wildlife refuge by the Mokoia Island Trust, which represents four sub-tribal owner groups. Natural re-growth of vegetation, which began in the 1960s, was given a major boost in more recent years by clearing the island of all pests.

Species since released on the island include saddleback (from Tiritiri Matangi Island), stitchbird/hihi (from Little Barrier Island), robin (from the nearby Mamaku Ranges), brown kiwi (from Whirinaki Forest Park and Ohope Scenic Reserve) and weka (from the Gisborne region). The stitchbird were subsequently moved to Kapiti Island, while saddleback and robin have flourished so greatly that a surplus has been transferred to other areas. Seven male kōkako were transferred here from Tiritiri Matangi Island and are regularly seen and heard. Meanwhile, the island's resident populations of tūī, grey warbler/riroriro and fantail/pīwakawaka have flourished.

Bird Spa

The Rotorua Lakes region, with its geothermal heating, provides added niches for wildlife. The most significant of these is Sulphur Point, on the edge of Rotorua city, where the water is warm, milky, sulphurous and shallow, and attracts so many birds it has been designated a wildlife refuge. Over 60 bird species have been recorded here, including 45 native species. Threatened New Zealand dabchick/weiweia, plus banded dotterel/tuturiwhatu, Caspian tern/taranui, New Zealand scaup, pied stilt/poaka, spur-winged plover, several species of shag, paradise shelduck/pūtangitangi and other duck species are generally present. A small silica inlet at Sulphur Point provides habitat for one of the few North Island colonies of black-billed gull/tarāpunga: about 60 pairs breed here each year.

A walkway to Sulphur Point leads eastwards along the Rotorua shoreline from Lakefront Reserve. Views of the Government Gardens, steaming thermal vents around the lake shore, and orange/red tinged silica flats make a most unusual setting for birdwatching.

Other species present, though less likely to be seen, include bellbird/korimako, tomtit/miromiro and shining cuckoo/pīpīwharauroa (in spring and summer). Black and little shag/kōau are often seen around the shoreline, while black swan, Canada goose and mallard nest on the foreshore.

DoC, in a close working partnership with the Trust, has been largely responsible for the restoration of Mokoia, assisted by other groups including Conservation Corps, schools, universities, volunteer bird organisations and visiting enthusiasts. Day-to-day management is vested in Mokoia Island Wai Ora Experiences, which is the principal concessionaire. They operate tours to the island, which have a strong historic and Māori cultural focus. You will undoubtedly hear the famous story of forbidden lovers Hinemoa and Tutanekai. Pack a towel to dry your feet if you wish to soak them in Hinemoa's pool. Birding groups can make special arrangements in advance to stay longer on the island than the regular 3-hour tours.

Getting there Rotorua is a busy tourist destination served by several daily Air New Zealand flights within New Zealand and twice weekly from Sydney, and daily bus services from all major North Island cities.

Boat trips to Mokoia Island take 15–20 minutes. Mokoia Island Wai Ora Experiences are licensed to take tours to the island. Access by private boats is not permitted, to help prevent re-invasions of rats and mice.

Getting around There is a small network of tracks and visitors can take self-guided walks or join a guided tour.

Accommodation and facilities Rotorua is one of New Zealand's major tourist centres, with a full range of accommodation and facilities. On Mokoia Island there is a public shelter and toilets.

Information

Rotorua i-SITE Visitor Centre – 1167 Fenton Street, 07 348 5179, rotorua@i-SITE.org, www.rotoruanz.co.nz.

Licensed guiding companies

Mokoia Island Wai Ora Experiences offer two daily scheduled trips, leaving from the Rotorua lakeshore at 9.30 am and 2 pm, each lasting three hours. Pre-booking is advisable and tours are for a minimum of four people. Specialist birding groups can pre-arrange longer tours. Large groups of more than 50 can be accommodated on the paddle-wheeler the *Lakeland Queen*. Three-hour scheduled tours cost $69/adult, $30/child. Phone 07 345 7456, 021 741 786 or the *Lakeland Queen* ticket office (for all Mokoia Island tours) 0800 572 784, www.mokoiaisland.co.nz.

Recommended reading

Mokoia, A Brief History, Philip Andrews. Rotorua: Bibliophil, 1992.

Te Arawa, Don Stafford. Auckland: Reed Books, 2003.

10

Pureora Forest to Manganui o te Ao River

Where Central North Island.

What's special Three sites: Pureora Forest Park, with abundant forest birds in magnificent podocarp forests; Mapara Wildlife Reserve, location of a kōkako management programme; and the Manganui o te Ao River, a North Island stronghold for blue duck/whio. All are on comparatively remote country roads, but once there viewing the birds is remarkably easy.

Birds to look for Kākā, yellow-crowned parakeet/kākāriki, rifleman/tītīpounamu, North Island robin/toutouwai, New Zealand falcon/kārearea, kōkako, blue duck/whio.

Birdwatching options Self-guided walks and roadside watching.

Top spots

- Pureora Forest Park (Tōtara Walk and forest tower)
- Mapara Wildlife Reserve (loop walk)
- Manganui o te Ao (Ruatiti Domain and road bridge).

When to go Year-round. Early morning or twilight is best for kōkako and blue duck.

Background

This geographically rather spread-out chapter covers three distinctly different yet significant birding spots, well worth including in any self-drive birding itinerary through the central North Island. They are rather

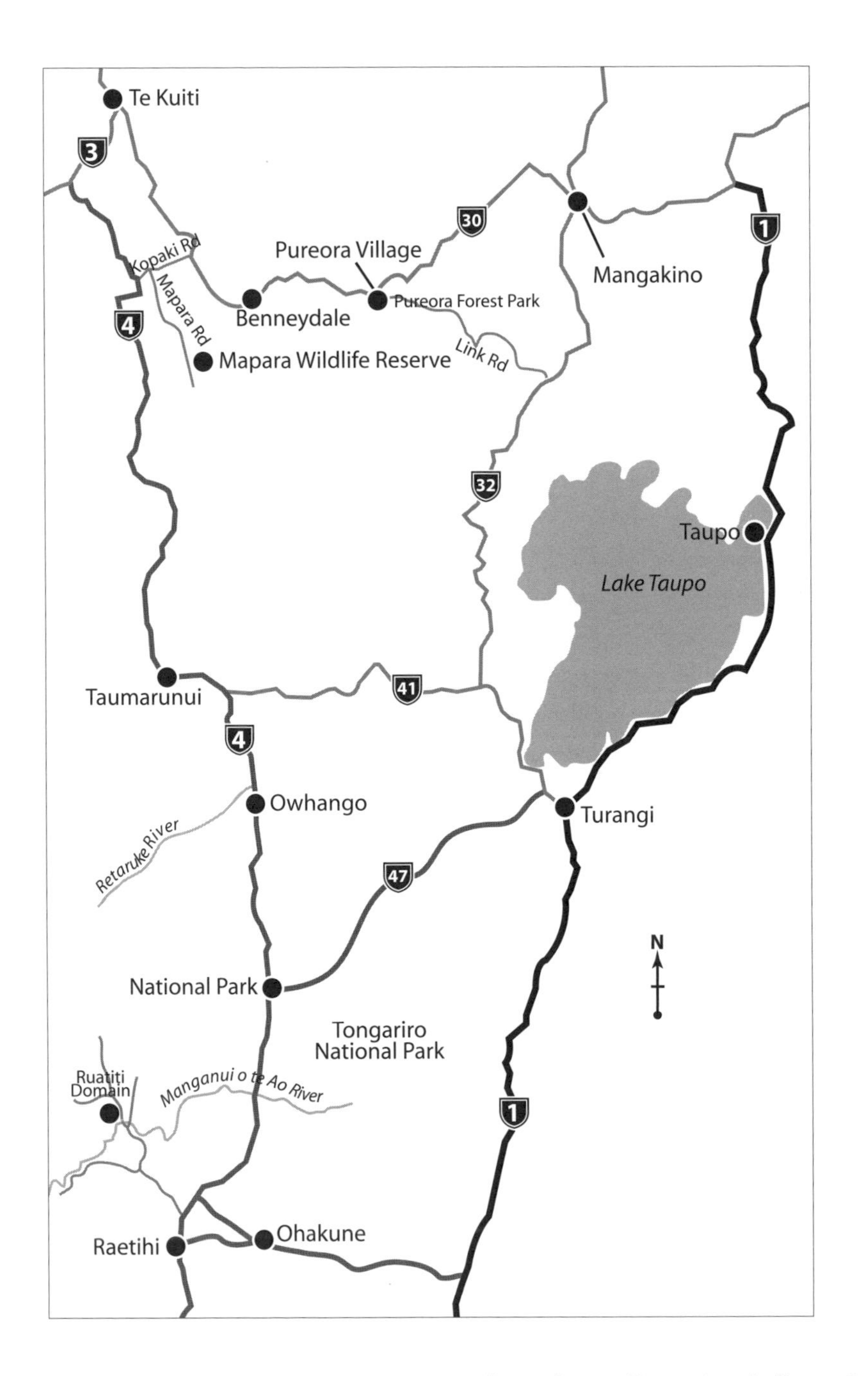
Te Kuiti
3
30
Pureora Village
Mangakino
1
Kopaki Rd
Mapara Rd
Benneydale
Pureora Forest Park
4
Link Rd
Mapara Wildlife Reserve
32
Taupo
Lake Taupo
Taumarunui
41
4
Owhango
Turangi
Retaruke River
47
N
National Park
Tongariro
National Park
Ruatiti
Domain
Manganui o te Ao River
1
Ohakune
Raetihi

off the beaten track, but the roads pass through some magnificent native forest and farmland, often with views of the Tongariro National Park volcanoes.

Pureora Forest Park is known for its magnificent tōtara, rimu, mataī and kahikatea trees. In 1978, Pureora was the scene of a major conservation victory when 'tree-sitters' thwarted logging and a government moratorium was imposed on clear-felling.

Such protection safeguarded habitats for populations of threatened species including kākā, yellow-crowned parakeet, brown kiwi, New Zealand falcon, New Zealand pigeon/kūku and whitehead/pōpokatea, along with other forest birds. Pureora is also one of the last North Island strongholds for the kōkako, with good numbers in remote northern areas of the park.

Close by, at Mapara Wildlife Reserve, a kōkako recovery management programme has been underway since 1992. Well over 100 kōkako now live here, and some have been relocated to islands and other reserves.

Another of New Zealand's most ancient and endangered endemics found near here is the blue duck, the only member of the genus *Hymenolaimus*. Once widespread, this distinctive slate-blue bird, with its exceptionally large webbed feet designed to manoeuvre in fast-moving water, is now generally restricted to remote headwater streams. In the North Island, small populations live in the eastern Raukumara, Kaweka and Ruahine Ranges and in Tongariro National Park.

The Manganui o te Ao River starts on the steep western slopes of Mt Ruapehu and flows into the Whanganui River. With 21 pairs of blue duck recorded along 10 km of river, it is the most reliable and easily accessible North Island site to see these iconic birds.

Best birding areas

▷ Puerora Forest Park (forest tower and Tōtara Walk)

Pureora village, a former logging village turned DoC base, has a visitor centre and accommodation cabins and is the best base for birding here.

There are several clearly signposted short walks close by, which are excellent for observing yellow-crowned parakeet and kākā, plus North Island robin, rifleman, whitehead, tūī, bellbird/korimako and New Zealand pigeon.

The 12-m-high forest tower (with enclosed ladder) was built to enable closer viewing of the birds in this tall forest. The tower is an easy 5-minute walk from the car park on Bismark Road, which turns off Pikiariki Road 3 km from Pureora Village. It does tend to be a bit hit-or-miss for bird sightings, but kākā and parakeet are sometimes present and one lone kōkako is sometimes seen. Probably more reliable is Tōtara Walk, a 30-minute wheelchair-accessible loop track opposite the Ngaherenga camping area, 100 m from the village.

The camping area and the village itself are also excellent spots, especially for kākā, often seen wheeling above the forest. New Zealand falcon are occasionally seen in the park.

▷ Mapara Wildlife Reserve (Loop Track)

Note that Mapara is essentially a conservation management facility in a remote rural area, with no particular focus on providing visitor facilities. There is one loop track through the reserve, at least an hour's walking time. It is steep, slippery when wet, and at times parts are likely to be overgrown with blackberry. Nevertheless the track is obvious (follow the orange markers) and if visiting just after dawn or in the late evening, you are almost guaranteed to hear the melodious, haunting chimes of the kōkako.

By walking slowly and staying alert, especially along the top ridge, there's every chance of spotting a bird running and hopping, as they do, through the branches of the trees or gliding across the valley. Other bird life flourishes in the reserve, notably tūī, bellbird, whitehead, New Zealand pigeon and the occasional North Island robin.

The reserve is located on Mapara Road (unsealed), off Kopaki Road which runs between SH30 and SH4, 26 km south of Te Kuiti and 56 km north of Taumarunui. After 3 km the reserve comes into view and after 5.5 km there is a car park, information panel and a small bridge marking the start of the loop track. This crosses the bridge, climbs an old vehicle track up the side of a small forested valley, then turns right into tall tawa forest and descends a steep ridge back to the vehicle track.

> Manganui o te Ao River (Ruatiti Bridge and Domain)

From SH4, 30 km south of National Park and 4 km north of Raetihi, Raetihi-Ohura Road (signposted to Ruatiti) turns west into the Manganui o te Ao Valley. The road descends steeply and negotiates several hairpin bends (keep left), through farmland and native forest, and meets the river 12 km from SH4. Along the way there are some good views down to potential blue duck territory in the river, but the best place to look is from the bridge, 15 km from SH4.

Directly across the bridge and signposted on the left is the unsealed road to Ruatiti Domain, a large riverside picnic and camping area. Follow this for 1 km and turn left very sharply, drive past a farmhouse, into the Domain and continue a few hundred metres to where you can walk alongside the river. With luck the distinctive whistling call of the male blue duck (hence the Māori name whio), will announce the bird's presence.

Other river access points cross private land and should not be used without permission. Several legal fishing accesses are shown on an info-map just inside the entrance to the Domain. Other river views are possible along Pukekaha Road, signposted off Raetihi-Ohura Road by a small bridge 12 km from SH4. Travel past the small Orautoha School about 7 km along Pukekaha Road, where there are occasional roadside views of the river, as far as Hoihenga Bridge, which crosses the Manganui o te Ao.

Remember that blue duck are most active at around dawn and dusk, reflecting the habits of the aquatic insects they feed on. During the day they hide. Other birds often seen here include New Zealand falcon, grey warbler/riroriro, tūī, New Zealand pigeon, long-tailed cuckoo/koekoeā and shining cuckoo/pīpīwharauroa (in summer), North Island robin and paradise shelduck/pūtangitangi.

Note: other easily accessible and very likely blue duck viewing spots in the central North Island are the angler pools on Tongariro River, close to Turangi township. Red Hut Pool is signposted beside SH1, 5 km south of the town. Park here and walk 2 minutes to the bridge, where birds are sometimes seen. Alternatively, cross the bridge and turn left onto the Tongariro River Walkway, which follows the true right, passing more angling pools along the way back to Turangi.

Getting there Self-driving or touring with a birding group is the only way to reach these places. Pureora Forest Park is to the west of Lake Taupo, an easy hour's drive from either Te Kuiti or Taupo. Pureora Village and the DoC Visitor Centre are located on Village Road, 4 km off SH30, 56 km from Te Kuiti and 27 km from Whakamaru.

Mapara Wildlife Reserve is located on Mapara Road (off Kopaki Road, which links SH30 and SH4), 26 km south of Te Kuiti.

Manganui o te Ao River is accessed via Raetihi-Ohura Road, which turns off SH4, 4 km north of Raetihi and 30 km south of National Park.

Getting around From Pureora Forest Park, via Mapara Wildife Reserve, to the Manganui o te Ao River is just over 180 km. Planning is required to be in place at optimal viewing times for the kōkako and blue duck.

Driving from Pureora to Mapara takes about 30 minutes. From Pureora Village follow SH30 towards Te Kuiti and after 26 km turn left onto Kopaki Road, then after 9 km turn left onto Mapara Road. To continue from here to the Manganui o te Ao River, turn left out of Mapara Road onto Kopaki Road, then left again onto SH4, which passes through Taumarunui and National Park townships. Raetihi–Ohura Road, which leads to the Manganui o te Ao River, is 30 km from National Park.

Accommodation DoC self-contained cabin and lodge accommodation (bookings required) and two self-registration camping areas are available at Pureora Forest Park. There is no accommodation at Mapara, although Pureora, Whakamaru (backpackers) and Te Kuiti (backpackers, motels and bed-and-breakfasts), are all within 30–45 minutes' drive.

Ruapehu District Council manages an informal camping area (with toilets and barbecues) at Ruatiti Domain beside the Manganui o te Ao River. The river is close to Tongariro National Park and there is a range of accommodation, from heritage hotel to backpackers, at Ohakune, National Park and Whakapapa, all within 30–45 minutes' drive. There are also roadside camping areas in the park.

Well worth considering is Blue Duck Lodge, at Whakahoro on the Retaruke River, another blue duck habitat. Whakahoro is reached from SH4, turning onto Oio Road near Ōwhango. The lodge owners run a huge conservation project that involves predator trapping throughout 2050 ha of private land. This includes kiwi habitat and headwater streams feeding the Retaruke River. To help with this they run an international volunteer programme. Blue duck can be observed while kayaking on the Retaruke. www.blueducklodge.co.nz.

Facilities The major towns in the region are Te Kuiti, Taumarunui and Ohakune. These have shopping, supermarkets, banks, ATMs and fuel. Fuel is also available at National Park village on SH4, and Bennydale and Whakamaru, on SH30, 15 minutes' from Pureora.

Information

Pureora DoC Visitor Centre: 07 878 1080, pureorafc@doc.govt.nz.

Central North Island Blue Duck Trust: aims to enhance, protect and promote blue duck populations and habitat, www.genesisenergy.co.nz/genesis/our-environment/environmental-initiatives/en/blue-duck.cfm.

Recommended reading

Whio, Saving New Zealand's Blue Duck, David Young. Nelson: Craig Potton Publishing, 2006.

11

Boundary Stream

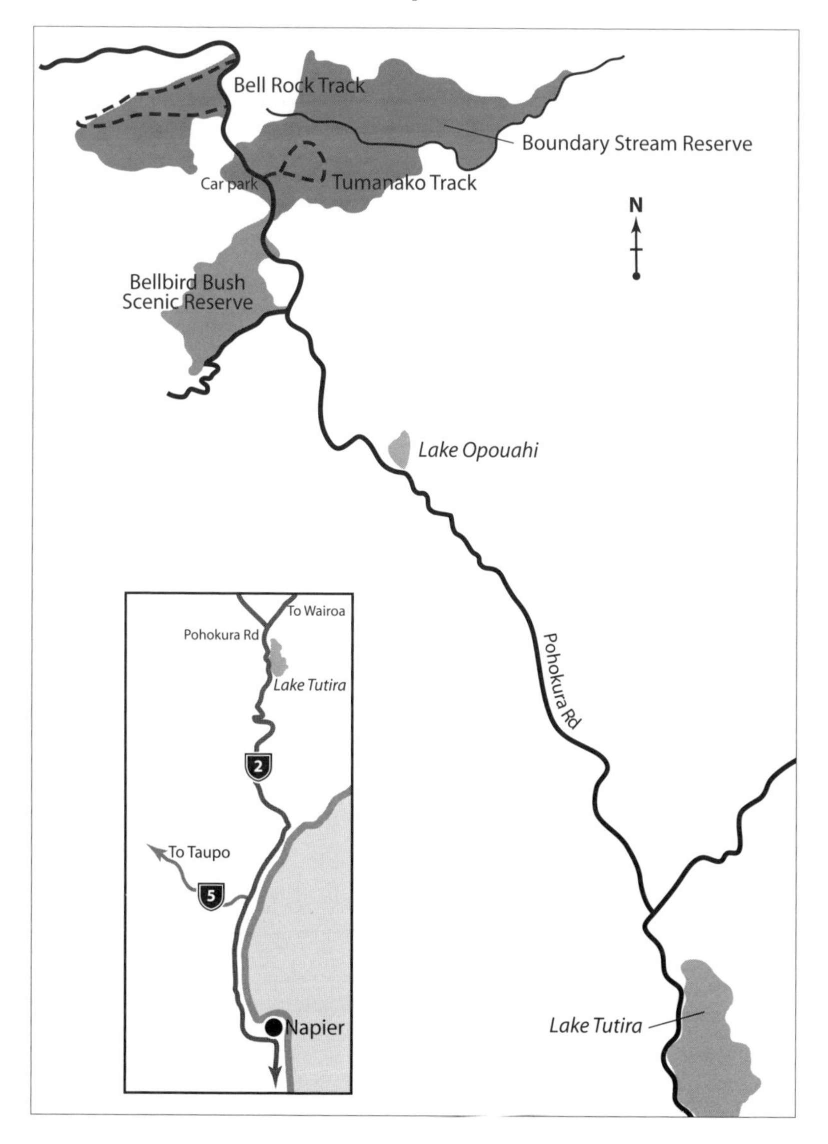

Where Northern Hawke's Bay, east coast of the North Island, an hour's drive north of Napier.

What's special Forested 'mainland island' reserve. Prolific birdlife and birdsong.

Birds to look for Kōkako, robin/toutouwai, tūī, bellbird/korimako, New Zealand pigeon/kererū, whitehead/pōpokatea, grey warbler/riroriro, tomtit/miromiro, rifleman/tītipounamu, New Zealand falcon/kārearea, shining cuckoo/pīpīwharauroa and long-tailed cuckoo/koekoeā (spring and summer). Brown kiwi are here but nocturnal and unlikely to be seen.

Birdwatching options Self-guided walks, guided walks.

Top spots

- Tumanako Loop Track (1 hour) and adjoining Kāmahi Loop Track (2 hours)
- Bell Rock Track.
- Lake Opouahi Reserve.

How long to go Half to one day (including time driving from Napier). In a 2-day visit to Hawke's Bay, you can visit Boundary Stream (and Lake Tūtira and Ahuriri Estuary en route) and Cape Kidnappers, as well as have time for other tourist activities.

When to go Year-round (occasionally snow falls in winter.) The birds are particularly active in early spring and autumn.

Background

It's a comparatively long drive to Boundary Stream from Napier, the nearest city, but the birdsong as you step from the car is probably as good as you will hear anywhere in New Zealand.

Generally, the songs of the honeyeaters, tūī and bellbird, dominate above the constant chatter of whitehead, grey warbler, tomtit, fantail and rifleman, especially in spring and summer when nectar-bearing trees are flowering. The beating wings of a pigeon might contrast with the call of a hunting falcon, or the occasional spine-tingling sound of a kōkako.

Boundary Stream, an 800-ha reserve surrounded by steep farm country, is one of New Zealand's 'mainland islands'. As conservation scientists perfected island restoration techniques their attention turned to the mainland, where the challenges were different. Here, by selecting areas with 'defendable' boundaries, for example waterways, mountain tops or farmland, several 'mainland islands' have been successfully cleared of browsing and predatory pests. As with offshore islands, the forests have quickly recovered, bird numbers increased and the choice of safe habitats in which to release endangered species increased.

After being partially logged of its original podocarp forest, the Boundary Stream forest became infested with introduced animals such as deer, goats, mustelids, possums, rats and cats. Since 1996 an intensive control programme run by conservation staff and volunteers has eliminated these and thwarted re-invasion. The forest has responded well, palatable vegetation has recovered and young seedlings cover the previously bare forest floor. Introduced robin, kiwi and kōkako have settled and are now breeding in the reserve, and the resident birdlife is flourishing.

Best birding areas

⊳ Tumanako Walk and Kāmahi Loop

These adjoining forest walks have good outlooks across the main valley. There's a good chance of seeing kōkako here, even from the car park. Tumanako Walk is gently graded and negotiable by pushchairs and wheelchairs. It passes through a variety of forest types, including rare plants such as kākā beak and yellow mistletoe, then links with Kāmahi Loop. Whitehead, robin, bellbird, tūī, New Zealand pigeon, rifleman, fantail, tomtit and grey warbler are present on both tracks. Kāmahi Loop is a little steeper, but leads to great outlooks and frequent sightings of New Zealand pigeon and New Zealand falcon diving and flying across the valley.

⊳ Bell Rock Loop Track

This is a rather more strenuous 3-hour walk, but good numbers of tūī, bellbird, pigeon and rifleman are present in the lower section. There are great views across the Mōhaka River valley and the broad sweep of Hawke Bay, from Māhia Peninsula to Cape Kidnappers. The bell-shaped rock is a feature in its own right.

The track climbs through forest then follows the open ridgeline of the Maungaharuru Range to Bell Rock. The return loop descends a farm track to Pohokura Road, at Pohokura Saddle, which is about 700 m from the car park.

Hawke's Bay wetlands

Two wetland birding areas worth a quick look on the way to Boundary Stream are neighbouring lakes Tūtira and Waikopiro. They are home to New Zealand scaup, pūkeko, New Zealand dabchick/weiweia, grey teal/tētē, Australasian shoveler/kuruwhengu, paradise shelduck/pūtangitangi and introduced mallard and black swan.

The lake has been protected for its wildlife values since 1929, at the behest of local farmer and ardent conservationist Herbert Guthrie-Smith. His book *Tutira: The Story of a New Zealand Sheep Station*, describing the effects of farming on the local ecology, is considered a New Zealand classic. Sadly, the introduction of grass carp has affected the lake's natural qualities.

Located 45 km north of Napier, right beside SH2, Lake Tūtira also has a pleasant picnic area, informal camping site, several walking tracks and is a popular fishing spot. There are plenty of obvious and easily accessed spots to observe birds around the lakeshore.

Ahuriri Estuary, near Napier, is a significant area for migrant waders

▷ Lake Opouahi Reserve

Clearly signposted on the right, halfway from Lake Tūtira to Boundary Stream, is this fully fenced 'kiwi crèche', where young kiwi are kept safe until strong enough to withstand predators in larger forest areas. You probably won't see the kiwi but the 20-minute easy track around the lakeside is a great place for fernbirds, as is the little jetty right by the car park.

Getting there Boundary Stream is about an hour's drive north of Napier. From Napier drive north along SH2 towards Gisborne. After 37 km, immediately after passing Lake Tūtira, turn left beside the Tūtira Store.

and waterfowl although its once more extensive wetlands have largely disappeared through reclamation and the dramatic uplift that occurred in the great earthquake of 1931. Arctic migrants that visit each spring and summer include bar-tailed godwit/kūaka, lesser knot/huahou, Pacific golden plover, Asiatic whimbrel, turnstone and red-necked stint. In winter royal spoonbill/kōtuku-ngutupapa (around 100 in number), black-fronted tern/tarapiroe and occasional white heron/kōtuku travel here from their South Island breeding grounds. Year-round residents include little black shag/kōau, black-fronted dotterel, banded dotterel, Caspian tern/taranui, Australasian bittern/matuku, grey teal and marsh crake. More than 70 species have been recorded here.

The estuary is just north of Napier city and is crossed by SH2. A well-used walkway starting either side of the SH2 bridge, marked by large interpretation panels, provides easy access to and views across the tidal flats. Dogs are not permitted in the middle and lower estuary wildlife refuge.

Boundary Stream is signposted from here. After 6 km turn left onto Pohokura Road, which becomes winding and unsealed before reaching the signposted Boundary Stream car park.

There is no public transport to the reserve.

Getting around Walking tracks are the only means of exploring the reserve. Bell Rock Loop track is signposted 2 km further up Pohokura Road from the Tumanako car park.

Be sure to keep to the main walking tracks, which are clearly marked with directions signs, interpretation panels and orange triangles. An extensive network of other tracks through the reserve is used by conservation staff monitoring traps and bait stations, and lead into steep gullies and thick forest.

Accommodation There is no accommodation at Boundary Stream. There is a DoC camping ground at Lake Tūtira and a cottage available for rent nearby. Napier and its outlying areas offer a range of luxury lodges, hotels, motels, holiday parks, bed-and-breakfasts, self-contained accommodation and backpackers.

Facilities Napier is served daily by the national air network and inter-city coach services. There are toilets and a day shelter at the Tumanako Walk car park. Visitors will need to be self-sufficient for food and drinks. The tiny Tūtira Store is the closest shop; Bay View, a few kilometres from Napier, has the closest fuel station.

Information

Department of Conservation, Conservation House, 59 Marine Parade, Napier, 06 834 3111, napier-ao@doc.govt.nz.

Napier i-SITE Visitor Centre, 100 Marine Parade, 06 834 1911, napier@i-SITE.org.

Recommended reading

Birdwatching in Hawke's Bay – A Guide to Prime Birding Locations, P.W. Twydle. Napier: P. Twydle, 1993.

12
Cape Kidnappers

Where Hawke's Bay, North Island east coast.

What's special Large easily accessible gannet colonies in a dramatic seascape; opportunities to get very close to the birds and their chicks.

Birds to look for Australasian gannet/tākapu, also gulls and shags and possibly white-fronted tern/tara, variable oystercatcher/tōrea, New Zealand dotterel/tuturiwhatu and reef heron/matuku moana.

Birdwatching options Self-guided walk (5–6 hours), guided tours by 4WD vehicle (3 hours) overland or tractor/trailer tour along beach (4 hours).

Top spots

- Black Reef colony
- Plateau colony.

When to go Late November to April. The birds are mostly absent in winter and the colonies are closed to visitors during nesting and breeding from July to October. Chicks are present from around late November. Public access is feasible only during mid- to low tides.

Background

The world's largest mainland concentration of Australasian gannet has established its summertime nesting residence here in a spectacular setting of sea cliffs, reefs and rock stacks. Most gannet colonies are on islands or offshore rocks, so this mainland location, with good public access, is one of the easiest places anywhere to see them. Around 8000 pairs nest in four colonies on and close to the prominent headland that juts into southern Hawke Bay. Some colonies are in the Cape Kidnappers Nature

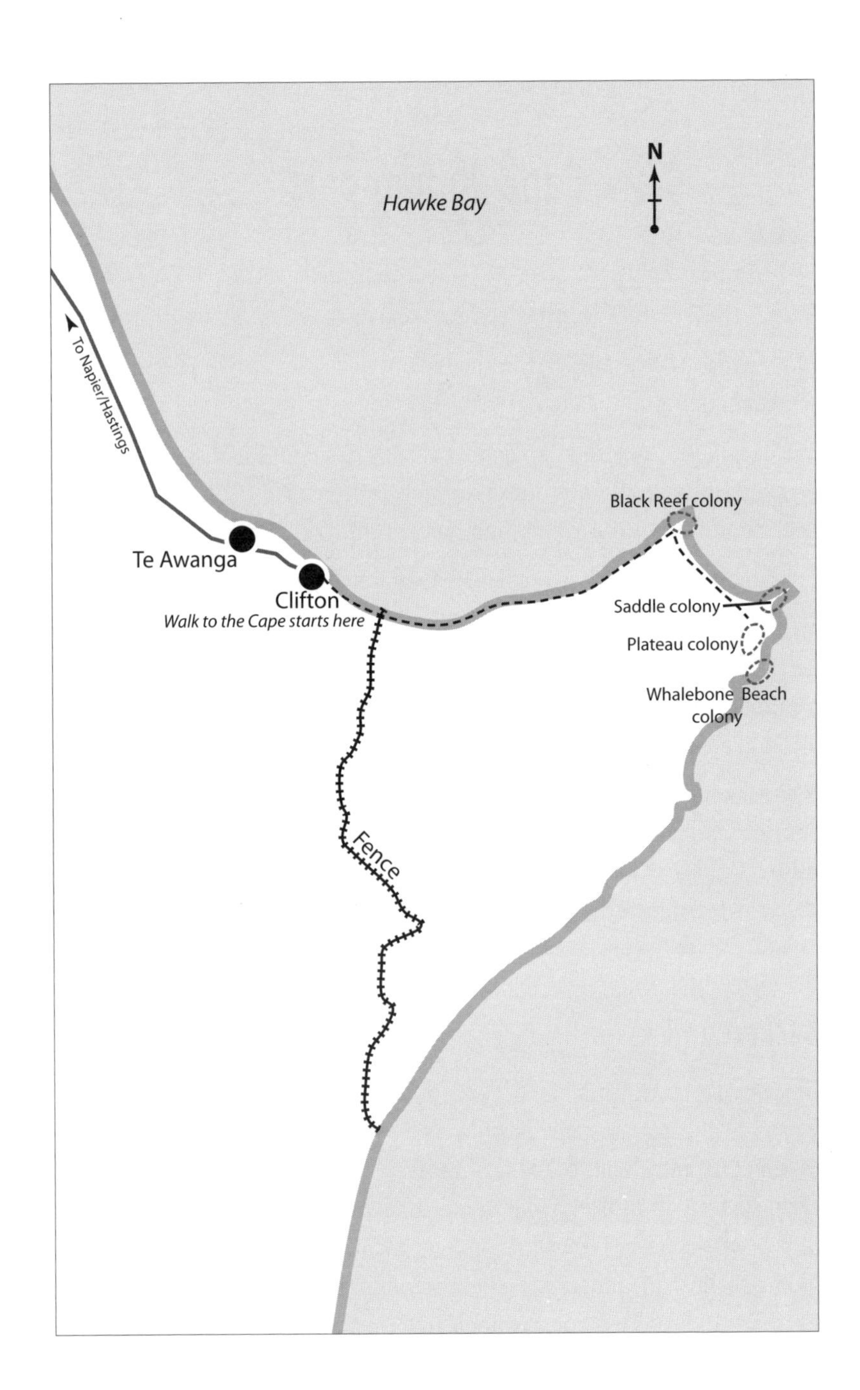
N
Hawke Bay
To Napier/Hastings
Te Awanga
Clifton
Walk to the Cape starts here
Fence
Black Reef colony
Saddle colony
Plateau colony
Whalebone Beach colony

Reserve; others occupy adjacent farmland as their numbers continue to increase. The Black Reef and Plateau colonies are particularly accessible.

Watching a gannet colony is a memorable experience, with the constant comings-and-goings of adults, the clumsy crash-landings so at odds with their graceful flight, and the bonding rituals with their life-long mates. Also memorable are the fluffy white chicks, the speckled juveniles testing their wings, and the chicks' excitement as adults disgorge their fishy catch into eager mouths.

Australasian gannets were first recorded here in 1856, when just 50 birds lived on what is now known as the Saddle colony, above the sea cliffs near the very tip of the Cape. As their numbers increased, the birds established three more colonies.

The gannets are present from July, through summer until April/May. The rest of the year most disperse around coastal waters, while almost all the juveniles fly to Australia. Those that survive the journey stay across the Tasman for 3–7 years, after which they return to breed. Chicks are hatched from around early November, then mature through stages of white fluffy down to grey, speckled juvenile birds. Although they have been known to forage up to 200 km away, resident birds usually fish close by and can often be seen diving for small fish and squid.

The coastal route to the Cape is hemmed by cliffs on which distinctive patterns tell the story of their geological history. Layers of coloured sand, silt and shells contrast with darker river gravels, fossilised plants and pale volcanic ash from the central North Island volcanoes. These patterns are broken by vertical fault lines that cut through the entire height of the cliffs.

At Black Reef, the gannets nest atop dark rocks of old erosion-resistant sandstone, while at the Cape itself, the towering cliffs are made of softer, readily-erodable siltstones. Keep to marked tracks and away from the cliff edges. Other birds here include red-billed gull/tarāpunga, black-backed gull/karoro and black shag/kōau. Sometimes present are white-fronted tern, variable oystercatcher, New Zealand dotterel, spotted shag/pārekareka and reef heron. New Zealand fur seals also haul out at the Cape over winter.

Best birding areas

▷ Black Reef

The coastal route to Cape Kidnappers passes through the Black Reef colony, probably the best viewing spot and definitely the best for photography.

Gannets and their chicks crowd onto huge rocks that lie at the base of steep cliffs. An increasing number of birds nest precariously on little ledges among eroding bluffs that tower behind the beach. Looking seaward, just metres from the beach, several rock stacks are crowded with nesting birds. Black rocks, white birds and blue sea behind – it makes an impressive scene, much enhanced by sunsets if the tide allows an evening visit.

▷ Plateau colony

One of the oldest colonies sits high on the edge of a plateau, beside the lighthouse near the tip of the Cape. This is private land but public access is permitted via a walking track that climbs steeply from sea level. Overland tours also drive to this colony, where only a low fence separates onlookers from the hundreds of adult birds and chicks. From the lighthouse there is a view of the original saddle colony, its numbers now reduced, and from the southern end of the plateau colony it is possible to see the newest, growing colony about 200 m away near the base of the cliffs on the south side of the Cape. Gannets aside, the high plateau offers a panoramic view across Hawke's Bay to the Kaweka Ranges.

Getting there Napier and Hastings are the closest cities, both served by Intercity coach services while Napier is served daily by the national air network.

Public walking access follows the narrow strip of coastline at the base of the cliffs on the north side of the Cape, negotiable only between mid- and low tide. This access starts at Clifton, 20 minutes' drive from Napier. From Napier follow SH2 along the coast to Clive, then follow the Cape Kidnappers signposts, through Te Awanga Village to the road end and car park, just before the Clifton Motor Camp. An information board here displays tide times. Departure for the Cape should be at least 3 hours after high tide, as any earlier the narrow coastal route is blocked by the sea. The return trip should be started no later than 1.5 hours after low tide. Tide times are also available in daily newspapers and at visitor information centres.

Shuttle transport to Clifton can be arranged from Napier or Hastings.

The coastal journey to the Cape is an outing in its own right, an interesting and easy walk over sandy beach, mudstone platforms and rocky shore. Allow 4–5 hours return plus time spent at the Cape. The downside is the likely presence of off-road vehicles, in particular during summer holidays and weekends.

Commercial tour operators are licensed by DoC to travel along the beach. Most notable is Gannet Beach Adventures, a family operation that has been running tours using vintage tractors and trailers for over 50 years. This is an iconic Kiwi trip. Alternative access is by Gannet Safaris overland tours, who travel by 4WD over the farmland of Cape Kidnappers Station direct to the Plateau colony. This trip is not affected by tides.

Getting around From Clifton, the route follows the beach to Black Reef, then turns a corner where the Cape itself comes into view. A few hundred metres along the beach from Black Reef a clearly signposted track leaves the beach and leads through a strip of native vegetation for 200 m to a public shelter and picnic area. The tractor tours carry passengers to the start of this track; from here walking is the only option.

If climbing hills doesn't suit you, relaxing at the picnic area or on the beach, or spending longer observing the gannets at Black Reef is a perfectly pleasant option.

From the shelter the track to the Plateau colony climbs steeply from the beach, crosses farm paddocks, possibly occupied by grazing sheep or cattle (keep to the track), then climbs again to the colony. Allow 30 minutes from the shelter to the top, add plenty of rest stops to enjoy the ever-expanding view.

Accommodation Hawke's Bay is a busy tourism and holiday region, known for its wine and food and art deco architecture, and has an excellent range of accommodation. There are also several self-contained holiday homes near Clifton and Te Awanga.

Facilities There is an information board and car park at the Clifton departure point. At the Cape there is a public shelter, with water, an information panel and toilets. There is no shop, and no fires or camp stoves are permitted, so visitors must carry their own picnic food. There is no accommodation at the Cape itself, and camping is not permitted.

At Clifton there is a cafe beside the departure point. There are also wineries with lunch restaurants at nearby Te Awanga.

Information

Department of Conservation, Conservation House, 59 Marine Parade,

Cape Sanctuary

Three local landowners have funded the construction of a 10.5-km predator-proof fence across the base of the Cape Kidnappers peninsula from Clifton to Ocean Beach. The fence protects a total area of 2500 ha including 200 ha of dune systems and 180 ha of mature kānuka forest, and its 17-km coastal perimeter also encloses farmland and an international golf course.

The fence was completed in early 2007 and a predator-control programme begun to prepare for transfers of several seabird species to a 2 ha ring-fenced pest-free area intended for species vulnerable to mice, such as lizards, tuatara and large-bodied invertebrates. Transfers and artificial rearing of grey-faced petrel/oi chicks began in 2008 and, in 2010, of Cook's petrel chicks. These species used to nest here until driven out. Seabirds tend to return to their natal colonies to breed, so it's expected that chicks that fledge from the Sanctuary will lead

Napier, 06 834 3111, napier-ao@doc.govt.nz.

Napier i-SITE Visitor Centre, 100 Marine Parade, 06 834 1911, napier@i-SITE.org.

Hastings i-SITE Visitor Centre, corner of Russell Street and Heretaunga Street East, 06 873 5526, hastings@i-SITE.org.

Licensed guiding operators

Gannet Beach Adventures: travel along the beach by tractor/trailer; daily from October to March/April, tour times according to tides. Adults $38, children $23, family and group rates available. 0800 426 638 or 06 875 0898, www.gannets.com.

Gannet Safaris: overland tours to the Plateau colony twice daily; 3 hours duration; adults $60, children $30, tour and group rates available. 0800 427 232 or 06 875 0888, www.gannetsafaris.co.nz.

---

to new colonies establishing here. Playing shearwater and petrel calls from a sound system on the cliff tops will provide an added lure.

Over 100 nesting boxes for blue penguin have been installed around the headland and beaches. In 2008 the first brown kiwi were reintroduced to the Sanctuary forest; it is hoped this will create a secure population to boost other declining Hawke's Bay kiwi populations.

Other forest birds introduced include North Island robin/toutouwai, brown teal/pateke, banded rail, tomtit, rifleman/tītīpounamu and whitehead/pōpokatea. Some of the common species are present elsewhere in Hawke's Bay but have long been absent from the Cape. Resident forest species, bellbird/korimako, tomtit/miromiro, New Zealand pigeon/kererū, fantail/pīwakawaka and grey warbler/riroriro, are expected to flourish in the absence of predators. To visit the Sanctuary, contact Kidnappers Safaris, www.kidnapperssafaris.co.nz or Gannet Safaris, www.gannetsafaris.co.nz.

13

Manawatu Estuary

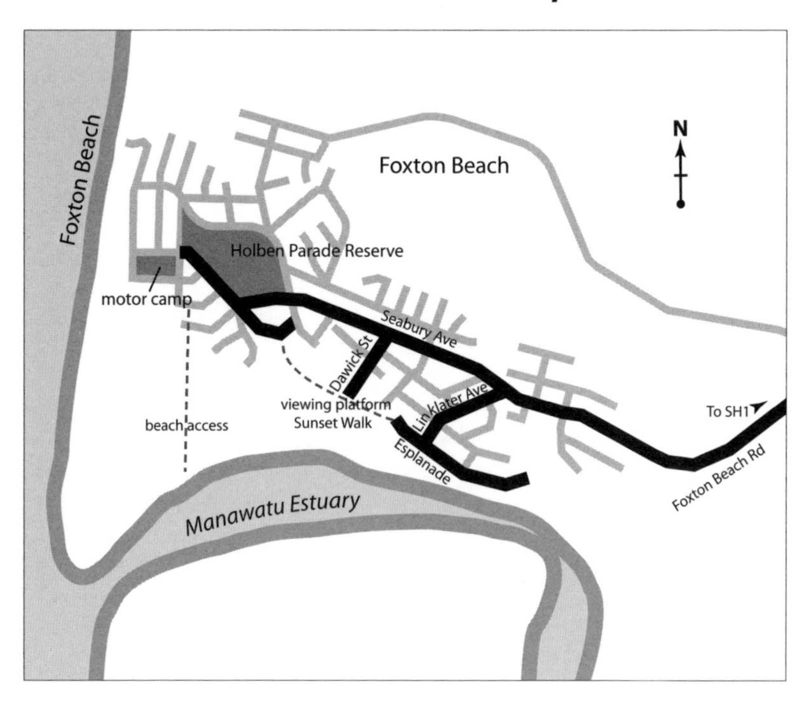

Where South-west coast of the North Island, 1.5 hours' drive from Wellington.

What's special The largest estuary in the lower North Island and an 'armchair viewing' spot for birders. Tidal mudflats and a high-tide roost are conveniently close to road access and viewing areas. In 2005 this estuary was declared a wetland of international importance under the Ramsar Convention.

Birds to look for Wrybill/ngutuparore, royal spoonbill/kōtuku-ngutupapa, banded dotterel/tuturiwhatu, black-billed gull/tarāpunga and South Island pied oystercatcher/tōrea (winter), bar-tailed godwit/kūaka, lesser knot/huahou, Pacific golden plover, sharp-tailed sandpiper (spring and summer), Caspian tern/taranui, white-fronted tern/tara, white-faced heron, red-billed gull/tarāpunga, black-backed gull/karoro, paradise shelduck/pūtangitangi and other duck species.

Birdwatching options Self-guided, easy walks.

Top spots

- Dawick Street viewing platform and Sunset Walk
- Sand bank from Holben Parade beach access.

How long to go 2–3 hours.

When to go Year-round: October to March for godwit, golden plover, lesser knots and other international waders (best around and through high tide), winter for South Island waders and royal spoonbill (on a falling tide).

Background

Manawatu Estuary is known more for its diversity of species than great numbers of birds. While 38 species are recorded as visiting each year, a total of 93 species have been recorded, so there is a good chance of spotting rarities. Mudflats provide habitat for international migratory shorebirds during spring and summer, in particular bar-tailed godwit and lesser knot, plus Pacific golden plover and sharp-tailed sandpiper. Less common visitors recorded include Asiatic whimbrel, Siberian tattler, terek sandpiper and great knot.

From late March to early September the estuary is important for native birds wintering after migrating from South Island braided riverbeds and wetlands, in particular wrybill, banded dotterel and royal spoonbill. Flocks of up to 70 spoonbill have been seen, and a small number stay all year.

Throughout the year, quite large flocks of variable oystercatcher and white-fronted tern gather on the sand flats, and Caspian terns feed in the water. In the upper reaches, salt marshes with ponds and channels support the North Island fernbird/mātātā subspecies, Australasian bittern/matuku and marsh crake. However, there is no public access to this area. Kayaking up the river channel offers a chance of seeing these particularly shy birds.

The estuary is closed to game bird hunting, so large numbers of birds flock here in May during the open season. Australasian shoveler/kuruwhengu, grey teal/tētē, paradise shelduck, mallard and Canada goose can be seen, often around the reedy ponds between Dawick Street and Holben Reserve.

Best birding spots

▷ Dawick Street viewing platform and Sunset Walk

The viewing platform looks directly on to the sandbank, which provides a roost at high tide. In summer, this is used by migratory birds from Alaska and Siberia; in winter, by South Island migrants, in particular wrybill and royal spoonbill and smaller numbers of banded dotterel and black-billed gull. Year-round, white-faced heron, Caspian and white-fronted tern and red-billed and black-backed gull often roost on the sand in large flocks.

Dawick Street is signposted on the left from the main road part-way through Foxton Beach settlement. The viewing platform is directly in front of the road-end car park, and has an information panel.

Sunset Walk follows the shoreline from Dawick Street to Foxton Beach Esplanade, where there is a foreshore picnic area and boating club. The 200-m walk overlooks the high-tide sand-bank roost and tidal mudflats. The surface is flat and sealed.

▷ Sand bank from Holben Parade beach access

Birds can be more closely observed, and with care can be approached to within 20 m by walking out onto the sand bank itself. Park in Holben Reserve and walk about 10 minutes through the signposted beach access by Foxton Beach Motor Camp, then turn inland and walk along the sand for about 10 minutes.

Getting there The turn-off to Foxton Beach settlement is signposted on SH1 at Foxton township, 20 km north of Levin. Daily Intercity bus services pass through Foxton township but there is no public transport to Foxton Beach.

Accommodation Options at Foxton Beach settlement include two motels (one right on the foreshore on Dawick Street). Foxton Beach Motor Camp has tent sites, powered sites and cabins a few minutes' walk from the estuary. There are also two motels in Foxton township, and several more just south in the larger town of Levin.

Facilities Public toilets by the boating club on Foxton Beach Esplanade and at Holben Parade Reserve beside the main road beyond Dawick Street. On the far side of the reserve (turn down Nash then right into Holben Parade) there is a small shelter with an information display.

There are a cafe and wine bar, ice-cream shop, grocery store and two takeaway food outlets at the beach settlement. Foxton has more cafes, fuel, an information centre and craft shops.

Information

Manawatu Estuary Trust, a community organisation to promote and protect the natural values of the estuary, is involved in regular bird counts, clean ups, newsletters and promotions. www.environmentnetwork.org.nz/80.html.

Foxton Information Centre: de Molen (The Mill), 06 363 5601, www.demolenfoxton.org.nz.

Levin i-SITE Visitor Centre, 06 367 8440, levin@i-SITE.org, www.naturecoast.co.nz.

14

Pukaha Mt Bruce

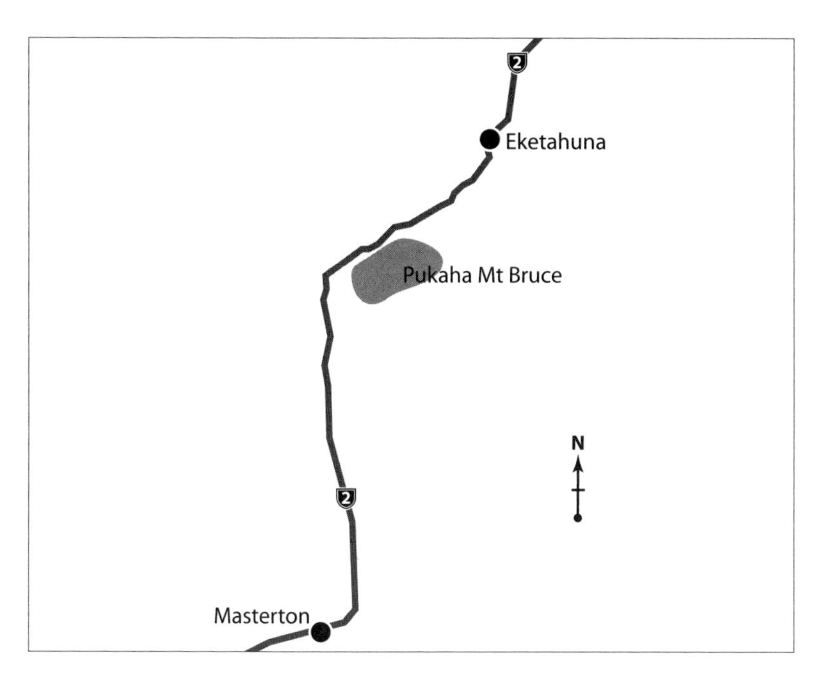

Where South-east North Island, 30 km north of Masterton.

What's special National Wildlife Centre, a breeding facility for threatened species, with walkways, aviaries, kiwi house, forest and wetland areas and visitor and education facilities. Pukaha Mt Bruce Forest is a focus of habitat restoration and bird population recovery.

Birds to look for In captivity: kākā, kōkako, brown kiwi, stitchbird/hihi, yellow-crowned parakeet/kākāriki, takahē, New Zealand scaup, shore plover.

In the forest (with some species visiting the centre): kākā, New Zealand falcon/kārearea, kōkako, New Zealand pigeon/kererū, tūī, fantail/pīwakawaka, rifleman/tītīpounamu, silvereye/tauhou, brown kiwi.

Birdwatching options Guided tours, daily feeding and educational talks, self-guided walks, nest cameras.

Top spots

➢ Kākā feeding station, 3 pm daily.

When to go Year-round. Open 9 am to 4.30 pm daily, except Christmas Day. There are talks daily on takahē (11.30 am), eels (with feeding) (1.30 pm) and kākā (3 pm). There are also guided tours (1.5 hours) on weekends and public holidays at 10.30 am and 2 pm.

Background

Captive breeding techniques were pioneered here in the 1960s and the National Wildlife Centre has since played a major role in saving many of the country's most threatened species.

Takahē, thought to be extinct, were rediscovered in 1948 in the Murchison Mountains, Fiordland. Ten years later a local Wairarapa farmer and bird enthusiast, Elwyn Welch, secretly raised four chicks in aviaries on his farm until 1960, when the public was invited to see what were by then healthy adult birds.

This success led to what was then the NZ Wildlife Service employing his expertise with other endangered birds. In 1962 all birds being raised on his farm were moved to Mt Bruce and the National Wildlife Centre was established.

Since then the centre has successfully bred some of New Zealand's most threatened species, including Campbell Island teal, stitchbird, shore plover, kōkako and saddleback. Once old and strong enough to fend for themselves, the offspring have been released into the wild, usually to predator-free islands or 'mainland islands'.

Mt Bruce Forest

The magnificent podocarp forest backing onto the centre is a remnant of what was once called the 70 Mile Bush, extending along the eastern foothills of the Tararua Ranges. Early travellers praised the Pukaha Mt Bruce forest for its primeval nature and glorious bird song, but forest clearance and animal pests soon led to the disappearance of entire species, for example kākā, kōkako and brown kiwi. In recent years, the tide has turned.

In 1996 kākā were released into the forest and settled well, encouraging a partnership between local Māori people, DoC, landowners and the National Wildlife Centre Trust to undertake a major forest restoration project. In 2003, 2004 and 2010 brown kiwi and kōkako were also reintroduced and, along with the kākā, are now breeding in the wild. It is now expected that the total bird population will double each year for at least five years.

The Visitor Centre has just been upgraded and an interactive gallery added to tell the Centre's conservation story.

Best birding spots

- The daily kākā talk and feeding session at 3 pm brings a flurry of colourful action. The birds fly in from the Pukaha Mt Bruce Forest, perform in their characteristically boisterous way, and great photo opportunities are guaranteed.

Getting there Pukaka Mt Bruce is on SH2, 30 km north of Masterton and 10 km south of Eketahuna, 2 hours' drive from Wellington or Napier and 1 hour's drive from Palmerston North. Public transport is available on Tranzit coaches travelling daily between Masterton and Palmerston North.

Getting around The National Wildlife Centre has 2 km of gently graded walking tracks and boardwalks, mostly wheelchair accessible. A 2-hour loop walk, Te Arapiki o Tawhaki, climbs steadily (steepish) in places through the forest reserve to the Pukaha Mt Bruce summit. Forest birds and great views of the Tararua Range are the rewards.

Accommodation There is a range of hotels, motels, holiday parks, farmstays and homestays in the nearby towns and district.

Facilities At the centre there is a shop, educational displays and interactive gallery, toilets, large car park and Cafe Takahe (open 9.30 am to 4 pm).

Information

Pukaha Mt Bruce National Wildlife Centre, entry $15/adult, $4/children, under five free, 06 375 8004, info@pukaha.org.nz, www.pukaha.org.nz.

Wairarapa i-SITE Visitor Centre, 316 Queen Street, Masterton, 06 370 0900, info@wairarapanz.com, www.wairarapanz.co.

Recommended reading

Pukaha – Songs from the Forest includes a history of Pukaha Mt Bruce, bird photos, whakatauaki (Māori proverbs) and a CD of birdsong. Available from the shop at the centre.

15

Kapiti Island

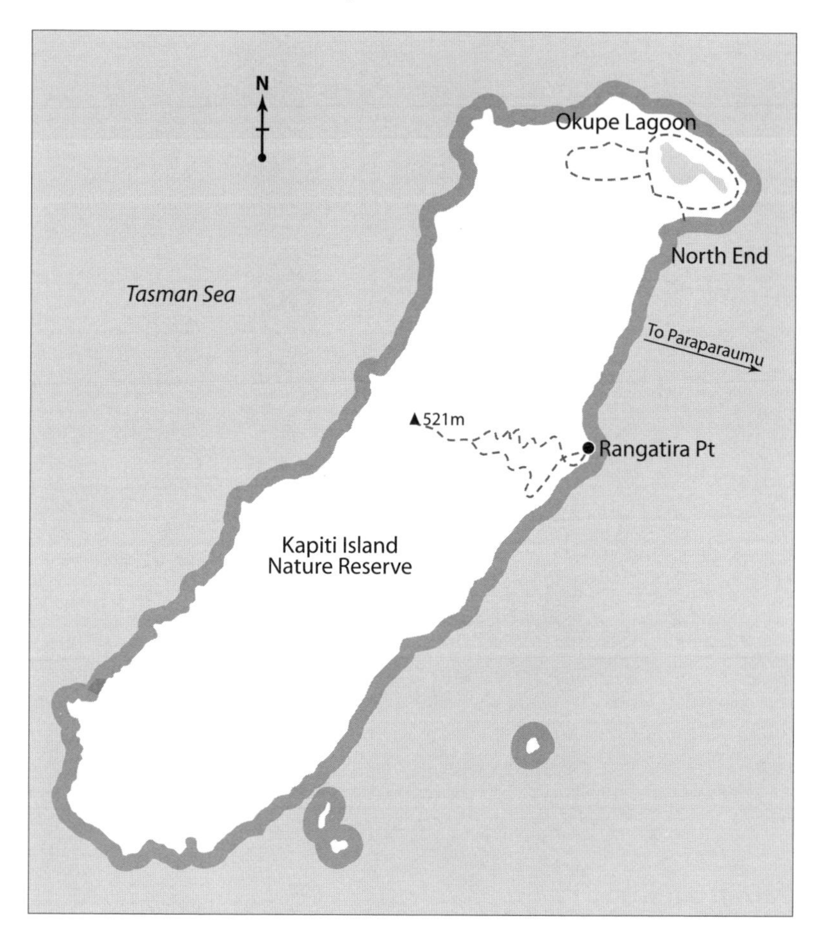

Where Five kilometres off the North Island west coast, just north of Wellington.

What's special Prolific birdlife, including some of New Zealand's rarest species. One of the few nature reserves open to the public.

Birds to look for Kākā, saddleback/tīeke, takahē, stitchbird/hihi, red-crowned parakeet/ kākāriki, New Zealand pigeon/kererū, North Island robin/toutouwai, whitehead/pōpokatea, little spotted kiwi/pukupuku, long-tailed cuckoo/koekoeā (spring and summer), plus coastal and seabirds and common forest birds.

Birdwatching options Self-guided walks, guided walks, evening kiwi spotting (for Kapiti Island Lodge guests).

Top spots

- Rangatira landing – lower-level forest tracks and Rangatira Flat near the public shelter (walks of up to 3 hours return)
- North End landing – Okupe Lagoon and forest tracks (walks of up to 2 hours return)
- Evening kiwi tours (lodge guests only).

How long to go Day trip, or overnight stay at Kapiti Lodge. Day trippers have around 6 hours on the island – plenty of time for relaxed birding.

When Year-round. Summer is more popular but the birds are generally more active in autumn and winter.

Background

Kapiti is one of the first islands of its size in the world to have all predators removed. This 1965-ha island now provides safe refuge for some of New Zealand's most endangered species, including some absent from the mainland. It is one of the country's most accessible island nature reserves, with daily boat trips from the mainland, albeit with careful controls.

The bar-tailed godwit is New Zealand's most prolific arctic migrant.

Banded dotterel nest in shallow scrapes on beaches and shingle river beds.

Left
Thought to have been extinct for 150 years, the New Zealand storm petrel was rediscovered in the Hauraki Gulf in 2003, and is sometimes seen there on birding cruises.

Opposite
South Island pied oystercatchers on a shellbank roost at the RAMSAR site, Miranda, in the Firth of Thames.

Below
Grey ternlet are occasionally seen around the North Island's eastern coastline, where they breed on offshore islands.

Above

Wrybill, the only bird in the world with a bill bent sideways, breed on the braided river beds of inland Canterbury and disperse to northern tidal harbours from late summer to winter.

Left

The variable oystercatcher, an endemic shorebird, lives on beaches and estuaries in many parts of New Zealand.

Above
About 1600 Australasian gannets form the largest mainland concentration of these birds in New Zealand, in four colonies on the bluffs and reefs of Cape Kidnappers, Hawke's Bay.

Right
The tūī, seen here feeding on kōwhai flowers, is one of New Zealand's most prolific and loved native birds, noted for its melodious song and distinctive white tuft of neck feathers.

Left
Kōkako, a member of the ancient wattlebird family, is known for its haunting, chime-like song.

Opposite
Work to save declining kiwi populations includes captive breeding and transferring birds to safe refuges.

Below
The endangered blue duck, one of the world's four species of torrent duck, evolved early in New Zealand's isolated history.

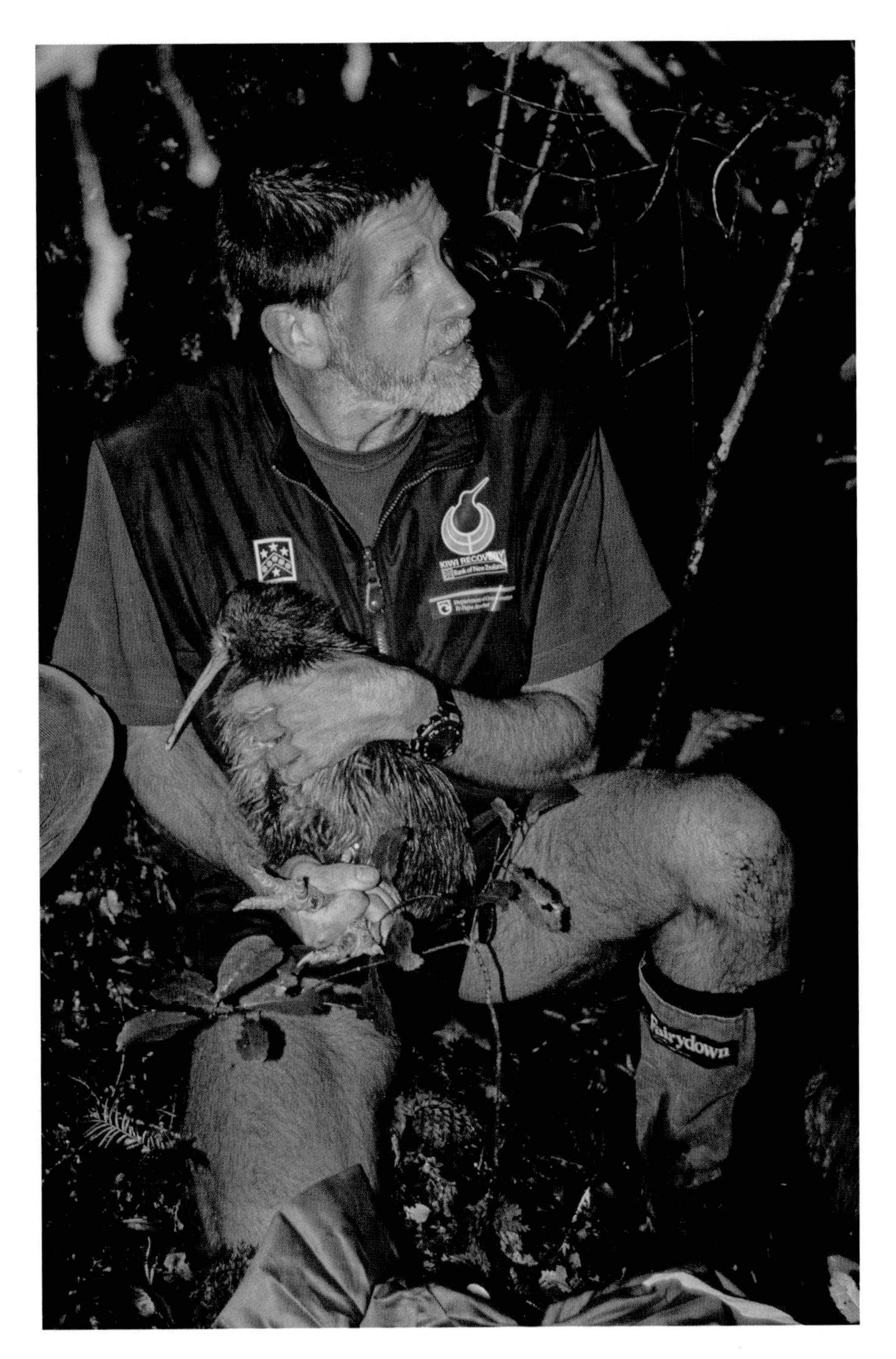
Fairydown

Left
Takahē, considered extinct until rediscovered in 1948, now survive only on predator-free island reserves.

Below
Saddleback were among the first birds to be re-located on predator-free islands, and experience with this initial work has made it possible to save other endangered species in the same way.

The island has a long history of occupation, first by Māori whose descendants, including Kapiti Island Lodge operator John Barrett, still own a small enclave of private land near the island's northern end. During the early 19th century whalers and sealers based themselves on Kapiti, followed by farmers who drained wetlands and destroyed much of the forest. In 1897 far-sighted conservationists persuaded the government to declare Kapiti a reserve. Farm animals, deer and goats were removed and the island is now covered in regenerated rainforest.

In the early 1900s little spotted kiwi were released on Kapiti. Except for its presence in Karori Wildlife Sanctuary, this species has become extinct on the mainland. Later successful introductions include kōkako, takahē, saddleback and stitchbird. During the 1980s possums were eradicated, followed by rats in 1996. This paved the way for more highly endangered birds, plus reptiles and invertebrates, to be released.

Today, Kapiti is managed as a nature reserve by DoC. Visitor access is permitted at two landing points, each with a small network of tracks. Most forest birds are present in both areas, but saddleback and stitchbird are most likely to be seen at Rangatira.

Best birding areas

▷ Rangatira landing

Most visitors disembark at Rangatira, where within 10 minutes' walk, on Rangatira Flat, there are good chances of seeing kākā, New Zealand pigeon, tūī, bellbird, red-crowned parakeet, takahē and weka. In early summer, tūī and bellbird can be particularly vociferous as they feed on the flowering rātā, just behind the stony beach. Be warned that kākā are bold, quick and wily – and interested in any food scraps they can steal, though feeding them is prohibited.

Trig Track and Wilkinson Track head uphill from Rangatira Point through some impressive mature forest, and link up just below the summit, Tuteremoana (521 m). The round trip takes about 3 hours but you are most likely to see North Island robin, saddleback, stitchbird and the more common forest birds along the first 300 m. The slower you walk, the more birds you are likely to see. Keep an eye open for feeding stations, sometimes frequented by stitchbird. Kōkako are present but very rarely seen or heard near any public tracks.

▷ North End landing

Tracks here explore a variety of habitats: the boulder-bank, lagoon, open grass and shrub lands and regenerating forest. Species here include weka, kākā, red-crowned parakeet, New Zealand pigeon, common forest birds and takahē. New Zealand scaup, grey teal/tētē and black swan are often seen on the lagoon and during winter there's also a good chance of seeing royal spoonbill/kōtuku-ngutupapa. Brown teal are present on the lagoon but rarely seen during the day. Shags, gulls, white-fronted tern/tara and reef heron/matuku-moana frequent the coast, although the coastal track is closed during the gulls' breeding season (November–March).

Kapiti Marine Reserve

The short boat trip to Kapiti Island passes through one of the first marine reserves created in New Zealand. Marine scientists have recorded significant increases in the sizes and numbers of fish and shellfish since the reserve was established in 1992. Divers report some of the finest underwater scenery in the Wellington region, and fish and crayfish have become quite tame in the presence of divers and snorkellers.

On the surface, dolphins, orca and whales are occasional visitors, seals come and go from small colonies on Kapiti Island, and seabirds are prolific. Keep an eye open for Australasian gannet/tākapu, blue penguin/kororā, sooty shearwater/tītī, shags, gulls and terns.

▷ Kapiti Island Lodge evening tour

Guided evening walks are a highlight of overnight stays with the only licensed accommodation and tour operator on the island. A delightful mixture of wildlife interpretation, Māori history and hospitality is offered by the convivial hosts, and chances of hearing and seeing kiwi near the lodge are very high.

Getting there Kapiti Island is a 20-minute launch trip from Paraparaumu Beach, about 1 hour's drive north of Wellington on SH1. Two DoC-licensed operators provide daily launch services (depending on the weather) for passengers with DoC permits. Private boats are not permitted.

Before visiting the island, you must obtain a permit from DoC (see below) then make a booking with one of the launch operators. Fifty permits are allocated per day for Rangatira Point and 18 for North End. A further allocation is available for overnight guests at Kapiti Island Lodge, and arranged through the company Kapiti Island Alive.

It pays to book well ahead for the summer months and public holidays when permits can quickly sell out. There are usually plenty of spaces available during winter, spring and autumn (when the birds are generally more active).

Launches depart from the Kapiti Boat Club, Paraparaumu Beach, about 3.5 km from the town centre and SH1. Departure times are 9–9.30 am, returning between 3 and 4 pm. Trips are occasionally cancelled because of weather or sea conditions so you must confirm travel with the skipper by phone, before 7.30 am on the day.

Permits cost $11/adult and $5/child, boat fares are approximately $55/adult and $30/child, varying slightly between operators and according to the group size. Bags and packs are inspected to ensure no stowaways like mice or rats are accidentally carried to the island. On arrival there is a compulsory introductory talk on track conditions and safety issues, as well as information on the special values of Kapiti, its forests, birdlife and human history. This talk significantly enhances the island experience.

Getting around By walking only. Tracks are clearly signposted and well formed but sturdy footwear is necessary. The tracks around Rangatira Flat and Ōkupe Lagoon are flat, other tracks climb on steady grades. Guided walks are available but must be pre-booked.

Accommodation Kapiti Island Lodge must be pre-booked. There is a good range of accommodation on the Kapiti Coast, including holiday parks, motels, bed-and-breakfasts, backpackers and luxury lodges. Major hotels are in Wellington, 1 hour by car or train from Paraparaumu.

Facilities At the two landing points there are public shelters, toilets and interpretation displays. Visitors need to bring their own picnic lunch and drinking water. Fires and camping stoves are not permitted.

Permits and information

Department of Conservation Visitor Centre, Manners Street, Wellington, 04 384 7770, wellingtonvc@doc.govt.nz or online booking at www.doc.govt.nz.

Licensed guiding companies

Kapiti Island Alive and Kapiti Island Lodge: accommodation, guided walks, evening kiwi walks, 06 362 6606, minnie@kapitiislandalive.co.nz, www.kapitiislandalive.co.nz.

Launch services: Kapiti Marine Charter freephone 0800 433 779, 04 297 2585, www.kapitimarinecharter.co.nz.

Kapiti Tours Ltd freephone 0800 527 484, www.kapititours.co.nz.

Recommended reading

Kapiti, Chris Maclean, Wellington: The Whitcombe Press, 1999.

16

ZEALANDIA: The Karori Sanctuary Experience

Where Wellington, 5 minutes' drive from downtown.

What's special A major urban conservation project: over 200 ha of forest, lakes and wetlands behind a predator-proof fence, supporting some of New Zealand's most endangered wildlife.

Birds to look for Little spotted kiwi/pukupuku, kākā, saddleback/tīeke, weka, stitchbird/hihi, whitehead/pōpokatea, North Island robin/toutouwai, grey warbler/riroriro, fantail/pīwakawaka, bellbird/korimako, tūī, New Zealand pigeon/kererū, shining cuckoo/pīpīwharauroa (spring and summer) brown teal/pāteke, New Zealand scaup, four species of shag/kōau, New Zealand falcon/kārearea, kingfisher/kōtare, welcome swallow.

Birdwatching options Self-guided walks, evening guided tours, electric boat cruise, wetland hides.

Top spots

- Lower reservoir and wetlands
- Te Mahanga Track
- Feeding stations
- Round the Lake Track
- 'Sanctuary by Night' tour.

When to go Year-round. The sanctuary is open daily 10 am to 5 pm (no entry after 4 pm), closed Christmas Day.

How long to go Two hours to half a day.

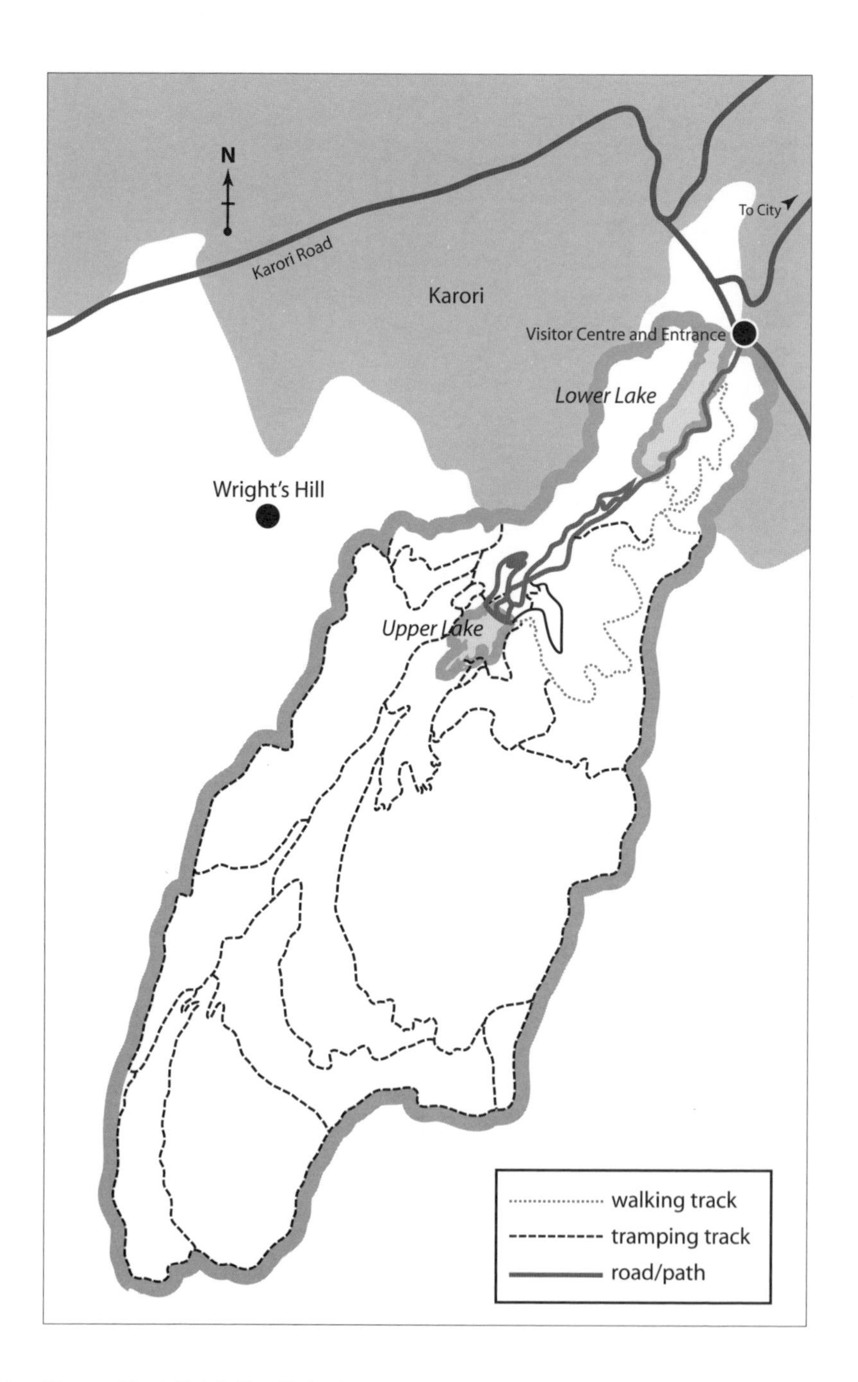
N
Karori Road
Karori
To City
Visitor Centre and Entrance
Lower Lake
Wright's Hill
Upper Lake
walking track
tramping track
road/path

Background

ZEALANDIA pioneered the concept in New Zealand of safeguarding conservation areas from mammalian pests by predator-proof fence. More remarkable is that the forest-filled sanctuary is just 2 km from downtown Wellington.

The 225-ha valley lost much of its original forest in the 19th century through farm clearance and fire. In 1908 it was made a water-catchment area and for 90 years neither farmed nor open to public access, while the city expanded around its boundaries. Two reservoirs in the valley were decommissioned in the 1990s and the valley was re-opened to the public, by which time the forest had significantly re-grown.

In 1995 the community-based Karori Wildlife Sanctuary Trust took over management of the valley and set in place ambitious plans to restore the forest to its original state and establish a native wildlife sanctuary. The Trust secured the support of thousands of community members and volunteers, as well as community-funding agencies and corporate sponsors. The Trust has worked with the city council, regional council and DoC.

A major component has been the completion, in 1999, of an 8.6-km fence to exclude all mammalian pests. Pests within the boundary were then removed, allowing unimpeded restoration of the ecosystem.

The way was also cleared for some of New Zealand's endangered species to be released into this safe refuge. Robin, weka, brown teal, New Zealand pigeon and little spotted kiwi (the first on the mainland in 100 years) were first released, then flying species including whitehead, saddleback, bellbird, kākā, tomtit, New Zealand scaup and stitchbird.

While flighted birds are free to come and go over the fence, in general they have settled well, establishing territories and breeding in their new home. Supplementary feeding for some species has been provided while the forest regenerates but recovery has been so rapid that already the birds have quickly shown preference for the native fruit and flowers.

Other native bird populations have also taken off, helped not only by restoration work in the valley but also by possum control in neighbouring reserves. The town belt, Otari–Wilton's Bush (one of New Zealand's most significant native botanical gardens) and Ngaio Gorge make up a sizeable, almost contiguous area of forest, all within the city boundary, where native birdlife is flourishing.

Other endangered species, tuatara, Maud Island frog and Cook Strait giant wētā have also been released into the sanctuary, back on their natural mainland habitat for the first time in over 100 years.

The sanctuary has focused on sharing its conservation successes; education and tourism is a key component of the Trust's long-term plans. In 2008 the sanctuary name was changed to ZEALANDIA, and a multi-level Visitor Centre, including the Exhibition which showcases New Zealand's natural history and conservation story, was opened in 2010.

Best birding areas

▷ Lower reservoir

The first feature that greets visitors is a small lake, originally a reservoir. Brown teal, New Zealand scaup, paradise shelduck/pūtangitangi, welcome swallow, Australasian shoveler/kuruwhengi, mallard and several shag species can be seen here and on the wetlands at the head of the reservoir. These wetlands were created as part of the restoration programme, and are favoured by brown teal.

Waterfowl viewing options include a walking track alongside and overlooking the reservoir (Lake Road), a pontoon walkway across the head of the lake, the picnic area by the wetlands, and a cruise on the whisper-quiet electric boat *Ara Kawau*. (This operates during weekends, weather dependent.) The vessel's name, meaning 'path of the shag', is appropriate. Black, little and little black shags, and more recently pied shag/kāruhiruhi, fly in from sea to roost in the sanctuary. During late afternoon and early morning they can be seen – up to 200 in winter – in huge macrocarpa trees beside the water. Little black shag, seen from September to January, have more recently moved to lower-growing lemonwood and matipo vegetation, where they are hidden from potential attack by Australasian harriers.

Walking beside or cruising on the reservoir there are also good vantage points to watch kākā, tūī and New Zealand pigeon perform their characteristic swooping dives across the valley.

⊳ Te Mahanga Track

From the lower reservoir, Te Mahanga Track winds its way along the valley floor over boardwalks in the shelter of regenerating forest. This track is one of the better places to encounter bellbird, stitchbird, tūī and possibly saddleback, especially from around July–November when the fuchsia is flowering. The birds are also most vocal during this time, their song continuing on through summer. During spring and summer, young shining cuckoo are often seen along this track.

⊳ Kākā, stitchbird and bellbird feeders

Close encounters with kākā are likely around their feeding stations, near the base of the upper dam. The feeders are designed so only the kākā can access the specially formulated pellets and beverages to supplement their food. Kākā may also be seen along the track as they fly beneath the foliage from one feeder to another. As a rule they use the feeders at any time of day during summer, but only towards the evenings in winter. There are also feeders for stitchbird and bellbird on Te Mahanga and other tracks. These are placed inside cages to exclude the more dominant and larger tūī.

⊳ Round the Lake Track

Further into the sanctuary, the upper reservoir is where saddleback and whitehead are most conspicuous, especially from March to May. Stitchbird and robin are also likely to be encountered here. Near the start of the track is a 10-m-high lookout with a grand view of the valley. Near the eastern end of the track, hides overlook the upper reservoir where scaup, brown teal and mallard are likely to be seen. The upper dam also provides a good view over the lower sanctuary.

⊳ 'Sanctuary by Night' tour

The sanctuary closes at 5 pm, so this guided evening tour provides a chance to hear the 'dusk chorus', watch the shags fly to their evening roosts, and hear the calls of nocturnal birds such as morepork/ruru and little spotted kiwi. Anecdotal evidence suggests there's almost a 50 per cent chance of actually seeing a kiwi out feeding, and that should increase as the population grows. Whether seen or not, they will usually be heard calling across the valley.

Getting there Several bus routes pass the start of Waiapu Road, which is a five-minute walk from ZEALANDIA. From the city take any of numbers 3, 13, 18, 21, 22 or 23, disembark at the first stop after the Karori road tunnel, and walk along Waiapu Road to ZEALANDIA.

By car, drive from the city up Bowen Street, turn left onto Glenmore Road and follow the signs. Waiapu Road is the first on the left immediately after exiting the Karori Tunnel. There is ample parking space.

The taxi fare from the city is about $20. There is a complimentary pick-up from Wellington i-SITE Visitor Centre, in Wakefield Street for those booked on some guided tours. Bookings are essential.

Getting around Access is through a gate at the Visitor Centre, at the end of Waiapu Road. For biosecurity reasons this is the only public entry point, and visitors are requested to check their bags for unwanted stowaways, such as mice, before entering.

Tracks are suitable for all ages, with many negotiable by wheelchairs and pushchairs. Most bird species are likely to be encountered in the lower third of the sanctuary, involving walks from about 1–3 hours' duration.

Visitors are free to wander at their own pace and encouraged to ask roving guides questions and seek advice on tracks and trails.

Accommodation Wellington has all of the accommodation options one would expect of a major city.

Facilities The Visitor Centre encompasses the Exhibition, a two-level interactive showcase of New Zealand's natural history and conservation story, plus Rata Cafe, toilets and a retail store. Inside the Sanctuary there is a small under-cover information display and several signs are located along the walking tracks. There are toilets just beyond the end of the lower reservoir, and seats and picnic tables in several areas. Of special interest are the 'bird tapes' hidden in the trees, designed to help visitors identify bird calls.

Information

General admission to the Exhibition and the sanctuary valley $28/adult, $14/child. Entry to sanctuary valley only $18/adult, $9/child. This includes access to Rata Cafe and the retail store. Family passes are available and entry is free for Trust members. 'ZEALANDIA by Night' tour $75/adult, $35/child, bookings essential. Group tours for more than 10 can also be booked. Small boat cruises operate on the lower reservoir in the weekends, weather permitting, $3/adult, 04 920 9200, info@visitzealandia.com, www.visitzealandia.com.

17

Farewell Spit

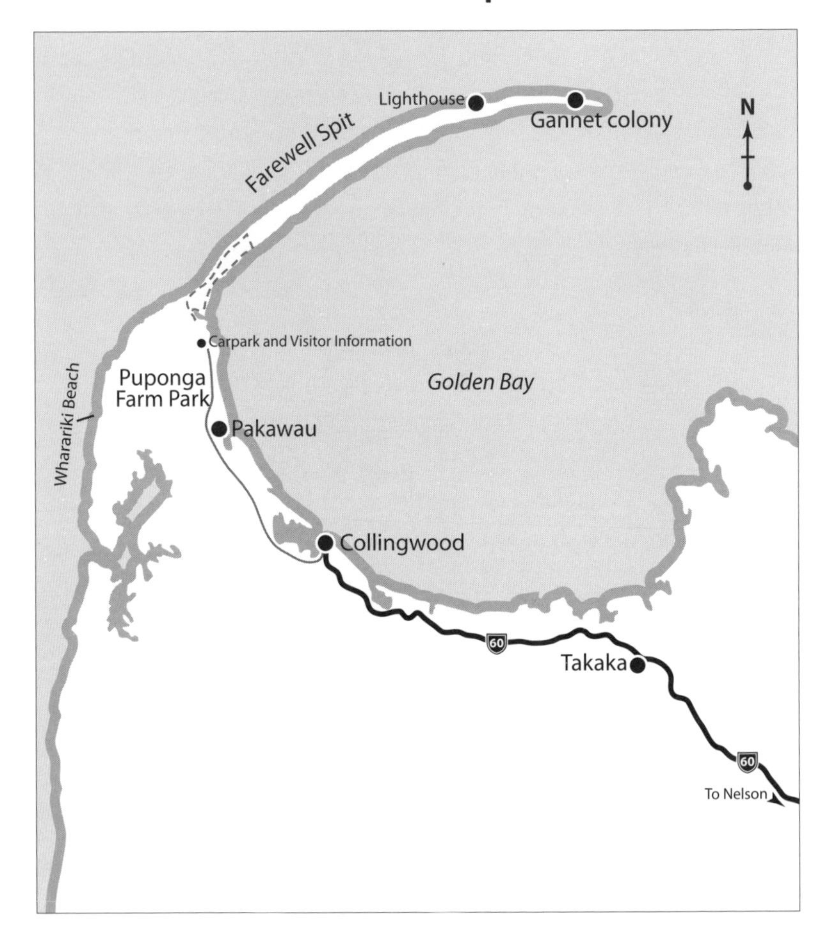

Where North-west tip of the South Island.

What's special Ramsar Wetland of International Importance and Nature Reserve. A massive sand spit, plus tidal flats that provide a summer home to thousands of Arctic waders and winter feeding grounds for native migrant waders, plus local estuaries.

Birds to look for Huge flocks of lesser knot/huahou and bar-tailed godwit/kūaka, as well as turnstone, eastern curlew, Asiatic whimbrel and other Arctic waders (in summer), banded dotterel/tuturiwhatu, South Island pied oystercatcher/tōrea, white heron/kōtuku, royal spoonbill/kōtuku-ngutupapa (from late summer to winter), Australasian gannet/tākapu, Caspian tern/taranui, black-backed gull/karoro, red-billed gull/tarāpunga, variable oystercatcher/tōrea, blue penguin/kororā and black swan (year-round).

Birdwatching options Guided 4WD tours, self-guided walks (base of Spit and Puponga Farm Park) or drives.

Top spots

- Farewell Spit tidal flats (3–4 hour guided tour or self-guided)
- Gannet colony (6.5-hour guided tour)
- Farewell Spit base (up to 6 hours' walking)
- Puponga Farm Park (up to a day)
- Puponga Inlet and Collingwood to Farewell Spit road (15-minute drive).

When September–March for Arctic waders, winter for New Zealand migrants; year-round for Australasian gannet, variable oystercatcher, terns and gulls.

Background

Farewell Spit extends some 30 km from the north-western tip of the South Island, its area increasing at least tenfold at low tide. Of the hundreds of thousands of Arctic waders that fly to New Zealand each summer, around a third base themselves at Farewell Spit.

Apart from the first few kilometres at the base of the Spit, where walking access is permitted, travel along the spit into the nature reserve is restricted to 4WD tours with licensed operators. By necessity, these travel at low tide when most waders are away out feeding on the extensive mudflats and only sightings of common species are likely. Nevertheless, these trips are spectacular for the landscape they traverse.

Tours to the gannet colony, at the very tip of the Spit, return later on the tide, when more birds are likely to be back on the Spit. Some wader tours travel along the inside of the Spit on the incoming tide, when it is possible to see the birds being driven back towards their roosts by the rising water. Walking around the base of the Spit is often most productive.

Each receding tide uncovers a 10-km-wide expanse of sand flats, mudflats, salt marsh and shell banks, prime habitats for waders and other birds. Over 90 species have been recorded, ranging from Arctic waders to kea from the South Island mountains.

Of the summer-visiting migrants, by far the most prolific are bar-tailed godwit (12,000–19,000 birds) and lesser knot (16,000–27,000 birds). Smaller numbers of Asiatic whimbrel, turnstone and eastern curlew are also usually present. Other waders occasionally recorded here include Siberian tattler, curlew sandpiper, red-necked stint, sanderling, sharp-tailed sandpiper, greenshank and Mongolian dotterel.

The Australasian gannet colony, on shell banks close to sea level, is unusual, as gannet colonies are normally located on high cliffs and rock stacks. At Farewell Spit, storms and spring-tide floods take their toll on this low-lying colony. Only 50 chicks survived a cyclone in 1997. However, the population has since recovered to over 3000 pairs. Both Caspian and white-fronted terns also nest on these shell banks.

The Spit is a winter home to New Zealand migrants, in particular South Island pied oystercatcher, banded dotterel, and resident variable oystercatcher and pied stilt. The tidal flats also provide a moulting site for around 12,000 black swan. Two tour operators are licensed to take visitors into the Farewell Spit Nature Reserve. They use 4WD coaches with sound systems and air conditioning, and tours take up to 7 hours..

Aside from the birds there are other, notable features to a Farewell Spit safari: the lighthouse history, the stories of shipwrecks and whale strandings (for which the Spit is notorious), the exhilaration of careering down a giant sand dune (optional) and the sheer drama of the landscape.

Best birding areas

⊳ Inland side of the Spit

From September to March Farewell Spit Eco Tours occasionally runs a 2-hour tour about 4 km along the inland side of the Spit, with views across the tidal flats where the waders feed, and which is timed to see the birds pushed toward the shore by the incoming tide. This is a short and restricted, tide-dependent tour for small groups in an all-terrain Argo vehicle. Bookings strongly advised.

⊳ Base of the Spit

Walking access is permitted at the base of the Spit for 2 km along the ocean beach and up to 4 km along the inner beach. The boundaries of this area are well signposted, as are walking tracks at the road end car park, just beyond the Farewell Spit Information Centre at Puponga Farm Park.

For the best bird viewing, leave the car about 1.5 hours before high tide (preferably a spring tide) and cross the farm park to the ocean beach. Fossil Point, 10 minutes' walk to the west, is worth a look for blue penguin, fluttering shearwater and white-fronted tern, all of which breed here. To see waders, walk eastwards along the beach to the clearly marked limit of public access. At high tide, several thousand bar-tailed godwit, lesser knot, turnstone and South Island pied oystercatcher usually roost along here.

Follow the signs and red-dot markers and walk back across the Spit to the inner beach and tidal flats. As the tide recedes, birds start to feed on the exposed mudflats and there can be good viewing. The mud is generally firm enough to walk on for some distance to watch the birds as they move further onto the flats. Alternatively, walk along the inner beach first, to see the waders working up the mudflats as the tide pushes them in, then cross to see the high-tide roost on the ocean side of the Spit.

Gannet colony

Farewell Spit Eco Tours is licensed to take visitors to the Australasian gannet colony at the very tip of the Spit. Tours are limited to 20 people and do not run every day, so pre-booking is essential.

To reach the colony, visitors need to walk about 20 minutes beyond the lighthouse (where the vehicle stops), across sand, often in very windy conditions, and can expect to get their feet wet. The up-close encounter with frenetic gannet activity is, however, ample reward.

Puponga Farm Park

The varied habitats of this working farm park, which spreads across the base of the Spit and forms a buffer for Farewell Spit Nature Reserve, are well worth a look. Waders sometimes roost in the open paddocks, while wetlands and shrub lands provide habitats for forest birds, fernbird, marsh crake and Australasian bittern/matuku. New Zealand scaup, paradise shelduck/pūtangitangi, Australasian little grebe and other waterbirds frequent small lakes in the park. Two of these lakes are found on Wharariki Farm Track, accessible from the car park at the western end of the park. A second track here descends to Wharariki Beach, where seabirds present are likely to include blue penguin, fluttering shearwater and white-fronted tern, all of which breed along this coast.

Puponga Inlet and Collingwood to Farewell Spit

While travelling the 30 km from Collingwood to Farewell Spit, keep an eye out for white heron and royal spoonbill, particularly in winter. White heron are often seen in Puponga Inlet, while royal spoonbill are regularly seen right beside the road – one tour operator claims to have counted up to 50, lined up like a white picket fence. It's also worth checking high-tide wader roosts at the end of Totara Avenue, the beach at Pakawau (easily visible from the road) and Taupata Point (pull over by the trig just over Taupata Creek). Hundreds of black swan can usually be seen in the bay, closer to the base of the spit.

At Collingwood, the beach directly in front of the town is a top spot to see sheer numbers of South Island pied oystercatcher – at times there will be a hundred or more.

Getting there The nearest town to Farewell Spit is Collingwood, 2.5 hours by road from Nelson on SH60. The road continues 30 km from Collingwood to Puponga Farm Park, where the public road ends at a car park at the base of Farewell Spit.

Golden Bay Coachlines provides daily a service (two in summer) from Nelson to Takaka, plus a daily 9-am connection to Collingwood (23 km from Takaka). 03 525 8352 or www.goldenbaycoachlines.co.nz.

Golden Bay Air runs scheduled daily flights from Wellington to Takaka during summer and chartered flights during winter (www.capitalair.co.nz or freephone 0800 588 885). Remote Adventures Scenic Flights offer scheduled flights to Takaka from Paraparaumu (north of Wellington), Nelson and other local towns (www.remoteadventures.co.nz, 03 525 6167).

Getting around Tours to Farewell Spit leave either from Collingwood or Pakawau (between Collingwood and Farewell Spit). If flying direct to Takaka, a rental vehicle can be arranged through the Golden Bay i-SITE. The road to Farewell Spit and Puponga Farm Park is sealed and well signposted. Walking tracks over the park and in the public access area of the Spit are also well marked.

Accommodation Golden Bay has an excellent range: motel, holiday park, backpacker, farmstay, bed-and-breakfasts and self-contained.

Facilities Takaka has supermarket shopping, banking and ATM machines, service stations, i-SITE visitor information centre, cafes, taverns and a host of galleries selling local arts and crafts.

Collingwood has a tavern offering dine-in and takeaway meals, restaurant, cafe, small store and fuel.

The Mussel Inn (6 km towards Takaka) combines a brewery, music venue and country pub in one. There is a cafe at Pakawau and at Puponga Farm Park there is a cafe (open mainly during summer) and information display.

Information

Nelson i-SITE Visitor Information Centre, 03 548 2304, vin@nelsonnz.com, or www.nelsonnz.com.

Golden Bay i-SITE, 03 525 9136, or gb.vin@goldenbaynz.com.

Licensed guiding companies

Farewell Spit Eco Tours: Eco tour to lighthouse $120/adult, $55/child, Waderwatch $110/adult, Gannet Colony $135/adult, $55/child. www.farewellspit.com.

Kahurangi Nature Experiences: lighthouse and Cape Farewell tours. Costs range from $45–90/adult, $45–55/child. www.farewell-spit.co.nz.

Recommended reading

Farewell Spit and Puponga Farm Park, brochure, Department of Conservation.

Farewell Spit – A Changing Landscape, Chris Petyt, Terracotta Books (available locally in Collingwood and Takaka or cpetyt@xtra.co.nz).

Birds of the Nelson Region and Where to Find Them, Peter Gaze, David Butler, Jenny Hawkins. Nelson: in association with the Ornithological Society of New Zealand, 1990.

18

Marlborough Sounds

Where North-eastern region of the South Island.

What's special Forest-lined waterways and predator-free island reserves with prolific seabirds and some endangered forest species. Dolphins and sometimes whales present.

Birds to look for New Zealand king shag/kōau and other shags, Australasian gannet/tākapu, fluttering shearwater/pakahā, blue penguin/kororā, terns, gulls and occasional albatross species. Saddleback/tīeke, South Island robin/toutouwai, weka, New Zealand pigeon/kererū, tūī, bellbird/korimako, fantail/pīwakawaka (the black form of the South Island subspecies).

Birdwatching options Guided nature cruises, guided and self-guided forest walks, sea kayaking.

Top spots

- Queen Charlotte Sound (half-day nature cruise or multi-day kayak trip)
- Motuara Island (1-hour walk)
- Queen Charlotte Sound and White Rocks (half-day cruise)
- Queen Charlotte Track (short walks and up to 5 days' hiking)
- Lochmara Lodge (overnight)
- French Pass (day or overnight).

When to go Year-round. During winter the weather is generally more settled and the area less crowded, though this does mean some operators cut back on services. Spring is a good time to see spotted shag in breeding plumage, and nesting blue penguin.

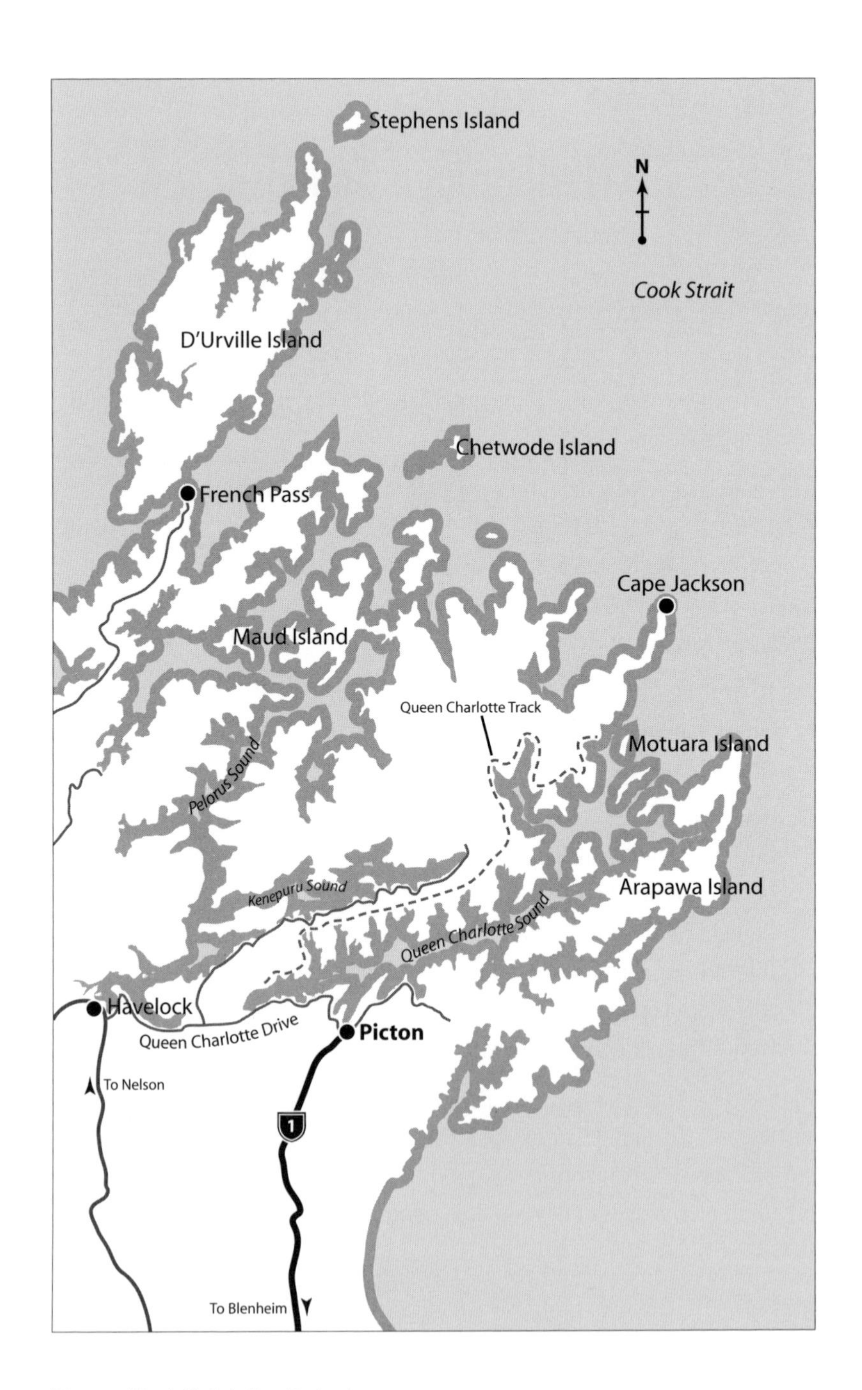
Stephens Island
N
Cook Strait
D'Urville Island
Chetwode Island
French Pass
Cape Jackson
Maud Island
Queen Charlotte Track
Motuara Island
Pelorus Sound
Kenepuru Sound
Arapawa Island
Queen Charlotte Sound
Havelock
Queen Charlotte Drive
Picton
To Nelson
1
To Blenheim

Background

The Marlborough Sounds are a maze of waterways, bays, inlets, forest-covered islands and promontories, largely backed by bush-clad hills. There are 1400 km of coastline and more than 50 reserves including a number of island wildlife sanctuaries and a marine reserve. These safeguard over 50,000 ha of regenerating and mature native forest, varied wildlife habitats and marine environments.

Picton, at the head of Queen Charlotte Sound, is the southern inter-island ferryport. The town of Havelock, between Blenheim and Nelson, is gateway to Pelorus and Kenepuru Sounds. The region is sparsely populated and relatively poorly roaded, so that much travel is by boat, but tourism draws many visitors each year and a wide range of tourist accommodation is available. Marine farming of green-lipped mussels and salmon is a major industry and the neighbouring Marlborough wine-producing region adds to the appeal.

With such a variety of habitat, the Sounds attract a great range of both resident and migratory sea and land birds including the endemic New Zealand king shag, which with a population of around 500 rates as one of the world's rarest aquatic birds. The shags breed in only five colonies, all located on tiny islands and reefs in the outer Sounds.

Many of the islands provide safe refuge for wildlife and plants that no longer survive on the mainland because of habitat destruction and introduced predators. Some of these islands are designated nature or scientific reserves, with restricted access to protect the rare species they support, for example the tuatara, fairy prion and giant wētā on Stephens Island. Other island reserves are open to visitors, including Motuara, where several threatened species have been reintroduced since rats were eradicated in 1992.

More recent island restoration projects have been undertaken on Blumine and Long Islands, also in Queen Charlotte Sound. Resident bird populations, for example weka, tomtit/miromiro, tūī, bellbird/korimako and New Zealand pigeon have since flourished.

Best birding spots

▷ Queen Charlotte Sound

A nature cruise or kayak expedition here is guaranteed to reveal a good variety of seabirds and shorebirds. (So will travel on an inter-island ferry or a water taxi in the Sounds, though these don't stop for birdwatchers.)

There's a reasonable chance of seeing king shag in the middle and outer Sounds, feeding alone or roosting in flocks. Local guides also know where to find the nesting spots of pied shag/kāruhiruhi, little shag/kōau and spotted shag/pārekareka.

Other seabirds and shorebirds likely to be seen include Australasian gannet, fluttering shearwater, blue penguin, white-fronted tern/tara, variable oystercatcher/tōrea, black-backed gull/karoro and red-billed gull/tarāpunga. There's also a reasonable chance of seeing Caspian tern/taranui, Arctic skua, reef heron/matuku-moana and white-faced heron. Very occasional visitors include various albatross, giant petrel, fairy prion and sooty shearwater/tītī.

Boat trips can be organised to see a small gannet colony established on Arapawa Island, in the outer Sound.

A likely bonus in the Sound is meeting the resident pod of Hector's dolphins, along with other dolphin species and orca that occasionally visit.

Guided sea-kayaking companies focus on all wildlife, marine mammals and birds, as they paddle around the Sound, calling on their local knowledge to show clients where the birds are likely to be nesting, moulting, roosting or feeding, depending on the weather and time of day or year.

▷ Motuara Island

Near the head of Queen Charlotte Sound, about 50 minutes by boat from Picton, Motuara's native forest has regenerated and birdlife flourished since rats were eradicated in 1992. Bellbird, New Zealand pigeon and fantail are prolific, while reintroduced robin, yellow-crowned parakeet and saddleback have settled well. The island also serves a valuable role as a safe nursery for young Ōkārito brown kiwi/rowi transferred here for two to three months until they grow big and strong enough to survive in their home forest in South Westland (see Chapter 26).

From the jetty a walking track wends its way gently to a lookout on the island's summit. Allow about 20 minutes' walking time each way, longer to watch the birds, in particular the robins that will be sure to engage with any passers-by. There is a good chance of seeing blue penguin, with nesting boxes close to the jetty. Look, too, for parakeet, saddleback and robin bathing in the natural stone bath 150 m from the jetty.

Access to Motuara is unrestricted, but visitors are urged to be vigilant against accidental reintroduction of animal pests. Guided walks are available with DoC concessionaires Dolphin Watch Ecotours, while Anakiwa Kayaks, Marlborough Sounds Adventure and Wilderness Guides all incorporate an island visit into their walking and sea-kayaking trips.

▷ Outer Queen Charlotte Sound

Colonies of the rare king shag are established on exposed, low-lying islands and reefs in the outer Sounds at White Rocks, Duffers Reef, Sentinel Rock and North Trio Island. These shags are particularly vulnerable to human disturbance and will leave their nests to the mercy of gulls if people land or boats approach too close. Thus boat operators are required to keep at least 100 m away, especially during the breeding season (March–August).

▷ Queen Charlotte Track

This popular multi-day walking track encompasses a variety of habitats and a range of forest and seabirds are usually encountered. The track runs for 71 km along the peninsula between Queen Charlotte Sound in the south and Kenepuru and Pelorus Sounds to the north. It passes through a variety of regenerating and mature forest, sometimes following high ridgelines and sometimes sidling close to the water around bays and inlets.

Forest birds most likely to be encountered (depending on fruiting and flowering seasons) include bellbird, tūī, fantail (the black form of the South Island subspecies), New Zealand pigeon, silvereye/tauhou and kingfisher/

kōtare. Less common but occasionally seen are tomtit, grey warbler/riroriro, robin, New Zealand falcon/kārearea and paradise shelduck/pūtangitangi.

The Sounds are also among the few remaining strongholds of weka, which have declined to the point of extinction in other regions. Here these inquisitive and nearly fearless birds are common around beaches and bays, and can be a nuisance as they will investigate anything left unattended for a moment and make off with whatever they can carry.

The track can be walked independently or with guides (allow for a small private land access charge added to their fee). Accommodation options range from DoC campsites to stylish lodges. Many people hire water taxis and walk small sections, perhaps a day or half-day at a time, or send their packs ahead to their following night's accommodation. With its mostly gentle grades, the track is also popular with mountain bikers.

▷ Lochmara Lodge

Owner Shane Olsen operates a predator-control and breeding programme for weka, red-crowned and yellow-crowned parakeet and other threatened wildlife, in association with DoC. Guests can see the parakeets in enclosures, along with Marlborough green gecko and local tree wētā. Seabirds are also conspicuous, including blue penguin which use the nesting boxes provided for them.

▷ French Pass

French Pass Sea Safaris and Beachfront Villas, run by the Bolton family. The company runs birding cruises which guarantee king shag sightings, and regularly see pied, spotted and little shag, blue penguin, Australasian gannet, white-fronted tern, fluttering shearwater, gulls, petrels, shearwaters, Arctic skua, Cape pigeon and others. The Boltons also run a pest-eradication programme at their property, where visitors can see weka, tūī, New Zealand pigeon, bellbird, kingfisher and possibly New Zealand falcon/kärearea during summer.

▷ Viewing birds from the ferry

The inter-island ferries (see below) cross the narrows of Cook Strait and pass through Queen Charlotte Sound during the 3-hour voyage between Picton and Wellington. This is an outstanding opportunity to watch for the albatross, shearwaters, petrels, prions, terns, shags, penguins and gulls that frequent these waters.

Getting there Picton is 20 minutes' drive from Blenheim, 2 hours' drive from Kaikōura, 4 hours' drive from Christchurch and 1.75 hours' drive from Nelson. Several daily Intercity coach services link Picton with other South Island towns and cities.

Passenger and vehicle ferry services make a number of daily crossings between Wellington and Picton. These services are the Interislander (www.interislander.co.nz) and the Bluebridge (www.bluebridge.co.nz). The website www.cookstraitferries.com provides an online booking service for both.

Sounds Air flies daily from Wellington direct to Picton (up to eight return flights per day, flight time 25 minutes), www.soundsair.com. Blenheim is on the national air network, with daily services from towns and cities throughout New Zealand. Shuttle services are available between Blenheim Airport and Picton.

The TranzCoastal passenger train travels daily between Christchurch and Picton. It's a scenic coastal trip taking just over five hours, with the option of breaking the journey at Kaikōura for some pelagic bird watching. www.tranzscenic.co.nz.

French Pass is located at the more isolated north-western end of the Sounds, about 3 hours' drive from Picton, or just minutes by helicopter (cost around $750) or floatplane.

Getting around Most nature cruises and guided kayaking and walking operations depart from Picton, and they will generally call for passengers staying at lodges around the Sounds. The Picton i-SITE Visitor Centre has contact details for several water-taxi companies, which operate regular services from Picton to accommodation lodges and drop-off points along the Queen Charlotte Track.

Accommodation Ranges from Qualmark five-star resorts to bed-and-breakfasts, backpackers and holiday parks. Picton has hotels, motels, backpackers, holiday parks, bed-and-breakfasts and luxury self-contained accommodation. Lodges and resorts nestled in picturesque bays throughout the Sounds offer self-contained or fully serviced options. DoC campsites are located along the Queen Charlotte Track. Blenheim and Marlborough offer motels, hotels, backpackers and luxury retreats.

Facilities Picton offers full shopping, supermarket, banking and pharmacy services, cafes, restaurants, bars and an i-SITE Visitor Centre. Most lodges in the Sounds have restaurants and welcome casual diners.

Information

Picton i-SITE Visitor Centre, The Foreshore, 03 520 3113, picton@i-SITE.org. www.destinationmarlborough.com.

Licensed guiding companies

Dolphin Watch Ecotours: marine mammal cruises combined with birding and a Motuara Island guided tour, plus a 'Birdwatchers' Expedition' that includes Motuara Island and an option to see the White Rocks king shag colony. Cost $120/adult, $60/child, additional $35/adult to see king shag colony, private charter only. 03 573 8040, info@naturetours.co.nz, www.naturetours.co.nz.

French Pass Sea Safaris and Beachfront Villas: specialist bird watching cruises to the Chetwode Islands (king shag and other seabirds), plus marine mammal encounters, diving, kayaking and accommodation. Birding cruises from $85/adult, king shag colony by arrangement, 03 576 5204, adventure@seasafaris.co.nz, www.seasafaris.co.nz.

Wilderness Guides: guided kayaking (packages start from $100 for a 1-day trip), guided Queen Charlotte Track walks including Motuara

Island. Also kayak/walk combinations and independent kayak hire. 03 573 5432, 0800 266 266, www.wildernessguidesnz.com.

Marlborough Sounds Adventure Company: guided kayaking (starting from $75 for a half-day trip), guided Queen Charlotte Track walks including Motuara Island. Also kayak/walk combinations and independent kayak hire. 0800 283 283 (NZ), 1800 007 083 (Australia), 03 573 8827, adventure@marlboroughsounds.co.nz, www.marlboroughsounds.co.nz.

Sea Kayaking Adventures: single and multi-day kayak trips, some including Motuara Island. 03 574 2765, info@nzseakayaking.com, www.nzseakayaking.com.

Lochmara Lodge, Wildlife Recovery and Arts Centre: accommodation, restaurant, bathhouse and massage suite, forest restoration, parakeet and weka breeding, art workshops. Overnight rates from $90 (twin units) to $260 (luxury chalets). Closed June to mid September. 03 573 4554, enquiries@lochmaralodge.co.nz, www.lochmaralodge.co.nz.

19

Rotoiti Nature Recovery Project

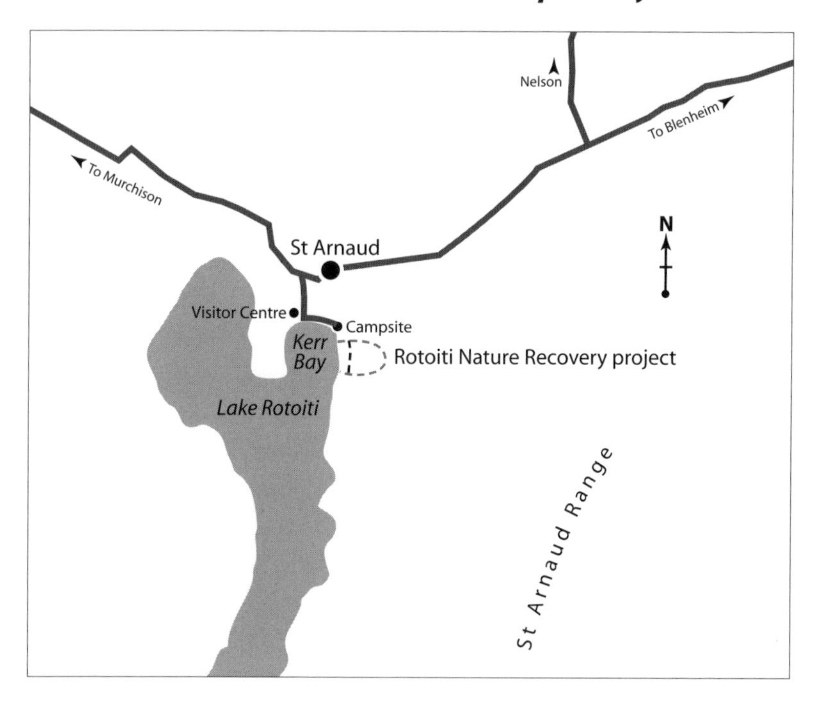

Where St Arnaud, Nelson Lakes National Park, northern South Island.

What's special An on-going conservation project in a South Island beech forest. Prolific forest birds, very easy access and a striking mountain and lake setting.

Birds to look for Kākā, red-crowned parakeet/kākāriki, South Island robin/kakaruai, tūī, bellbird/korimako, fantail/pīwakawaka, tomtit/miromiro, rifleman/tītīpounamu. Great spotted kiwi/roroa may be heard.

Birdwatching options Self-guided walks.

Top spots

- Bellbird Track and Honeydew Walk (1 hour's walk).

When to go Any time – during summer holidays St Arnaud is very busy, in winter snow-covered mountains add to the spectacle. Staying overnight provides opportunity to hear the notable dawn chorus.

Background

The Rotoiti Nature Recovery Project was established in 1997 to enhance and protect around 800 ha of the park's 'honeydew' beech forest. In 2001 the area was expanded and today encompasses 5000 ha of mountainside, from the Rotoiti lakeshore all the way to the summit ridge of the St Arnaud Range.

The project began as one of DoC's six 'mainland island' areas, where intensive predator control has resulted in forest recovery and a resurgence of native wildlife.

A sweet honeydew that gives the forest its distinctive character is produced by small sap-sucking insects living on the tree trunks. Where honeydew is present, a fungus grows and gives the trunks a distinctive blackened appearance. Native birds, insects and lizards depend upon the honeydew as a food source. This food has been monopolised by wasps, which were accidentally introduced to New Zealand last century and spread widely throughout many areas. However, within two years of starting a rigorous control campaign, wasp numbers at Rotoiti were seasonally reduced by 90 per cent. Other pests were also targeted, with possum numbers cut to nearly zero and an all-out, ongoing blitz launched against stoats and rats.

Early results have included record breeding seasons for kākā and increased numbers of robin. In 2004 great spotted kiwi, which had not been seen or heard in the park since the 1920s, were reintroduced from one of the species' last strongholds, Kahurangi National Park.

As well as forest recovery and reintroduction of birds, the Rotoiti project focuses on other rare species that were originally part of this natural ecosystem, such as native mistletoes, giant snails, lizards, bats and insects. The local community, though a volunteer group called Friends of Rotoiti, has also got behind the restoration efforts, and volunteers regularly monitor some 20 km of stoat trap lines.

One of the reasons for selecting Rotoiti as a 'mainland island' was its ease of access, making it an ideal site to showcase and share this successful conservation story. Already more than 100,000 visitors come each year, relishing the chance to hear the restored dawn chorus and enjoy the playful antics of the growing population of young kākā.

⊳ Bellbird Track and Honeydew Walk

Bellbird Track is a 15-minute pathway, easily negotiable by pushchairs and wheelchairs, that explores the lakeside forest. From the very start of the walk, the resident bird population generally makes itself known, with songs of the nectar-feeding tūī and bellbird, kākā likely to be screeching and swooping from the canopy, curious robin watching from the forest floor, and fantail and tomtit darting for insects. Interpretation panels describe the story of the recovery project and the flora and fauna.

Honeydew Walk, a 45-minute loop track, continues from Bellbird Track further among the honeydew-producing red beech and mountain beech trees. A longer loop track continues into the forest, taking about 1.5 hours to complete. However, it is not necessarily a matter of the further the walk, the more birds seen, as they are present throughout.

Note: Visitors should keep to the marked tracks and not tamper with bait stations or traps. Wasps can still be a nuisance, especially in late summer and autumn.

Getting there St Arnaud township is located on SH63, 1.5 hours' drive from both Blenheim and Nelson. Lake Rotoiti and the project area are beside the township. Daily bus services are available from all nearby towns and cities, though some run only three times weekly over the winter.

Getting around Walking tracks are clearly signposted near the lake, beside the camping ground. At the west end of St Arnaud township, turn off SH63 and head a few hundred metres to the lake, passing the Nelson Lakes Visitor Centre on the right. Turn left at the traffic island, cross the bridge and continue 100 m to the forest edge and car park.

Accommodation St Arnaud offers backpacker hostels, rental holiday homes, motels, a hotel and two camping areas, each with showers, toilets, laundry, powered sites and tent sites. If visiting during the busy summer months it would pay to book ahead.

Facilities There is a restaurant, cafe, shop, postal facilities and fuel at St Arnaud. The park visitor centre is worth a look for its excellent audiovisual presentation and displays about the park's natural and human history. By the lake there are public toilets and picnic areas.

Murchison, less than an hour's drive west of St Arnaud, has camping grounds, motels, hotels, cafes, restaurants and shops. Blenheim and Nelson have all services.

Information

Nelson Lakes Visitor Centre, View Road, 03 521 1806, nelsonlakesao@doc.govt.nz.

20

Kaikōura

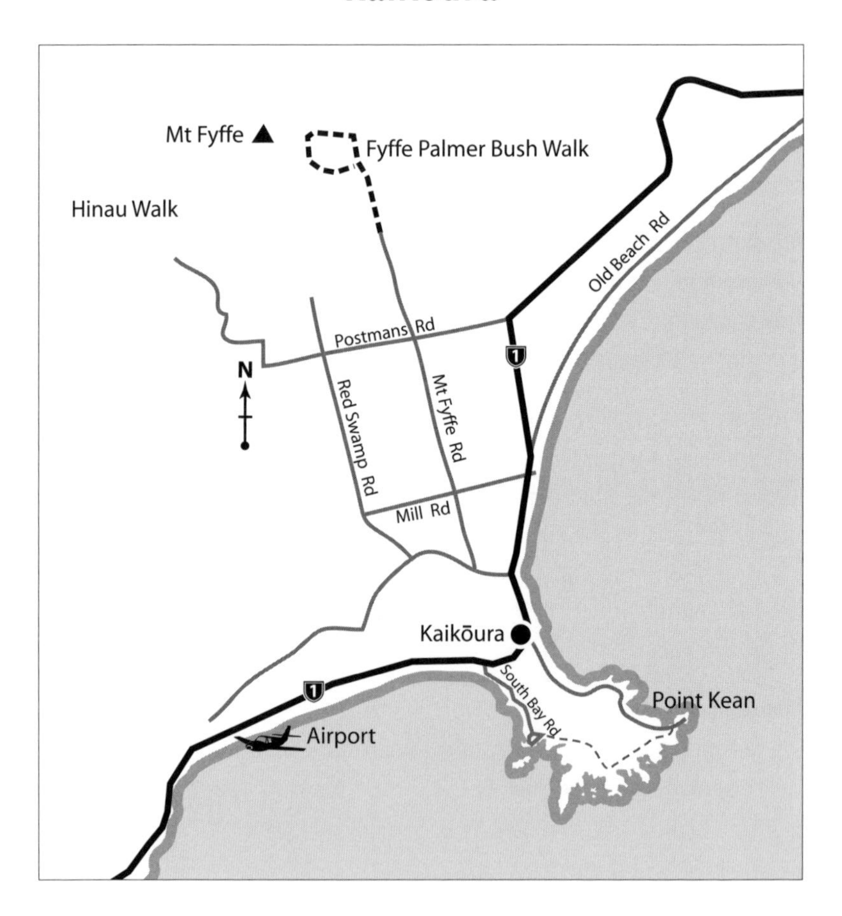

Mt Fyffe
Fyffe Palmer Bush Walk
Hinau Walk
Old Beach Rd
Postmans Rd
N
Red Swamp Rd
Mt Fyffe Rd
1
Mill Rd
Kaikōura
South Bay Rd
Point Kean
1
Airport

Where South Island east coast, north of Christchurch.

What's special Some of the most accessible pelagic birdwatching in the world, against an impressive mountain backdrop; also whale and dolphin watching.

Birds to look for Hutton's shearwater/tītī (spring and summer), northern and southern royal albatross/toroa, wandering albatross, Salvin's albatross (mainly summer), Buller's and white-capped albatross (winter); up to 10 other albatross species; fairy prion, Cape pigeon, giant petrel, Antarctic fulmar (winter), Westland petrel/tītī (summer) and several other petrels. Arctic skua, white-fronted tern/tara, black-fronted tern/tarapiroe (summer); red-billed gull/tarāpuna.

Birdwatching options Pelagic cruise, self-guided walk, guided walk.

Top spots

- Pelagic cruise (2–3 hours)
- Kaikōura Peninsula Walk (2–4 hours)
- Hinau Walk and Fyffe-Palmer Reserve (2–4 hours).

How long to go Half a day will suffice for the pelagic cruise, the main drawcard for birders at Kaikōura, but there is plenty more to do here too.

When to go Year-round. In winter there are higher numbers of pelagics; in summer there are smaller numbers of birds but more species, sometimes rarities. Spring to late summer for Hutton's shearwater. Spring and summer for red-billed gull colonies.

Background

Pelagic specialists say that when conditions are right, Kaikōura is the best place in the world for watching seabirds. It is also one of the most accessible, just 10 minutes by boat to the rich feeding grounds a few kilometres offshore. There are few places in the world where the continental slope lies so close to land, and in such a spectacular setting. Nutrient upwelling sets in motion a complex food chain above the Kaikōura Canyon, a 1500-m-deep submarine trench which is the home of giant squid and a feeding ground for whales as well as seabirds. Sperm whales, dolphins, orca, sharks, fish, crayfish (rock lobster), seals and birds of sea and shore come together in this cornucopia of marine life.

When Kaikōura was first settled by Europeans in the early 19th century, whaling was the town's main business. Fishing, in particular for crayfish, later became a major industry, but today the tide has turned and nature tourism has become the town's economic mainstay.

Gary Melville is one of many locals who have adapted to the new order. A fisherman for 25 years, he became knowledgeable about the birds following his fishing boat, to the point where visiting birders began asking to go fishing with him. Gary began running birdwatching cruises, and is now one of several skippers working for Albatross Encounter.

One special Kaikōura species is Hutton's shearwater, which disperses around the South Pacific but breeds only in the Seaward Kaikōura Range, at altitudes of 1200 to 2000 m. Once widespread throughout the ranges, the birds are now confined to two colonies, both closed to visitors. At Mt Fyffe Hut, a popular hiking and mountain-biking destination near Kaikōura, during the breeding season it's possible to hear them after dark, passing overhead en route to their nests, and on a still, moonlit night, to see their dark silhouettes against the sky. However, the best place to observe the birds is on the water, close to the shore, where they gather in rafts of thousands from September to mid-March.

Between 2005 and 2008, DoC scientists attempting to establish a new breeding area relocated nearly 300 chicks from their mountain colony to artificial nests on peninsula land managed by the Hutton's Shearwater Charitable Trust. Young birds have been seen returning to these nest boxes, which is positive news. In 2010 the Trust completed a predator-proof fence safeguarding 2.1 ha of these new nesting sites.

For their sheer numbers and frenzied activity and noise the colonies of red-billed gulls at the end of Kaikōura Peninsula are worth a visit.

Best birding areas

⊳ Pelagic cruise

Albatross Encounter is licensed to run pelagic cruises. The company offers three trips daily during summer (6 am, 9 am and 1 pm) and two daily during winter (9 am and 1 pm). Summer is the busier tourist season, though winter is better for seeing more birds.

Tours require a minimum of three people (or one paying three fares); bookings are advisable in winter and essential in summer. Boat capacity is limited to 12 passengers. Larger vessels and extended cruises can be pre-arranged, such as half- or full-day trips that travel up to 30 km offshore.

The standard cruise makes several stops along the edge of the Kaikōura Canyon, then moves further offshore. If susceptible to motion sickness, be sure to take pre-cruise medication. As a rule, the wilder and windier it is, the better the birding. They'll generally come in close to the boat and present good photographing opportunities.

Tour skippers are extremely knowledgeable and also provide a bird list for identification purposes. They're even confident enough to offer a refund if no albatross are seen!

Tours leave from Encounter Kaikōura, 96 The Esplanade, on the Kaikōura beachfront and start with a five-minute drive to the South Bay wharf. The tour is subject to weather and sea conditions. Albatross Encounter's parent company, Encounter Kaikōura, is Green Globe certified.

⊳ Peninsula Walkway – 'Gull City'

At the tip of Kaikōura Peninsula there is a circular walking track that crosses the grassy headland and returns (tides permitting) along the shoreline. Coastal birds will be seen and in late afternoons (from September to March) the prominent headlands are great vantage spots for watching rafts of Hutton's shearwater on the water.

The northern end of the walkway at Point Kean is 5 km from town at the end of Fyffe Quay. From the car park (and seal colony), the shoreline walk crosses tidal platforms and little beaches to reach two red-billed gull colonies, First Point (15 minutes) and Sugarloaf Point, on the north side of Whalers Bay (30 minutes).

These colonies have been well established for several generations, and birds number in the thousands. In winter the colonies are largely deserted; however, in spring and summer they present a cacophony of noise and activity. Keep your distance, as the gulls will attack if they think their eggs or chicks are threatened, or possibly desert their nests if disturbed.

The shoreline has no formed track and is impassable at high tide. Check with the Kaikōura i-SITE Visitor Centre for tide times. Alternatively, Whalers Bay can be reached via a short climb to the Clifftop Track, then a steep, clearly signposted descent. From the vantage point of this track, seabirds can often be seen feeding on shoals of small fish. The Clifftop Track passes beside the predator-proof fence safeguarding Hutton's shearwater nests. Interpretive signs here explain this conservation story.

Other birds likely to be seen around the Peninsula Walkway are white-fronted tern/tara, black-backed gull/karoro, little, pied shag/kāruhiruhi,

Southern Seabird Solutions

In the Southern Ocean alone, tens of thousands of seabirds are killed each year in fishing operations. Albatrosses and petrels are particularly vulnerable because they can dive beneath the surface and take baited hooks while long-lines are being set. The number of hooks on a line may be up to 35,000. Birds also get tangled in the lines and drown, or are injured or killed when struck by trawl warps (heavy wire ropes attached to a trawling net).

New Zealand has a major stake in this international conservation issue, with a large fishing zone and some of the most diverse seabird populations, and is at the forefront of addressing the problem. Some New Zealand fishing vessels have changed their practices, for example

spotted shag/pārekareka, South Island pied oystercatcher/tōrea, cirl bunting and white-faced heron. Blue penguin/kororā can sometimes be observed in the water. Be sure to keep a safe distance from the seals, and don't get between them and the water.

At the South Bay car park there is a DoC shelter with information panels and a viewing hide for watching waders on the mudflats at low tide. Turn onto South Bay Parade from SH1, immediately south of the township.

▷ Hinau Walk and Fyffe-Palmer Reserve

While the birding focus at Kaikōura leans towards the ocean, there is good viewing of forest birds in the foothills close to town. Recommended are the Fyffe-Palmer Reserve Forest Walk, a gentle, 2- to 3-hour circuit through regenerating and mature lowland podocarp forest, and Hinau Walk, a 45-minute loop track through coastal lowland broadleaf forest. Bellbird/korimako, New Zealand pigeon/kererū, grey warbler/riroriro and

setting their lines at night when seabirds are less active, and using bird-scaring devices that prevent seabirds getting close to the baits or warps.

Southern Seabird Solutions, an alliance between the New Zealand government, the fishing industry and WWF-NZ, promotes seabird-safe fishing practices throughout the southern hemisphere. However, the range covered by many of these birds means that conservation efforts must be globally coordinated. Southern Seabird Solutions' work also includes international projects, for example skipper exchanges with Chile, Peru and Reunion Island.

For more information visit www.southernseabirds.org.

brown creeper/pīpipi are all present. There's also good chance of seeing robin/toutouwai and rifleman/tītīpounamu and, from September to April, hearing shining cuckoo/pīpīwharauroa.

Fyffe-Palmer Reserve is on Mt Fyffe Road, 9 km northwest of Kaikōura. Hinau Walk is on Postmans Road, 15 km inland from Kaikōura at the start of the 4WD road to Mt Fyffe.

Getting there Kaikōura is located on SH1, 183 km (2.5 hours' drive) north of Christchurch and 154 km (2 hours' drive) south of Picton. Daily rail and coach services pass through the town.

Getting around Kaikōura is a small town, with most accommodation and cafes within easy walking distance although tour operators and accommodation providers offer transport as required. Kaikōura Shuttles kaikoura.taxis@xtra.co.nz, 03 319 6166 run daily sightseeing tours also. There's also moped and scooter hire at the Kaikoura Woolshed Gallery (03 319 7979) and bicycle hire from R&R Sports (03 319 5028).

Accommodation Kaikōura has an excellent range of lodge, hotel, boutique, motel, holiday park, backpacker, bed-and-breakfast, farmstay and self-contained accommodation, including several Qualmark five-star motels, apartments and lodges.

Facilities There are several restaurants, cafes and bars, a number of craft galleries, two supermarkets, an internet cafe, laundromat, museum and i-SITE Visitor Centre.

Information

Kaikōura i-SITE Visitor Centre, Westend, 03 319 5641, kaikoura@i-SITE.org, www.kaikouranz.co.nz.

Hutton's Shearwater Charitable Trust, www.huttonsshearwater.org.nz.

Guiding companies

Albatross Encounter: daily pelagic cruises, $110/adult, $55/child.
03 319 6777, info@oceanwings.co.nz, www.albatrossencounter.co.nz.

Bush Birding Kaikōura: local conservationist and author Barry Dunnett offers low-key guided walks in regenerating lowland forest, 8 km from Kaikōura. Tours last 2–3 hours and birds are easy to spot in the low-growing canopy. Cost $60 for 2 people, discounts for large groups.
bjdunnett@xtra.co.nz, http://www.virtual-kaikoura.com/birding.

21

Arthur's Pass

Where Central Southern Alps/Kā Tiritiri o te Moana.

What's special Easy access to alpine birds in Arthur's Pass National Park, which also encompasses braided rivers, beech forest and mixed rātā and podocarp rainforest habitats. Also Lake Pearson Wildlife Refuge.

Birds to look for Australasian crested grebe/kāmana, kea, New Zealand pipit/pihoipihoi, kākā and common forest birds, , rock wren/pīwauwau (summer), braided river birds, wrybill/ngutuparore, black-fronted tern/tara, black-billed gull/tarāpunga and banded dotterel/tuturiwhatu (spring and summer).

Birdwatching options Self-guided walks, roadside watching.

Top spots

- Arthur's Pass village and local walks (up to half a day)
- Ōtira Viaduct viewpoint (5 minutes)
- Lake Pearson/Moana Rua (1 hour)
- Waimakariri River (1–2 hours)
- Upper Ōtira (2 hours' walk return, best in summer).

When to go Year-round, although the road is sometimes closed by snow during winter.

Background

Arthur's Pass National Park straddles the Southern Alps/Kā Tiritiri o te Moana and is one of New Zealand's alpine national parks. Beech forests and wide braided rivers on the park's drier eastern side contrast with dense,

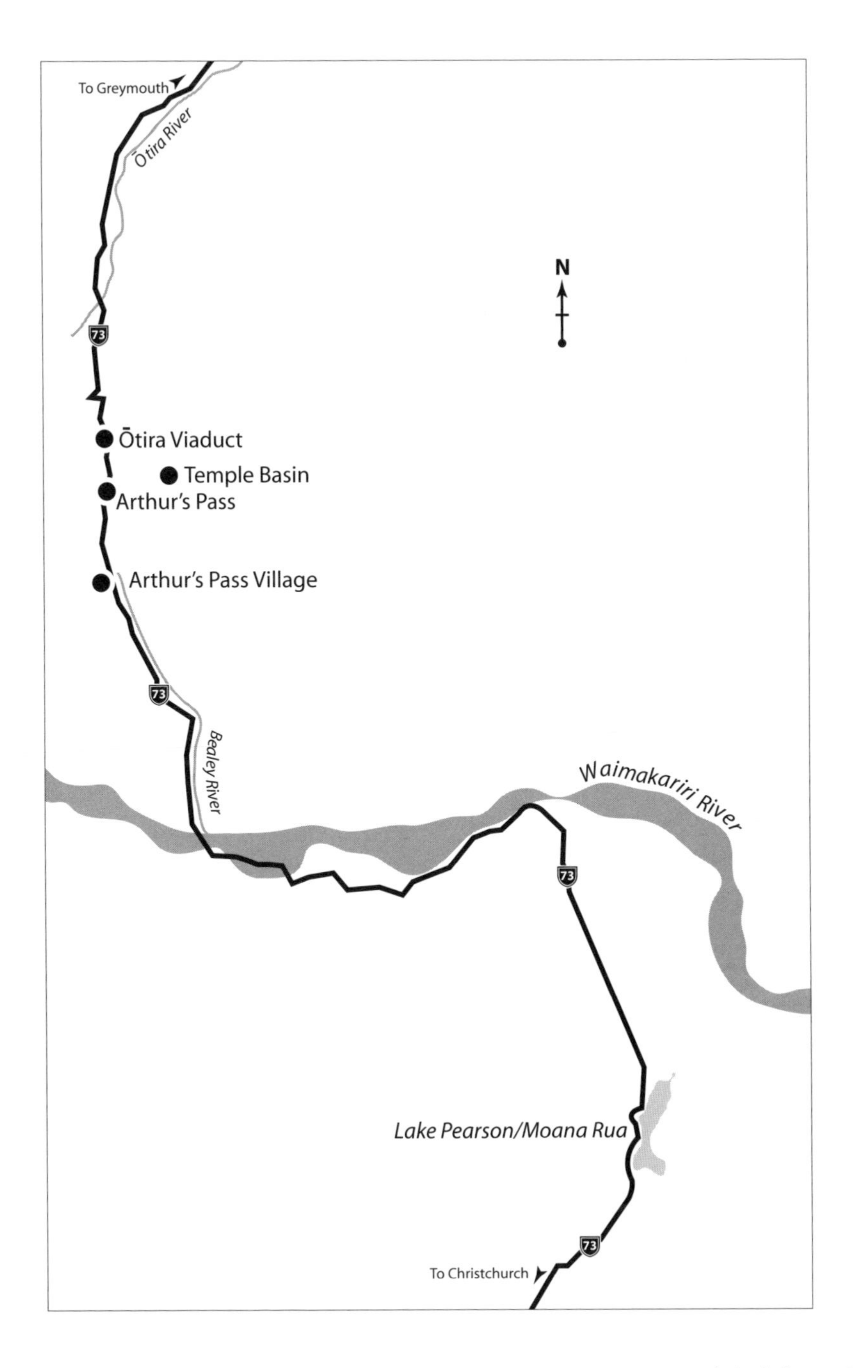
To Greymouth
Ōtira River
N
73
Ōtira Viaduct
Temple Basin
Arthur's Pass
Arthur's Pass Village
73
Bealey River
Waimakariri River
73
Lake Pearson/Moana Rua
73
To Christchurch

tangled rainforests and steep creeks on the much wetter western side of the main divide.

The highway that crosses the main divide at Arthur's Pass is the highest pass over the alps. The road climbs above the forest line, passing tussock-filled subalpine valleys, steep scree slopes and towering rock bluffs.

This is the domain of the kea, New Zealand's endemic mountain parrot, a colourful, brash and at times destructive bird. Watching flocks of young kea at car parks, tearing the rubber from windscreen wipers, belies this bird's endangered status.

New Zealand's only true alpine bird, the endemic rock wren spends its entire life above the bush line, surviving winters by hiding in rock crevices beneath the snow. Aside from the effort usually involved to reach its territory, the bird's patchy occurrence in South Island alpine areas, tiny size and ground-feeding habits make it difficult to find.

Kākā, the kea's equally raucous bush-parrot cousin, are most commonly seen in the park's western rainforests, along with tūī and New Zealand pigeon/kererū, where they find fruit, nectar and bark (for the kākā) more abundant than in the drier eastern forests.

The eastern braided rivers, with their many channels and wide grassy flats, provide breeding grounds for South Island migrant waders, along with paradise shelduck/pūtangitangi, pipit, the introduced skylark, and the self-introduced Australian spur-winged plover. Australasian harrier/kāhu are also present in these valleys and, in lesser numbers, New Zealand falcon/kārearea.

While these rivers provide routes for multi-day walking trips in the park, birds are commonly seen close to the highway. Blue duck/kōwhiowhio are still seen occasionally, generally in the upper reaches of rivers such as the Ōtira and Bealey.

One particularly accessible spot to observe Australasian crested grebe is Lake Pearson/Moana Rua. This sits directly beside the highway on the eastern approach to Arthur's Pass National Park. The lake is one of the few remaining breeding sites for these birds, and numbers have remained stable here for several years despite declining in other regions. In 2004 the lake was declared a wildlife refuge, the use of motorised boats restricted and predator control intensified.

Best birding areas

▷ Arthur's Pass village and local walks

Kea may be endangered but they certainly aren't shy. One of the most likely spots to see these engaging and approachable birds is right in Arthur's Pass village, perhaps outside the cafe or park visitor centre. Visitors are asked not to feed the birds, as it is harmful to them.

Short walks starting from the village, which explore beech forests, mountain streams and waterfalls, are likely spots for seeing a variety of forest birds, such as the South Island robin/toutouwai, rifleman/tītīpounamu, tomtit/miromiro, bellbird/korimako and brown creeper. Recommended walks are Bridal Veil (1.5 hours return) and Devil's Punchbowl (1 hour return, steep in places).

Arthur's Pass is the southernmost limit for great spotted kiwi/roroa, and it's not uncommon to hear the bird's piercing calls at dusk. The DoC Visitor Centre keeps records of where the kiwi have most recently been heard, and these are available to the public. Sightings, however, are unlikely.

▷ Ōtira Viaduct viewpoint

Another good spot for seeing kea is the signposted viewpoint at Deaths Corner, overlooking Ōtira Viaduct, on SH73 about 7 km west of Arthur's Pass village. A dramatic outlook adds to the spectacle: mountains, massive rock falls, Ōtira Gorge and remarkable sloping Ōtira Viaduct.

▷ Upper Ōtira Valley

A walking track climbs reasonably steadily from the highway near Arthur's Pass itself, through open subalpine vegetation, into the upper Ōtira valley. Rock wren may be seen here, although they are hard to find (summer is the best season for them, or at least when there is no snow). New Zealand pipit are also present. The walk starts near the highway's highest point as it crosses the Alps and, even if no birds are seen, this is one spectacular and relatively easy walk in the mountains. Look for the track sign on the left, about 6 km west from Arthur's Pass village.

If the upper Ōtira yields no rock wren, an option close by is Temple Basin. Getting there involves a 1- to 2-hour walk on the old 4WD track to Temple Basin skifield, zigzagging beneath bluffs to the ski-field. There are also higher tracks from the ski-field to the tarns further up the mountain. The birds are hard to find but on a clear day the views will compensate. Temple Basin is signposted from the highway 4 km west of the village.

▷ Waimakariri River

The main highway (SH73) crosses the Waimakariri River at Klondyke Corner, 5 km east of Arthur's Pass village. On the western side of the bridge a short road turns off the highway and follows the true left bank between beech forest and the wide grassy flats, providing access to tramping routes in the park. This is the most accessible area to look for braided-river birds.

▷ Lake Pearson/Moana Rua

This stronghold for Australasian crested grebe sits right beside the highway (SH73) leading from Christchurch to Arthur's Pass. It is usually easy to see the birds from the roadside parking area, near the western (Arthur's Pass) end of the lake. The birds make their nests among the willows, some of them 50 m from the car park. Depending on the conditions and wind direction, grebe can also be present in any of the sheltered bays along the lake's edge. The birds breed from September to March (following their elaborate courting rituals). Later in the season, young chicks can sometimes been seen carried on a parent's back. There is a DoC camping area, with toilets and picnic table, at the lake.

Getting there By road, Lake Pearson/Moana Rua and Arthur's Pass village are located on SH73. Lake Pearson/Moana Rua is 109 km from Christchurch, 25 km past Porter's Pass. Arthur's Pass village is on SH73, 153 km from Christchurch and 98 km from Greymouth.

Between Arthur's Pass and Ōtira the highway is steep and winding. It can be slippery with ice in winter and sometimes closed by snow. If uncertain, call the DoC Visitor Centre or listen to local radio stations.

The TranzAlpine train crosses daily from Christchurch to Greymouth, with stops along the way, including Arthur's Pass village. Daily coach services also run between Christchurch and Greymouth.

Getting around Self-driving is the best option, allowing for stops at birding points along the highway.

Accommodation In Arthur's Pass village there are backpacker hostels, bed-and-breakfasts, motels, and a park campsite. Luxury lodge and hotel accommodation is available in nearby towns and on high-country stations. Free DoC camping areas are located at Lake Pearson/Moana Rua and Klondyke Corner (by the Waimakariri River).

Facilities In Arthur's Pass village there is a bar, cafe, restaurant, visitor centre, fuel and a shop. There is no bank or ATM.

Information

Arthur's Pass National Park Visitor Centre, open daily 8 am to 5 pm (summer), 8.30 am to 4.30 pm (winter), 03 318 9211, arthurspassvc@doc.govt.nz.

Arthur's Pass general information, www.arthurspass.com.

Licensed guiding companies

Wilderness Lodge Arthur's Pass: Naturalist-guided walks for guests with a strong focus on birding, the natural ecology and conservation. 03 318 9245, www.wildernesslodge.co.nz.

Home in the Hills offer specialist wilderness education and guiding, including birding tours from four hours to two days. Bookings essential, 03 318 9220, www.homeinthehills.co.nz.

Recommended reading Arthur's Pass park map.

22

Christchurch and environs

Where In and around Christchurch city, South Island.

What's special Large coastal lagoon, estuaries, harbours and headlands; more than 200 bird species have been recorded in the greater Christchurch/Lake Ellesmere area, and more than 90 species are found there, seasonally or permanently, each year.

Birds to look for Arctic waders, South Island waders, massive flocks of waterfowl, white-flippered blue penguin/kororā, spotted shag/pārekareka, Australasian crested grebe/kāmana.

Birdwatching options Self-guided walks and drives, guided penguin-colony tour.

Top spots

- Lake Ellesmere/Te Waihora (2–3 hours from Christchurch)
- Pohatu/Flea Bay penguin colony (3 hours from Akaroa)
- Avon–Heathcote Estuary/Ihutai and Bromley oxidation ponds (2–3 hours from Christchurch)
- Travis Wetland Nature Heritage Park (1-2 hours from Christchurch)
- Waimakariri River (1–2 hours from Christchurch).
- Lake Forsyth/Waiwera.

How long to go 1–2 days.

When to go September–January (white-flippered blue penguin), September–February (Arctic migratory waders), December–June for impressive waterfowl flocks.

Background

New Zealand's cities are comparatively small and this is possibly one reason why so many habitats and birding opportunities are found close to urban areas. In the Christchurch region, efforts to restore urban wetlands and estuaries have had significant benefits for the wildlife that rely on these habitats. Examples include improved management of treatment plant and oxidation ponds at the Avon–Heathcote Estuary, resulting in the return of masses of waterfowl. The subsequent stopping of effluent discharge into the estuary is further enhancing water quality. Estuarine habitats have been the focus of restoration work, with new reserves created at Bexley, Charlesworth, and Ferrymead on the shores of the estuary. The city council's purchase of the Travis Wetlands has prevented further urban subdivision in a valuable wetland remnant.

A trust and multi-agency plan is working to restore the water quality of Lake Ellesmere, and efforts have been made by individual Banks Peninsula landowners to keep predators from the Pohatu penguin colony.

Educational programmes in schools, community tree-plantings and clean-up days have all played their part. In 2006 a large new regional park was created along the Waimakariri River, offering a higher level of protection to threatened species such as wrybill/ngutuparore, black-fronted tern/tarapiroe and Australasian bittern/matuku, along with picnic areas and walking trails for the public.

These Christchurch examples are typical of many government, council and community efforts throughout New Zealand.

Best birding areas

▷ Avon–Heathcote Estuary and Bromley oxidation ponds

Just 12 km from the city centre, the Avon–Heathcote estuary and adjacent oxidation ponds support up to 30,000 wetland birds, with 136 species recorded. The 800-ha area is particularly good for waders, royal spoonbill/kōtuku-ngutupapa and waterfowl, with around 7000 Australasian

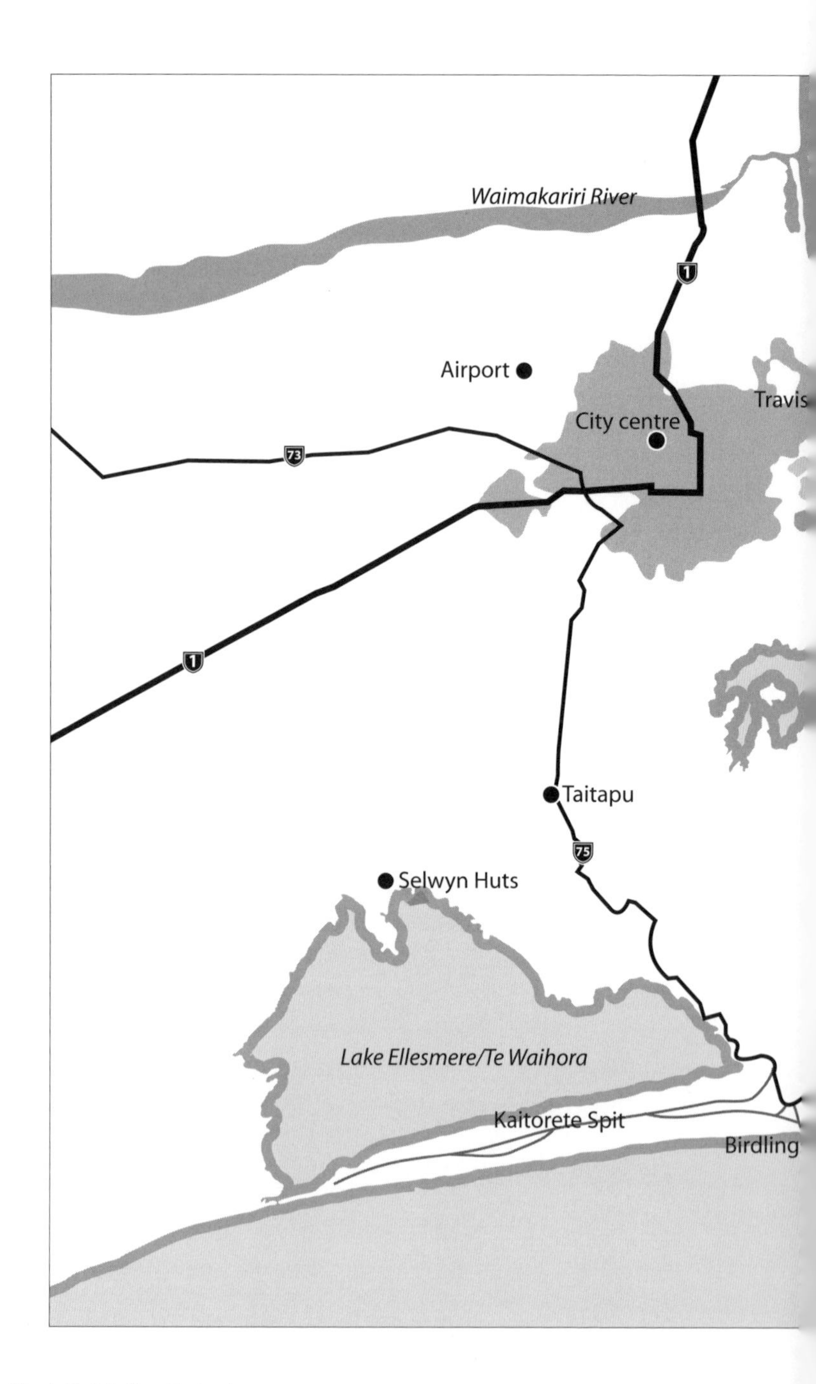
Waimakariri River
Airport
City centre
Travis
Taitapu
Selwyn Huts
Lake Ellesmere/Te Waihora
Kaitorete Spit
Birdling
1
73
1
75

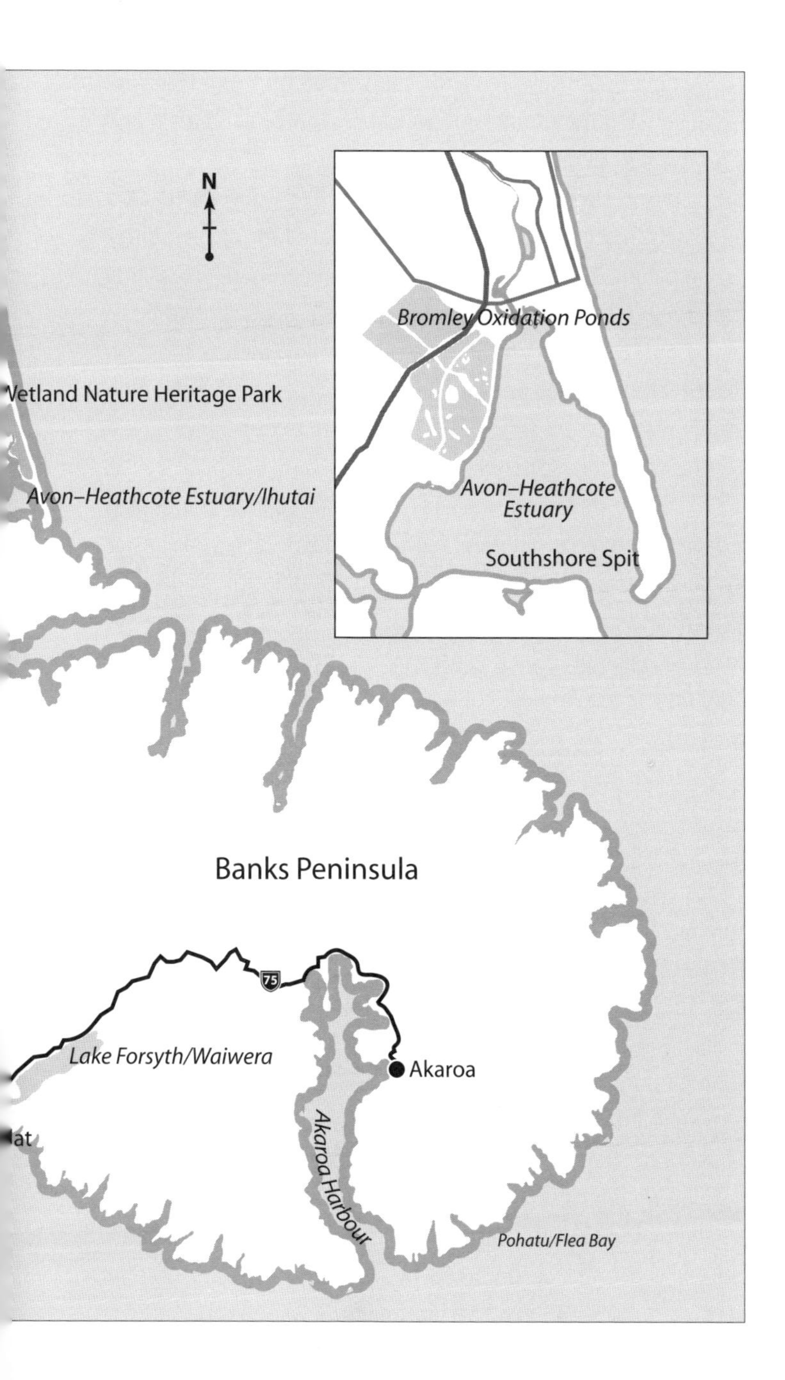
N
Bromley Oxidation Ponds
Avon–Heathcote
Estuary
Southshore Spit
Vetland Nature Heritage Park
Avon–Heathcote Estuary/Ihutai
Banks Peninsula
75
Lake Forsyth/Waiwera
Akaroa
Akaroa Harbour
Pohatu/Flea Bay

shoveler/kuruwhengu, 6000 New Zealand scaup, 4000 grey teal/tētē, and 2500 paradise shelduck/pūtangitangi. All five of the New Zealand mainland shag species are present here.

Beside the estuary, the oxidation ponds have been developed as a wildlife management reserve. Islands have been created for nesting birds, and a major shag colony has become established on one. There are several options for observing birds: the western shoreline is a good spot to be as the tide is going out. During high tide in winter, many waders roost on paddocks adjacent to the ponds and can be seen at close quarters feeding along the estuary margins.

The tip of the spit which shelters the estuary from the open sea is the best place to see bar-tailed godwit/kūaka (summer), South Island pied oystercatcher/tōrea, and terns. On these high-tide roosts congregations of around 2500 bar-tailed godwit (in summer), and 4000 South Island pied oystercatcher can be seen at close quarters.

McCormacks Bay, enclosed by a causeway on the southern shoreline, Bexley Wetland (in the north-west corner) and Charlesworth Wetland (in the south-west corner) are good places for pied stilt/poaka and flocks of grey teal. Little black shag/kōau roost on the pylons beside the canal adjacent to Linwood Avenue. Other shag species, gulls and terns can be found roosting around various parts of the estuary shoreline.

Several roads and city bus routes lead to the estuary. To reach the southern shoreline from the city centre head south on Colombo Street, then turn left and follow Moorhouse Avenue, which becomes Ferry Road and then Main Road, which leads towards Sumner Beach. To reach the western shoreline and the spit, turn off Ferry Road onto Dyers Road at the first major roundabout. After crossing the Avon River (at the mouth as it feeds into the estuary) turn right into Estuary Road at the next roundabout. The Sumner bus routes (30 and 31), lead directly to the estuary.

For the oxidation ponds, travel as described above to Dyers Road, which crosses the ponds. Note that the ponds are closed to public access; permission to walk in must be obtained by phoning Christchurch City Council call centre, 03 379 1660 and asking for the Sewage Works.

To reach the spit from the ponds, turn right onto Bridge Street, which leads to South New Brighton. Pine Avenue and Marine Parade turn right (south), then join as Rockinghorse Road, and continue almost to the end of the spit. From here, a walking track leads around the tip of the spit. The Southshore bus route (5) leads to the end of Rockinghorse Road, and the New Brighton bus routes (42 and 51) go as far as the pier at New Brighton Beach. Allow 40 minutes for the walk along the beach.

At the eastern end of Sumner Beach is Whitewash Head, an excellent place to see spotted shag (peak nesting time is September to November) and, in summer, white-fronted tern and red-billed gull. A walkway explores the headland here.

▷ Lake Ellesmere/Te Waihora

Waihora, or 'spreading water', is the Māori name for this vast shallow coastal lagoon. It is New Zealand's fifth-largest lake, and one of its most important wetland ecosystems, protected since 1990s by a National Water Conservation Order.

Peak summer/autumn bird numbers can range from 30,000 to 100,000 wetland birds on the lake, including impressive numbers of waterfowl and New Zealand waders. It is a popular stop-off point for migratory birds, both Arctic and New Zealand migrants, so populations and species do vary. Of 180 recorded species, 80 are regular users. Of particular interest are the thousands of banded dotterel/tuturiwhatu and pied stilt. Wrybill are also generally present and, very occasionally, black stilt/kakī are seen here.

The most regular international visitors are Pacific golden plover, sharp-tailed sandpiper, pectoral sandpiper, curlew sandpiper, red-necked stint and white-winged black tern. Both little and black shags can been seen roosting on trees around the shore and Australasian bittern live in the shore ribbonwood and sea rush marshes. Caspian tern/taranui, cattle egret and a few white heron/kōtuku are usually present. Pūkeko, black-backed gull and spur-winged plover are prolific. During November and December up to 30,000 ducks may be present including 10,000 each of grey teal and Australasian shoveler, thousands of mallard and hundreds of paradise shelduck and grey duck, along with black swan and Canada goose.

The brackish lake has extensive weed beds and is prone to algal blooms. It has 58 km of shoreline, including extensive areas of salt marsh and mudflats. Sheltering the lagoon from the open sea is Kaitorete Spit, which extends for nearly 30 km from Birdlings Flat, on the southern coast of Banks Peninsula. This spit has a harsh, dry and windy environment that supports the largest areas in New Zealand of the native sand-binding plant pingao, as well as sand tussock and shrubby tororaro. Several bird species nest in the dunes and grasslands, including banded dotterel, New Zealand pipit/pīhoihoi, white-fronted tern/tara and Caspian tern.

A good place to observe Arctic waders is the Greenpark sands, around 3000 ha of salt marsh where most waders gather. From Christchurch central city, drive south on SH75 for about 40 minutes to the settlement of Taitapu. Turn west into Lincoln–Taitapu Road, south-west into Davies Road, then south into River Road. Follow this for 500 m to the first junction and proceed south to Hudsons Road. About 2 km along Hudsons Road turn west into Davidsons Road, where three side-roads lead to good viewing points. These are Embankment, Wolfe and Days Roads (the last of which leads right to Selwyn Huts, on the lake edge).

There are good roadside points for observing birds along SH75 (the road to Akaroa). Continue past the settlements of Taitapu and Motukarara and look for the Blue Duck Cafe. Continue 8 km past the cafe to Ataahua Point. Although not clearly signposted, there is an obvious pulling-over spot with a view over the lagoon. A second spot is 4 km further along, just past the Kaituna Valley Road turn-off (be wary of the blind corner). Generally, good populations of birds, mostly black swan and pied stilt, are clearly visible from here on Kaituna Lagoon (a sheltered enclave of the larger lake). The Christchurch–Little River Rail Trail, a walking/biking trail that follows an old railway line, provides even closer viewing, in particular of marsh crake, which are likely to be present in the raupo. The trail is easily accessible from several points on the Akaroa highway.

Note: Midges that swarm around the lagoon, in particular on still warm days in spring and summer, can be particularly annoying.

Continuing around the lakeshore road, the turn-off to Birdlings Flat and Kaitorete Spit is signposted. It's worth a look on the ocean side for shorebirds, and close to shore for Australasian gannet/tākapu, giant petrel and Arctic skua.

▷ Lake Forsyth/Waiwera

Up to 300 Australasian crested grebe/kāmana winter here, and their numbers have markedly increased since the late 1980s. Grebes also now breed on the lake so are resident year round. Also impressive here and easy to observe are large flocks of waterfowl, including some 4000 scaup and 2000 each of grey teal, shoveler and black swan. The lake is a regular site for up to three white heron and occasional little egret.

The lake sits beside the Akaroa Road, just beyond the Birdlings Flat turn-off. Best spots are Catons Bay, halfway along the lake and right beside the road, and at the top end of the lake. The rail trail provides good viewing access along the western shoreline. Across from the lake is the settlement of Little River, with an information centre, cafe, craft gallery and public toilets.

▷ Pohatu penguin colony

Blue penguin, the smallest penguin species in the world, live throughout New Zealand. A recognised subspecies, the white-flippered blue penguin, breeds on Banks Peninsula and Motunau Island Nature Reserve off the northern Canterbury coast. This bird is distinguishable from the blue penguin by its slightly larger size, lighter colour and broader white band at the front base of its flipper.

The largest mainland colony is at Pohatu, a remote marine reserve near the volcanic headlands of Akaroa Harbour. Locals have worked over the past decade to protect the colony from introduced predators. Local residents and landowners, Francis and Shireen Helps, who run Pohatu Penguin Tours, are the only operators licensed to take tour groups to the colony. They share a wealth of knowledge about the birds and their spectacular environment. See their newsletter on www.pohatu.co.nz for updates on what's happening in the colony.

Because the habitat is so sensitive, only small guided groups are permitted. Tours are at dusk, when the birds come in from the sea. The best time to visit is during the breeding season, September–January. There are also brief viewing opportunities from April to September when the birds return periodically from sea.

Tours depart from Akaroa (83 km from Christchurch) and are of 2.5–3 hours' duration. Travel from Akaroa is in 4WD vehicle over rough terrain. People with suitable vehicles can join the guided tour at the colony. The Helps also offer self-contained cottage accommodation at Pohatu Bay and kayak hire, presenting more opportunities to observe penguins as well as the sea and shorebirds that frequent the area.

▷ Travis Wetland Nature Heritage Park

This 56-ha freshwater wetland sits in the middle of an urban environment, yet offers a number of good birding opportunities. Home to resident Australasian bittern, marsh crake, brown teal and pūkeko, the wetland is particularly known for the regular presence of glossy ibis, with one or two birds recorded here each winter since 1998. White heron and banded dotterel are also regular visitors.

Fifty-three species, including 30 natives and most native freshwater wetland birds of lowland Canterbury, have been recorded in the wetland, which also contains Canterbury's largest winter concentration of pūkeko, peaking at over 700 birds. The park is located in the north-east Christchurch suburb of Burwood, bounded by Travis, Frosts and Mairehau Roads. There is a bird hide and the Anne Flanagan Walkway provides an easy walking track around and through the park.

▷ Waimakariri River

If a trip to the braided rivers of the Canterbury high country is not an option, it may be worth taking a look around the Waimakariri River, about 15 km north of the city, for braided-river birds. Although the lower Waimakariri is less pristine, and has fewer birds than the high-country rivers, there are breeding populations of wrybill, banded dotterel, South Island pied oystercatcher, pied stilt, black-billed gull and black-fronted tern, as well as inland-nesting white-fronted tern and Caspian tern. Riparian wetlands also support Australasian bittern and marsh crake. The SH1 road bridge approximately marks the uppermost reaches of the tidal zone, so the birds tend to be upriver from here.

An unsealed access road follows the north bank about 20 km upriver from the old highway bridge. From Christchurch, drive north on SH1 to Belfast and just before joining the motorway turn off to Kaiapoi. Cross the Waimakariri River on the old highway bridge and immediately turn hard left onto a shingle track that crosses the stopbank. Drive under the motorway bridge, past a boat ramp, and continue along the riverside road.

The Old West Coast Road on the south side of the Waimakariri also offers access points, generally marked with blue-and-white 'Angler's Access' signs. Nature trails and picnic areas are currently under development.

Getting there Christchurch is a major international gateway. Air services connect with Australia, Asia, the Pacific and North America, and the domestic network links with major centres throughout New Zealand. Christchurch International Airport is 12 km from the city centre. By road, the city is located on SH1, and daily coach services connect with towns and cities in the South Island. Rail connections link with Kaikōura and Picton (Cook Strait ferry terminal) and Greymouth (West Coast).

Getting around The Avon/Heathcote Estuary is 12 km from the city centre, and easily accessible by private car, city bus service or taxi. Akaroa is 83 km from central Christchurch, following SH75. Allow 90 minutes' driving time, as some of the road climbs and turns steeply. The Akaroa Shuttle provides both a direct city-to-Akaroa service and a Banks Peninsula scenic tour, phone 0800 500 929 or visit www.akaroashuttle.co.nz. Lake Ellesmere is beside SH75, about halfway between Christchurch and Akaroa.

Accommodation Christchurch offers the full range of accommodation, from five-star hotels, lodges and bed-and-breakfasts, to hotels, motels, backpackers and holiday parks. In Akaroa and the surrounding Banks Peninsula area there is an excellent range of self-contained cottages, homestays, farmstays, motels and holiday parks.

Facilities Major stores, shopping malls, supermarkets and banks are located in the city centre and suburbs. Restaurants and cafes range from fine dining to pubs, casual cafes and eateries of various ethnicities. The road to Akaroa, and the township itself offers a charming selection of cafes, delis and craft galleries. There are visitor information centres in Christchurch City (Cathedral Square), at Christchurch Airport, Little River and Akaroa.

Information

Christchurch i-SITE Visitor Centre, Cathedral Square, 03 379 9629, christchurch@i-SITE.org, www.christchurchnz.net.

Akaroa Information Centre, 03 304 8600, www.akaroa.com.

Licensed guiding company

Pohatu Penguin Tours, 03 304 855, www.pohatu.co.nz.

23

Inland Canterbury lakes and braided rivers

Where Central South Island, 2–3 hours' drive from Christchurch.

What's special Braided rivers, high-country lakes, wetlands and wetland birds.

Birds to look for Wrybill/ngutuparore, black-fronted tern/tarapiroe, banded dotterel/tuturiwhatu, black-billed gull/tarāpunga, South Island pied oystercatcher/tōrea, Australasian crested grebe/kāmana, Australasian bittern/matuku, marsh crake, New Zealand scaup.

Birdwatching options Guided tour, self-driving tour.

Top spots

- Ashburton Lakes/Ō Tū Wharekai (including Lake Heron Nature Reserve, Māori Lakes Nature Reserve, Lake Emma, Lake Roundabout and Lake Clearwater Wildlife Refuge), and Rangitata/Potts River confluence (up to 1 day)
- Lake Coleridge and surrounding small lakes: 1–2 hours return, driving time only, from SH77
- Rakaia River: 50 minutes return, driving time only, from SH72.

How long to go 2–3 days.

When to go Summer for braided-river birds. Note that during the breeding season (August–December) they are highly vulnerable to disturbance. Year-round for other birds, although during winter snow may prevent access to some areas – check local radio stations and information centres.

In spring expect high river flows and floods owing to snow melt and heavy rainfall in the headwaters. Flow information is shown on www.ecan.govt.nz, but be aware that rivers can rise quickly at any time.

Background

Where the mountains meet the plains, there lies a vast hinterland of tussock-filled basins, chiselled by wide braided riverbeds and dotted with subalpine lakes and wetlands. These are the breeding grounds of two endangered endemics: wrybill and black-fronted tern. Australasian crested grebe, banded dotterel, black-billed gull and South Island pied oystercatcher also rely on braided-river habitats, while shags, ducks, pied stilt, spur-winged plover, New Zealand falcon and Australasian harrier frequent the rivers, lakes and open tussock areas.

On a world scale, braided rivers are scarce. Distinctive for their broad gravel beds, many channels, ever-changing shingle islands and variable flows, braided rivers are constantly undergoing change through erosion and build-up of alluvial outwash from the mountains. Sixty per cent of New Zealand's braided rivers are in Canterbury and, during spring and summer, at least 26 species of waterbirds feed or nest on these rivers.

In 2007, huge tracts of high country were incorporated into the new Hakatere Conservation Park. In the same year the Rangitata River, one of the important braided rivers for wading birds, was protected by a Water Conservation Order. These measures mean the future is looking brighter for these species.

Best birding areas

▷ Ashburton Lakes/Ō Tū Wharekai and Rangitata/Potts River confluence

Of the 11 lakes collectively known as the Ashburton Lakes, the main ones for observing birds are Heron, Emma, Roundabout and Clearwater. There are also smaller lakes and wetlands in the area worth checking.

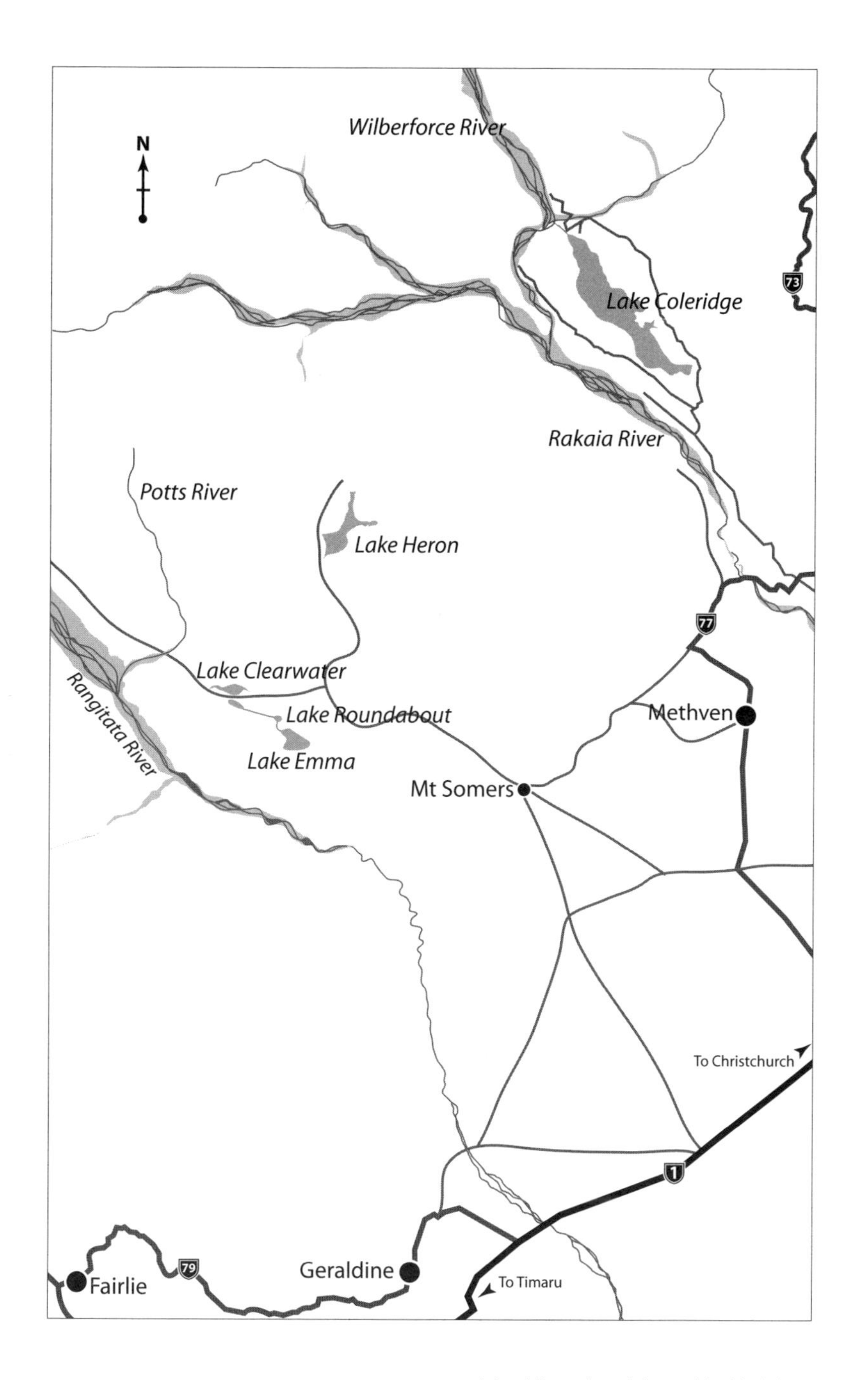
N
Wilberforce River
Lake Coleridge
73
Rakaia River
Potts River
Lake Heron
77
Lake Clearwater
Rangitata River
Lake Roundabout
Methven
Lake Emma
Mt Somers
To Christchurch
1
Geraldine
79
Fairlie
To Timaru

Access to the lakes is via Ashburton Gorge Road, which turns off the Inland Scenic Route (SH72) at Mt Somers village, about 1.5 hours' drive from Christchurch. The road is sealed for the first 24 km, from Mt Somers to Hakatere junction. From here, the right-hand fork leads 16 km to Lake Heron, and the road straight ahead leads to Lakes Emma and Roundabout (6 km), Lake Clearwater (10 km) and the Rangitata/Potts River confluence (19 km). All lakes are clearly signposted and the roads themselves traverse magnificent wide tussock valleys lined by snow-capped mountain ranges.

Lake Heron Nature Reserve

The largest and most pristine of the Ashburton Lakes, Lake Heron is afforded New Zealand's highest protected status of Nature Reserve, and supports the largest populations of Australasian crested grebe and New Zealand scaup, along with high numbers of Australasian coot, paradise shelduck/pūtangitangi, black swan, mallard, and both black and little shag/kōau and summer visiting black stilt/kakī.

From Hakatere, the road to Lake Heron traverses an expansive tussock valley. New Zealand falcon/kārearea are frequently seen here, often sitting on roadside fence posts. Look, too, for banded dotterel. As the road comes out into the open valley, keep an eye out for black-fronted tern, often present around a small wetland beside the bridge. About 5 km from Hakatere, the road passes Māori Lakes Nature Reserve on the left, a wetland area not signposted but worth a look for waterbirds including Australasian bittern/matuku. Just beyond the signposted Castle Ridge Station, on the right, is a smaller wetland.

At Lake Heron there is good vehicle access for 2 km along the southern shore to a car park and wetland board walk. However, if the wind is nor'westerly this can be an unpleasantly exposed spot. At such times Harrisons Bight, by the lake's outlet, provides shelter for hundreds of wetland birds. The Bight is 5 km past the car park along an obvious 4WD track that leads first along the lake edge then avoids swampy areas by cutting directly across to the Bight. Alternatively, look in the sheltered bays in the south-west corner of the lake. Follow the road that continues around the western shore past the entrance to Mt Arrowsmith Station homestead. New Zealand scaup, perhaps up to a thousand of them, as well as Australasian coot, Australasian shoveler/kuruwhengi, black swan and Australasian crested grebe are likely to be sheltering in these bays.

For the more energetic, continue 7 km along the shore and look for the gate on the right as the road straightens across the Cameron fan, before a pine tree shelter belt. There's no sign, but look for a fishing access track that leads to the magnficent Cameron wetland on the western lake shore. This 1-hour walk offers the possibility of seeing Australasian bittern, New Zealand falcon, marsh crake and, in summer, black stilt/kakī.

Lakes Emma, Roundabout and Clearwater

From Hakatere junction, continue straight ahead on Potts Road. Five kilometres from Hakatere a short access road on the left leads to Lake Emma/Kirikiri honu honu, Lake Roundabout and Mt Harper/Mahaanui. Lake Emma is the larger of the two lakes, but both have good numbers of waterbirds, including small populations of Australasian crested grebe. Raupo growing along the far side of Lake Emma is a good site to see marsh crake. Signs at both lakes provide information about the grebes, and advise birders to move quietly around the shoreline during nesting time (September–February) so as not to disturb them.

Lake Clearwater/Punataka

Ten kilometres from Hakatere is the holiday settlement of Lake Clearwater. Access to the lakeshore is clearly signposted. Turn right into the village and drive 200 m to a car park and picnic area. From here a 4WD road that follows the shoreline to the lake outlet is worth exploring. While there is not the same density of birds here as on Lake Emma, keep an eye open for the pair of grebe that usually nest close to the village.

Clearwater Village has a public phone, toilets and informal camping area. While Lake Clearwater is a wildlife refuge this is not the case for Lake Camp, across the road from the village, where recreational motorboats and jetskis have largely displaced the birds.

Rangitata River/Potts River

The Rangitata River is one of New Zealand's most unmodified braided river systems. One of the best accesses is by walking down the delta of its tributary (the Potts River) from the bridge, 9 km past Lake Clearwater. To reach the Rangitata from the bridge takes about an hour, and might involve wet feet and slippery stones. The channels here are ever-changing. This is a major wrybill breeding area, and they will be present from around September, while black-fronted tern can be seen from August onward. Finding these well-camouflaged birds requires stealth and patience. Banded dotterel and South Island pied oystercatcher are likely to be present. Black-billed gull may also be seen. Take care: these birds nest on the ground and their nests can be hard to see. Terns and gulls generally nest in colonies on the open shingle, and will fly up and call loudly to warn of any approaching threat. DoC recommends visiting outside the peak of the breeding season, perhaps after December when most chicks have fledged. The wrybill generally leave for their North Island estuarine feeding grounds in January.

▷ Lake Coleridge and surrounding lakes

The main braided-river species also breed along the upper Rakaia River and on the deltas feeding into Lake Coleridge. Australasian crested grebe are usually present on some small lakes in the area.

Lake Coleridge is signposted from SH77 north of the Rakaia Gorge, about 1 hour's drive from Christchurch. From the turn-off, follow Coleridge Road, turn right onto Homestead Road, then left onto Harper Road, which follows the north-eastern side of the lake. On the right-hand side of Harper Road, check Lakes Georgina, Evelyn and Selfe for Australasian crested grebe, scaup and marsh crake, which are most active around dusk.

A signposted rough walking track by Lake Evelyn leads 5 km across private land to Lake Ida, a good place to see crested grebe and bittern.

At the head of Lake Coleridge the delta formed by the diverted Harper and Wilberforce Rivers is worth a look for wrybill, black-billed gull, banded dotterel, black-fronted tern, Australasian crested grebe and South Island pied oystercatcher. To reach the Harper delta, pass through the small settlement of holiday homes, cross the Harper River bridge, then turn left and follow the public road towards the lake. To reach the Wilberforce riverbed, cross the Harper River bridge, turn right and continue, past the Glenthorne Station turn-off, to the canal. Follow the canal out onto the Wilberforce riverbed.

⊳ Rakaia River

Like the Rangitata, the Rakaia has such high natural values it is protected by a Water Conservation Order. On the south bank above the Rakaia Gorge (80 km from Christchurch on SH77) are two good access points to classical high-country braided-river habitat just a brief detour from the highway. On the south side of the gorge, turn off SH77 just before Mt Hutt Station onto Blackford Road, which follows the southern bank of the Rakaia. Follow this road for 11 km, past Cleardale Station to Hutt Stream. From here, walk along a signposted fishing-access track about 200 m to the Rakaia riverbed for possible sightings (in spring and summer) of wrybill, black-fronted tern, black-billed gull, and banded dotterel.

Continue along Blackford Road a further 6.5 km from Hutt Stream to a riverside flat and informal camping area known as Kowhai Flat. Access to the Rakaia is obvious and easy from here.

Getting there The lakes and rivers in this chapter are located in the mountains; the roads leading to them are mainly access roads leading through and to remote high-country sheep stations and conservation land. Nevertheless, they are easily accessible and within 2–3 hours' drive from Christchurch. Take the West Coast road (SH73) to Darfield, then follow the Inland Scenic Route (SH72) that passes through the small settlements of Rakaia Gorge and Mt Somers (and eventually to Geraldine). The main town in this region is Methven, 5 km off the Inland Scenic Route between Rakaia Gorge and Mt Somers. Alternatively, Mt Somers village is 30 minutes' drive from Ashburton.

Methven Travel offers a coach service linking Christchurch and Methven, departing daily in winter and 2–3 times a week during summer.

Getting around Roads are good, well signposted and with little traffic. Some of the more remote roads are unsealed, and at times during winter might be covered with snow. Methven Travel offers rental vehicles ($45/day) or charter services to birding spots. 03 302 8106 or email methventravel@xtra.co.nz.

Accommodation Methven has two hotels, a motel, several lodges and bed-and-breakfasts and two campervan parks. Rakaia Gorge has a lodge and campervan park. At Mt Somers and neighbouring township Staveley, there is self-contained cottage accommodation, plus two holiday parks. Terrace Downs High Country Resort is located near Lake Coleridge.

Facilities Methven has cafes and restaurants, fuel, supermarkets, pharmacy, ATM and information centre. Mt Somers village has fuel, general store, restaurant and a tavern. The Staveley Village Store has good coffee, excellent ice creams and cafe meals served by friendly locals in that endangered New Zealand species, the country store.

Information

Methven i-SITE Visitor Centre, 03 302 8955, info@methveninfo.co.nz, or www.methveninfo.co.nz.

Ashburton i-SITE Visitor Centre, 03 308 1050, ashburton@i-SITE.org, or www.ashburtoninfo.co.nz.

Licensed guiding company

Tussock and Beech Ecotours; Warren and Marita Jowett offer natural history tours, specialising in birdwatching by request. 03 303 0880, ecotour@nature.net.nz, or www.nature.net.nz.

Recommended reading

Wild Rivers, Neville Peat and Brian Patrick, Dunedin: Otago University Press, 2001.

White-fronted terns breed in coastal areas throughout New Zealand.

New Zealand wood pigeon. This large forest bird is widely distributed, but numbers have seriously declined in many regions.

Left
South Island robin, one of four New Zealand robin subspecies.

Opposite
Kaikōura is one of the world's most accessible spots to see pelagic birds. A southern royal albatross (above) soars close to the Seaward Kaikōura Range, and a Buller's albatross (below) flies above cape pigeons.

Below
Kayaking provides excellent birdwatching on Ōkarito Lagoon, South Westland.

Lake Rotoiti, Nelson Lakes National Park, where the forest teems with birds since a successful forest recovery project.

One of the world's rarest waders, the black stilt lives in the Mackenzie Basin, central South Island. Since 1981 a captive-breeding programme has increased its numbers from 23 to about 100.

The bold antics of the kea, New Zealand's mountain parrot, belie its endangered status.

Left
Yellow-eyed penguin, one of the world's rarest penguins, live around Otago Peninsula, the Catlins coast and Stewart Island/Rakiura.

Opposite
Grey-headed and Campbell Island albatross on Campbell Island. The subantarctic islands are noted for their great numbers of birds and many endemic species.

Below
Mason Bay, on Stewart Island/Rakiura, is a stronghold for Stewart Island tokoeka (kiwi). Pelagic and shore birds also frequent this remote coastline.

Left

Campbell Island albatross, one of the five albatross species that breed on Campbell Island. Only the Crozet Islands in the southern Indian Ocean boast a greater diversity of albatross species.

Below

A guided tour party gets up close to a southern royal albatross chick on Campbell Island. Only a few nature cruise operators are permitted to land on the World Heritage-listed subantarctic islands.

24

Mackenzie Basin and Ahuriri Valley

Where Central South Island, 3–4 hours' drive from Christchurch.

What's special Dramatic arid open subalpine country with numerous glacial lakes, ponds and braided rivers that are the main habitat of one of the world's rarest waders, black stilt/kakī (see Chapter 25), along with other wetland birds. Hydro-electric power development has destroyed much bird habitat by diverting rivers, but also created new habitat in the form of lakes and canals.

Birds to look for Black stilt/kakī, black-fronted tern/tarapiroe, banded dotterel/tuturiwhatu, black-billed gull/tarāpunga, wrybill/ngutuparore, South Island pied oystercatcher/tōrea, pied stilt/poaka, Australasian crested grebe/kāmana, New Zealand scaup, Australasian shoveler/kuruwhengi, kea, New Zealand falcon/kārearea, rifleman/tītīpounamu, Australasian harrier/kāhu, rock wren/pīwauwau, black-backed gull/karoro, white-faced heron.

Bird watching options Self-driving and walking, black stilt recovery centre hide (see Chapter 25).

Top spots

- Ahuriri Conservation Park and Ben Avon wetlands (1 hour's driving, return, from SH8)
- Ohau River wetlands, mouth and Lake Benmore (30 minute's drive from Twizel)
- Lake Ohau (1–2 hours' return, driving from Twizel)
- Tasman River delta (up to 1 hour's walk from SH80)
- Aoraki/Mt Cook Village (several short walks)
- Lakes Alexandrina and McGregor (30 minutes' return drive from SH8).

When to go Year-round for most birds including black stilt (note that during breeding season, August–December, they are highly vulnerable to disturbance); summer for other braided-river birds.

Background

Past glaciation is still clearly visible in the Mackenzie Country, with its vast areas of moraine, stony plains and tussock lands punctuated with icy-blue glacial lakes and kettle ponds and framed by some of New Zealand's highest mountains. Major hydro-electric development has created dams and diversion canals, altered lake levels and created several new lakes, and recently irrigated dairy farms have begun to further change the arid landscape.

In 1981 the black stilt recovery programme was established, marking the beginning of a significant turnaround in favour of the birds. Other braided-river birds migrate north during summer, but black stilt tend to stay year-round in the Mackenzie Basin. Only a very few migrate to coastal Canterbury and North Island estuaries, from February to June.

Project River Recovery, a habitat-restoration programme, has been undertaken by DoC and electricity suppliers Meridian Energy, in rivers and wetlands. Predator and weed control is making a difference, and huge tracts of high-country land have been retired from grazing and incorporated into new conservation parks.

Unfortunately there is now a new threat, the invasive freshwater alga known as didymo or 'rock snot', forming dense colonies that can smother life in streams and rivers. New Zealand biosecurity agencies are fighting a major battle to prevent the wider spread of this weed, which is thought to be transferred between waterways on boats and fishing gear.

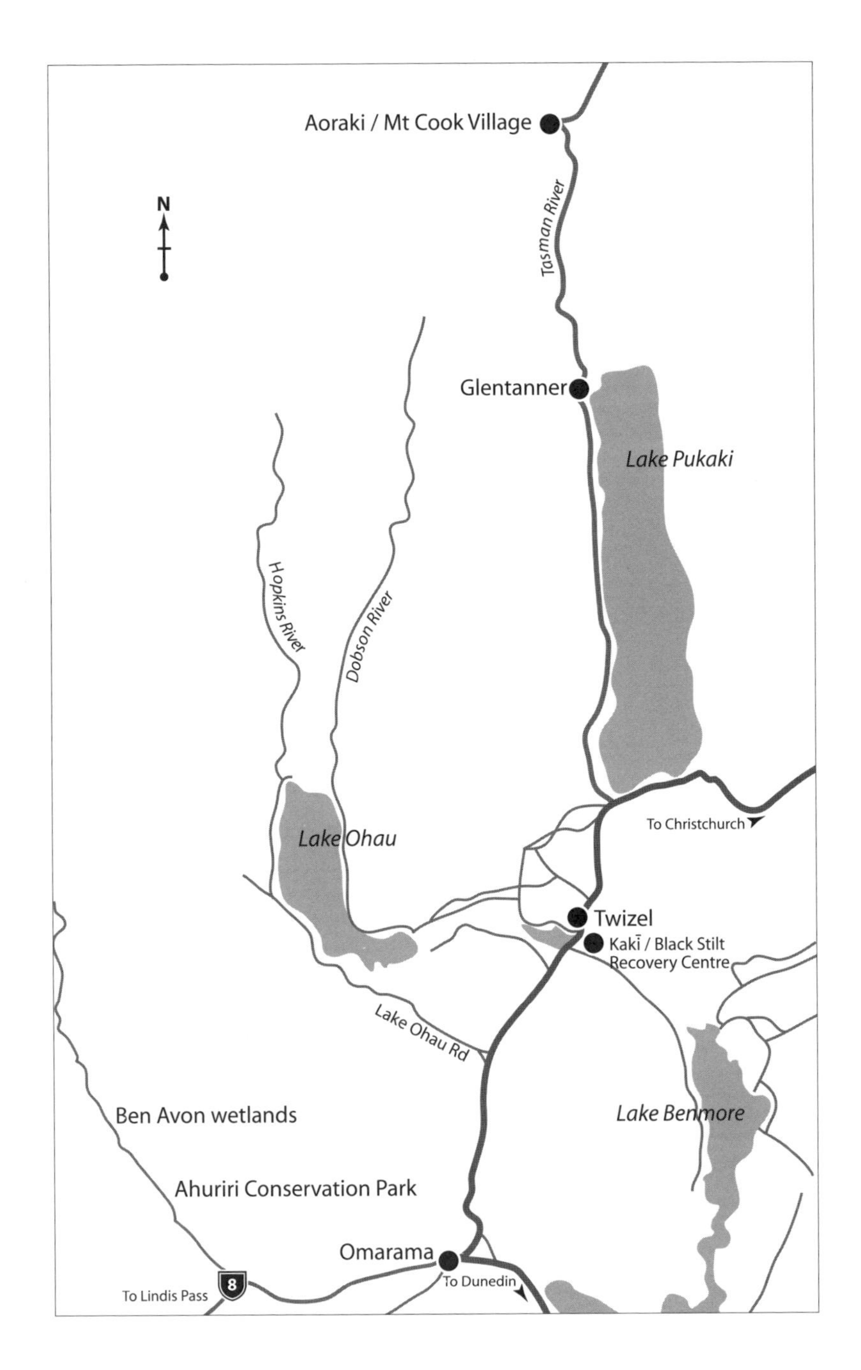
Aoraki / Mt Cook Village
N
Tasman River
Glentanner
Lake Pukaki
Hopkins River
Dobson River
Lake Ohau
To Christchurch
Twizel
Kakī / Black Stilt
Recovery Centre
Lake Ohau Rd
Lake Benmore
Ben Avon wetlands
Ahuriri Conservation Park
Omarama
To Dunedin
To Lindis Pass
8

Best birding areas

▷ Ahuriri Conservation Park and Ben Avon wetlands

Established in 2005, this park encompasses nearly 50,000 ha of mountains, fellfields and tussock lands, wetlands, rivers and streams and small remnant stands of beech forest. The Ben Avon wetlands sprawl across the Ahuriri Valley floor, beside the access road to the park.

At least one pair of black stilt is resident here, and numbers are likely to increase with subsequent releases. Other birds present include New Zealand scaup, grey teal/tētē, spur-winged plover, pied stilt, South Island pied oystercatcher, paradise shelduck/pūtangitangi, Australasian harrier and black swan. The more secretive Australasian bittern/matuku and marsh crake are also sometimes seen. Spring and summer residents include black-fronted tern, black-billed gull and banded dotterel.

Access is signposted on SH8, 24 km from Omarama. Follow the road up the valley for 18 km to a sign that overlooks the wetlands. The road is unsealed and there is a small ford just before the wetlands. There is walking access around the wetlands and to the Ahuriri River, although it may be possible to observe birds, including black stilt, while sitting in the car.

▷ Ohau River wetlands and mouth; Lake Benmore

Most of the Ohau River has been diverted for power generation, but the small stream and wetlands that remain still support some birds, including black stilt. Heading south from Twizel on SH8, cross the Lake Ruataniwha dam, turn left and drive 3 km to the Ohau B dam, with the hydro canal on your right and the dry bed of the Ohau River on your left . Cross the dam and continue along the south side of the canal. After 11 km turn left to cross the top of Ohau C dam, then turn right and drive down to the left of the power station. From here, several rough vehicle tracks meander around the Ohau wetlands and ponds. Drive or walk along the gravel track alongside the Ohau C tailrace to where the remnant of the Ohau River enters Lake Benmore – an excellent place to find scaup and waders, including black stilt, crested grebe and marsh crake.

Lake Ohau

The small lakes and waterways of the upper Ohau Valley are well worth exploring. From SH8 at Clearburn, about 15 km south of Twizel, turn right onto Lake Ohau Road. Small lakes along the way are possible sites to see Australasian crested grebe.

About halfway around the lake, 41 km from Twizel, the Parsons Creek–Freehold Creek walking track (2 hours one way, or 10 minutes to a viewpoint) passes through a mixture of forest and subalpine shrublands and is worth exploring for forest birds.

The road becomes unsealed and continues 15 km beyond the head of Lake Ohau to the Hopkins River delta, where wrybill and black-fronted tern may be seen. New Zealand falcon also live in the area, and forest birds including tomtit/miromiro, fantail/pīwakawaka, brown creeper and rifleman frequent the beech forests.

Tasman River delta

The mighty glaciers east of the main divide in Aoraki/Mt Cook National Park feed the Tasman River, whose channels spread across the wide valley floor as it flows towards Lake Pukaki. The biggest predator-control programme ever undertaken in a braided river system began here in 2005. The delta is well worth exploring for black stilt and, in spring and summer, banded dotterel, wrybill, black-billed gull and black-fronted tern.

A public walking track is signposted from Glentanner Park on SH80 to Aoraki/Mt Cook National Park, 15 minutes' drive from Aoraki/Mt Cook village and 45 minutes from SH8. Allow about an hour to walk to the delta, though birds are likely to be seen within 5 to 10 minutes.

Aoraki/Mt Cook village

The village is nestled in a most spectacular setting, surrounded by mountain, glaciers, snow fields and massive rocky buttresses. Community efforts to rid the village and adjacent Tasman and Hooker valleys of predators, such as stoats, have increased bird numbers.

Around the village and on short walks into small patches of forest you are likely to see at least rifleman, fantail, tomtit and kea. In open areas look for New Zealand falcon, Australasian harrier and New Zealand pipit/pīhoihoi. Introduced birds include chaffinch, greenfinch and sparrow. For the more energetic, a few rock wren live around Mueller Hut, a steep 3-hour climb from the village.

▷ Lakes Alexandrina and McGregor

These lakes, close to the western shore of Lake Tekapo, are among the better places to see Australasian crested grebe, marsh crake and other wetland birds. From SH8, 2 km west of Lake Tekapo township turn right onto Godley Peaks Road (signposted). Follow this sealed road for 3.5 km where an unsealed road turns left to the south end of Lake Alexandrina.

A further 5 km past this turn-off Godley Peaks Road runs beside Lake McGregor, and a second access road to Alexandrina turns left just past here. To reach the head of Lake Alexandrina, where marsh crake are abundant in the raupo, continue a further 5 km from Lake McGregor and follow the signposted fishing access through the deer paddocks of Glenmore Station. There are good walking access tracks around the lake edge. It may be worth continuing a few kilometres to the road end to see river birds on the Cass River delta.

Getting there The towns closest to the birding spots in this chapter are Omarama, Twizel and Lake Tekapo, all on SH8. Lake Tekapo is 3 hours' drive from Christchurch and 1.5 hours from Timaru. Omarama is within about 2 hours' drive from Timaru. Twizel is located between Lake Tekapo and Omarama. Daily coach services travel from Christchurch along SH8 en route to Queenstown, and link with Aoraki/Mt Cook village.

Getting around Most roads in the Mackenzie Basin are sealed, well signposted and generally carry little traffic. There is public transport to Glentanner Park and Aoraki/Mt Cook village, but not to the Ben Avon wetlands or Ohau wetlands. Rental vehicles are available in Twizel from High Country Auto Services, 03 4350 214.

Accommodation There is hotel, motel, holiday park, backpackers, bed-and-breakfast and self-contained accommodation at Twizel, Aoraki/Mt Cook, Omarama and also at Tekapo, 1 hour's drive north of Twizel. Glentanner Park offers cabins, camping and campervan sites.
A DoC camping area is located at Aoraki/Mt Cook National Park.

Facilities Twizel has a supermarket, restaurants, ATM, pharmacy, fuel and an information centre. Omarama township has fuel, shops, restaurants and cafes and an information centre. Aoraki/Mt Cook Village has cafes, hotel restaurants, fuel and an information centre.

Information

Lake Tekapo Information Centre, 03 680 6686.

Lake Pukaki Visitor Centre, SH8, Lake Pukaki, 03 435 3280, lake.pukaki@xtra.co.nz, www.mtcook.org.nz.

Twizel Information Centre, 03 435 3124, info@twizel.com, www.twizel.com.

Omarama Information Centre, 03 438 9818.

Department of Conservation, Wairepo Road, Twizel, 03 435 0802, www.doc.govt.nz.

25

Kakī/Black Stilt Recovery Centre

Where Mackenzie Basin, central South Island, 3 km from Twizel.

What's special Opportunity to see black stilt and learn about the programme that has rescued one of the world's rarest waders from the brink of extinction.

Birdwatching options Guided tours of the black stilt visitor hide (1 hour).

When to go October–April

Background

Once widespread throughout New Zealand's wetlands, black stilt are now largely restricted to the Mackenzie Basin after suffering from habitat loss and predation by introduced animals. In the 1970s the black stilt was dealt a further massive blow when hydro-power development destroyed habitat in their last remaining stronghold, the upper Waitaki Basin, and their population declined to a mere 23 adults.

Enter the Department of Conservation with its black stilt recovery programme, established in 1981 and focused largely around the captive breeding and rearing centre near Twizel. Each year about four black stilt pairs are held at the centre for captive breeding. Their eggs are artificially incubated and the chicks raised in captivity before being released into the wild as juveniles or sub-adults. Eggs are also collected from nests in the wild for incubation, to avoid predation and loss due to flooding. Most of these chicks are raised at the Centre, though some are returned for their parents to raise to help them maintain their breeding skills. Fortunately black stilt can produce up to four clutches with 3–4 eggs each per year.

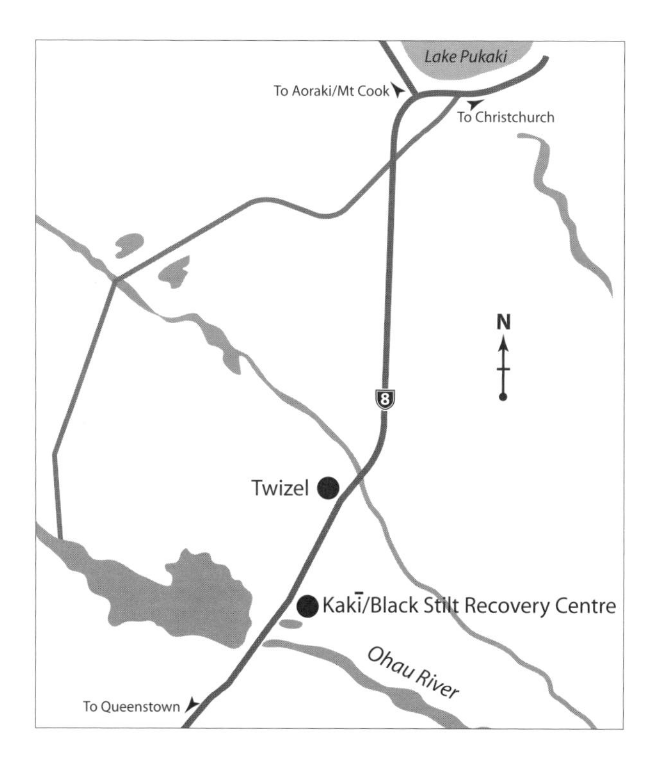

Today the black stilt's future is looking brighter. In 2006 there were 100 known adults, including 14 breeding pairs, living in the braided rivers and wetlands throughout the Mackenzie Basin. The number of breeding pairs in the wild is increasing every year and predator control is intensifying. The long-term aim is that the wild black stilt population will be sustainable without the need for releases of captive-raised birds.

Kakī/black stilt visitor hide

Located at the captive breeding centre, among wetlands and landscaped ponds beside the Ohau River, the hide overlooks aviaries where the black stilt breeding pairs are held and chicks are raised. Nest-building and egg-laying occurs in early summer and the chicks are transferred to outdoor aviaries when they are 35 days old. At times there are up to 60 chicks in these aviaries.

Guided tours offer the opportunity to see the birds and to learn about their ecology and conservation. Tours run from October to April, at 9.30 am and 4.30 pm daily, and include an audiovisual presentation and viewing and photography opportunities.

Bookings are essential and should be made at least 30 minutes before the tour is due to depart. While the tours start from the visitor hide itself, bookings must be made at either the Twizel Information Centre or the Lake Pukaki Visitor Centre. Visitors need to have their own transport to the hide. Charges are $15/adult and $7/child, with a minimum charge per tour of $30. Group and family discounts are available and large groups can be accommodated by prior arrangement with the DoC Twizel Area Office.

Getting there The hide is located 3 km south of Twizel on SH8. Daily coach services travel from Christchurch through SH8 en route to Queenstown, and link with Aoraki/Mt Cook Village. There is no public transport from Twizel to the hide.

Accommodation Twizel township has hotels, motels, bed-and-breakfasts, lodges and holiday park accommodation.

Facilities Twizel has a supermarket, restaurants, ATM, pharmacy, fuel and an information centre. Note that there is no toilet or shop at the hide.

Information

Twizel Information Centre, 61 Mackenzie Drive, 03 435 3124, info@twizel.com.

Lake Pukaki Visitor Centre, Lake Pukaki dam, SH8, 03 435 3280, lake.pukaki@xtra.co.nz, www.mtcook.org.nz.

Department of Conservation, Twizel, 03 435 0802, KakiVisitorHide@doc.govt.nz.

26

South Westland

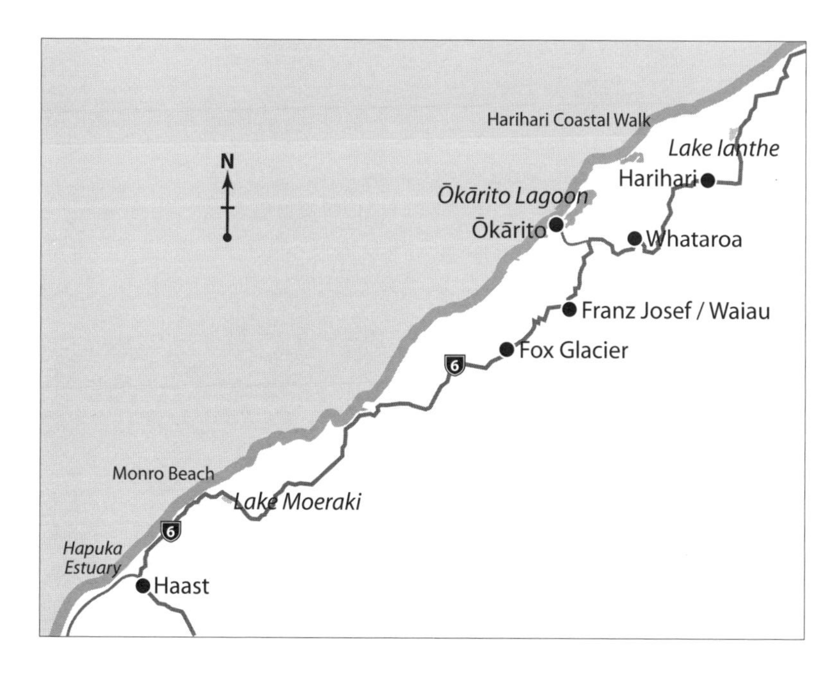

Where South Island west coast.

What's special Outstanding World Heritage landscapes and bird habitats – mountains, glaciers, rain forests, lakes, dune lakes, lagoons, pākihi swamps and secluded beaches.

Birds to look for Royal spoonbill/kōtuku-ngutupapa, white heron/kōtuku, fernbird/mātā, Fiordland crested penguin/tawaki, Australasian crested grebe/kāmana, Ōkārito brown kiwi/rowi and many species of forest birds, shorebirds, waders and waterbirds.

Birdwatching options Guided and self-guided walks, guided and independent kayaking tours, guided boat tours, night-time kiwi listening tours, lodge-based tours.

Top spots

- Lake Ianthe (20 minutes or longer with own boat)
- Harihari Coastal Walk (2–3 hours)
- Waitangiroto Nature Reserve/White Heron Sanctuary (2.5 hours)
- Ōkārito Lagoon coastal and forest walks (2 hours to full day)
- Monro Beach, Lake Moeraki (2–3 hours)
- Hapuka Estuary (30 minutes).

When to go Year-round. Winter weather is more settled and there are plenty of birds present, though the best birding is generally from September to April/May. From October to March white heron are resident at their breeding sanctuary, and although they feed year-round on Ōkārito Lagoon they are fewer in winter. Fiordland crested penguin nest from July to November.

Background

South Westland is one of the few places in the world where wilderness remains intact from mountains to the sea, and where glaciers meet with rainforests that in turn merge with lakes, lagoons and misty boulder beaches. It's a dramatic setting for observing and photographing birds.

Most places in this chapter are in or close to Westland/Tai Poutini National Park which, along with three adjacent national parks and other conservation land, makes up the 2.6 million ha Te Wāhipounamu South-West New Zealand World Heritage Area.

Two glaciers are the main visitor attractions here, gouging their way down from New Zealand's highest mountains and into the rainforest. Most of the landscape between the mountains and sea is glacially shaped, with kettle lakes and lagoons and forest-covered moraines. Closer to the sea, water rather than ice has further shaped the landscape, and in places there is a distinctive, swampy habitat called pākihi, consisting of tussocks, rushes, low shrubs, mosses and ferns on the flood plains. The coastline has dunes, shrublands, estuarine salt marshes and dune lakes with patches of forest. The result is myriad habitats for birds, so this region supports probably as many species as will be found anywhere in New Zealand.

Best birding areas

➢ Lake Ianthe

Surrounded by pristine rainforest, Lake Ianthe is one of New Zealand's oldest scenic reserves, with the largest resident population of Australasian crested grebe in Westland. There is a small DoC campground beside the lake. The best option if you have your own boat or kayak is a lake cruise, which can reward with close views, sometimes of adults with their chicks, perhaps being carried on the adult's back. Courtship displays occur in December and January and chicks will be seen during February and March, possibly from December if there has been a mild spring with no floods.

Other birds likely to be seen are little, pied shag/kāruhiruhi, black shag, paradise shelduck/pūtangitangi, grey teal/tētē, mallard and grey duck/pārera, New Zealand scaup, kingfisher/kōtare, black swan and the occasional white heron.

Lake Ianthe is located on SH6, 40 km south of Hokitika and 78 km north of Franz Josef/Waiau.

➢ Harihari Coastal Walk

This 2–3-hour walk passes through a variety of habitats so a good range of species can be observed, in particular in the lagoon and tidal mudflats by the Wanganui River mouth. At low tide walking along the beach is easy, and at high tide a short detour through the forest is signposted. Walking at low tide is likely to be more rewarding for seeing birds.

The circular, gently graded route passes through pākihi and regenerating kahikatea, over a low moraine covered in mature podocarp forest to the Poerua River and estuary, then north along a stony beach to Mt One One, a prominent headland and lookout point known as the Doughboy. The track returns to the starting point along the Wanganui River bank.

Common forest birds fantail, tūī, bellbird and New Zealand pigeon are bound to make their presence known. On the tidal flats South Island pied oystercatcher, possibly variable oystercatcher/torea, pied stilt/poaka, white-fronted tern, banded dotterel, shags, gulls, ducks, and occasionally white heron can possibly be seen feeding on small fish and shellfish. The swampy areas and mudflat margins of the Wanganui River are also worth a listen and look for fernbird.

From September to November, birders can also observe fishing for whitebait from the many stands along the river bank.

The walk is reached from Harihari township, on SH6, 78 km south of Hokitika and 61 km north of Franz Josef/Waiau. From Harihari, turn off SH6 on to Wanganui Flat Road and drive towards the coast for 20 km, first through farmland (look for spur-winged plover and Australasian harrier/kāhu) then through pākihi and kahikatea forest to the road end. The walk is clearly signposted.

▷ Waitangiroto Nature Reserve/White Heron Sanctuary

This is the only white heron breeding colony in New Zealand. Each year 30–40 pairs nest along just 60 m of the forest-lined Waitangiroto River. Adding to the crowded spectacle is a royal spoonbill colony, nesting directly above in tall kahikatea trees and, at a lower level, an increasing number of little shag. Three species, in three layers, stacked up in a delightful natural setting directly across the river from a secluded viewing hide.

White heron are rare in New Zealand, and especially revered by Māori. Worldwide, these birds were once hunted for their decorative feathers. By the 1940s only four nesting pairs remained in New Zealand. Today's population recovery is being largely helped by predator trapping and weed control carried out by the Arnold family, who since 1978 have held the sole concession to take visitors to the colony.

White Heron Sanctuary Tours issues entry permits on behalf of DoC. Tours take 2.5 hours and leave from Whataroa township (on SH6, 31 km north of Franz Josef/Waiau and 108 km south of Hokitika). A 20-minute minibus ride is followed by a 20-minute jet-boat trip and a 500-m walk along a boardwalk through the rainforest to the viewing hide. Around 40 minutes is spent at the hide. Tūī, bellbird, fantail and New Zealand pigeon are usually prolific along the boardwalk and at the hide.

Tour times and sizes are restricted, with usually four tours per day and a maximum of 12 people per tour. Trips go regardless of the weather – wet-weather gear is provided and there is shelter at the hide.

Nature tours on the beautiful Waitangiroto River run year-round, but white herons are only present from October to March. Tour times are 9 am, 11 am, 1 pm and 3 pm, and other times can be arranged if there is sufficient demand. Transport is available from Franz Josef/Waiau township. Bookings are advisable.

⊳ Ōkārito Lagoon

The largest and perhaps least-modified coastal wetland in New Zealand, Ōkārito is well known for its outstanding birdlife. Out of more than 80 bird species that have been recorded here, 54 are regularly seen, 42 are native species and 27 are endemic. The lagoon covers over 3000 ha of shallow open water, tidal flats, salt marsh and coastal shrub land, and is surrounded by magnificent kahikatea and rimu rainforest.

Kayaking is by far the most rewarding and least intrusive option for birding on the lagoon, gliding silently through tidal channels, close to waders feeding on the mudflats and perhaps with a curious fantail/pīwakawaka landing on your prow. White heron seem particularly unthreatened, preferring to concentrate on their fishing rather than worrying about a kayak gliding just metres away. Nowhere else in the world can they be photographed in such a setting, backed by rainforest and snow-covered mountains. White heron feed year-round at Ōkārito, but are most abundant from October to March when they are breeding on the nearby Waitangiroto River. Other species you are likely to see include white-fronted tern/tara, Caspian tern/taranui, banded dotterel/tuturiwhatu, black-billed gull/tarāpunga, kingfisher and Arctic waders, mainly bar-tailed godwit/kūaka.

Kayaking also provides access to the rainforest-lined channels of the

Ōkārito River delta that flow slowly into the lagoon, the domain of forest birds such tūī, bellbird/korimako, tomtit/miromiro, brown creeper and New Zealand pigeon/kererū.

Ōkārito Nature Tours is a small family-run company that provides guided kayaking tours or independent kayak hire. This comes with all paddling and safety equipment, map and resource kits about the lagoon, its birdlife and ecology, plus advice about tidal flows and navigable waterways. Book well in advance to plan the best timing for your trip: tides make a critical difference to the navigable channels and paddle-power required.

You can also paddle your own kayak on the lagoon. There's an obvious launch site beside the old wharf just as the road enters Ōkārito. The helpful folk at Ōkārito Nature Tours are happy to offer their maps, resource kits and navigation advice: they are genuinely keen to ensure all visitors have the best possible experience and approach birds without disturbing them.

If kayaking is not your preference, Ōkarito Boat Tours offer a quiet open-

Westland petrel/tītī

The Westland petrel, also known as Westland black petrel, is a threatened endemic that breeds only in the steep, forested foothills of the Paparoa Range, near Punakaiki (47 km north of Greymouth on SH6). The Westland species *Procellaria westlandica* is closely related to the threatened black petrel *P. parkinsoni* that breeds on Little and Great Barrier Islands, in Auckland's Hauraki Gulf.

The population probably numbered many hundreds of thousands before the arrival of humans, who harvested both adults and chicks for food, but the Westland petrel has suffered considerably. Today's major threats include dogs, cats, stoats and rats. The total breeding population is believed to be slowly increasing, but remains vulnerable at about 3000–4000 breeding pairs out of a total population of about 20,000. The petrels have learnt to scavenge offal discarded from fishing

air cruise for up to 12 passengers. Visibility and photography opportunities are good, with 360-degree viewing from all seats.

Moving on from the lagoon, the road continues about 1 km through the village to walking tracks to Ōkārito Trig (90 minutes return) and Three Mile Lagoon (3 hours return; a circuit via the coastline is possible at low tide). Forest, coastal and seabirds including banded dotterel and blue penguin are prolific here. From August to December, watch out for banded dotterel nests on the beach. The camouflaged eggs are hard to see among the sand and stones – walk below high-tide mark if possible.

At the start of these walks, just near the road end, the distinctive 'zit zit' call of the fernbird is likely to be heard from the coastal shrubbery. Another likely spot for fernbird is Pākihi Walk, signposted on the road to Ōkārito 5.7 km from the turn-off from SH6. This delightful 30-minute return walk crosses open pākihi swamp then climbs through rimu forest to a superb view of rainforest, mountains and sea.

vessels, which risks their being injured or killed when they are struck by trawl warps or take baited hooks.

During summer the birds disperse to eastern Australia and South America, returning to Punakaiki between mid-March and April. Chicks fledge from early November to mid-December.

Each day, as the birds fly in and out from their colony, there is an excellent viewing opportunity on the roadside beneath their flight path, 3 km south of Punakaiki settlement (at the northern boundary of Nikau Scenic Reserve). The best times are half an hour after sunset (all season) or half an hour before sunrise (April–October). Viewing can vary from day to day; sometimes several thousand can be seen flying just 30 m overhead.

A night-time venture at Ōkārito, started in 2006 by Ōkārito Kiwi Tours, involves listening for (with a promised 90 per cent chance of seeing) Ōkārito brown kiwi. There are some 250 kiwi living in the Ōkārito Forest area of Westland/Tai Poutini National Park. Tour guide Ian Cooper offers a range of 'low-key, low-impact' tours of 2.5–3 hours' duration, leaving just before dusk to catch the evening chorus of the day birds and the first calls of the nocturnal kiwi and morepork/ruru.

Ōkārito is located 13 km off the main highway (SH6) between Whataroa and Franz Josef/Waiau. Look for the signposted turn-off between Lakes Wahapo and Māpourika.

▷ Monro Beach, Lake Moeraki

The Fiordland crested penguin/tawaki is one of the rarest of New Zealand's mainland penguins. Several small colonies are established on secluded beaches, but these birds are particularly timid and sensitive to human presence so protective locals are tight-lipped about their locations.

One accessible population is at Monro Beach, close to Lake Moeraki. A 40-minute walking track is signposted beside SH6, 30 km north of Haast and 88 km south of Fox Glacier. The gently undulating track leads through splendid rainforest to a small sandy beach framed by rocky headlands and backed by windswept coastal shrubbery, stunted rātā trees and gorse (a noxious weed). About 15 pairs nest in the shrubby vegetation, some of them several hundred metres inland.

The penguins live at the colony during the breeding season (July–November) and occasionally during the moulting season (mid-January to early March). They feed at sea during the day, generally leaving their nests at daybreak and returning to shore at dusk, when it's possible to watch them come through the breakers and walk up the beach. It is essential to stay still and hidden: the beach is very confined and if the birds detect any human presence they are unlikely to come ashore. DoC has strict guidelines for viewing penguins, most of them patently obvious – for example, do not approach, follow, surround, obstruct, harass or feed the birds, or use flash photography.

New Zealand fur seals are also sometimes present on Monro Beach (stay well clear) and Hector's dolphin may be seen playing in the surf. While in the vicinity, it's well worth visiting Lake Moeraki, on the inland side of SH6 near the Monro Beach car park. Common forest birds and waterfowl are present here, plus there is a good chance of spotting Australasian crested grebe, kākā, and New Zealand falcon/kārearea.

▷ Hapuka Estuary

Here, a 30-minute walkway with boardwalks and viewing points circles through the coastal forest and along the estuary margins. At low tide, South Island pied oystercatcher, variable oystercatcher and pied stilt are likely to be feeding on the flats. Also present are pūkeko and several duck, shag and gull species. Common forest birds are prolific, particularly when certain plants are flowering, for example flax (December) and kōwhai (September). At such times the feeding frenzies of tūī, bellbird and New Zealand pigeon tend to render them oblivious to humans and cameras.

To reach the walkway turn off SH6 at Haast and drive south 15 km to Ōkuru. Just before crossing the Hapuka River bridge turn left (the track is signposted here) and drive 50 m to the car park.

Getting there South Westland is relatively remote, but being a major tourist destination it is well served by transport and visitor services.

Hokitika and Greymouth are the closest major towns, with connections to the national air network. Intercity (www.intercitycoach.co.nz) and Atomic Shuttles (www.atomictravel.co.nz) provide daily services from Wānaka, Christchurch, Nelson and Picton.

Alpine passes link South Westland with Christchurch (via Arthur's Pass, both road and rail) and Wānaka (via Haast Pass/Tioripatea). SH6 is the main road along the South Westland coast.

Getting around From Hokitika SH6 travels south to Lake Ianthe (40 km) Harihari (78 km), Whataroa (108 km), Franz Josef/Waiau (139 km), Lake

Moeraki and Monro Beach (252 km) and Haast (282 km).

Note that distances here can be deceptive, not least because of the magnificent landscapes, photo stops, DoC's excellent interpretative displays and short walks that entice travellers to dally along the way.

Accommodation The two glacier townships, Franz Josef/Waiau and Fox Glacier, have hotel, motel, bed-and-breakfast, backpacker and holiday-park accommodation. At Ōkārito there is a motel, YHA backpackers and community-run camping ground (toilets, showers but no powered sites).

Whataroa has farmstays, bed-and-breakfasts, two motels and a hotel with camping and campervan sites. Harihari offers lodge, motel, motor inn, campervan park and farmstay accommodation. Wilderness Lodge at Lake Moeraki has a strong focus on nature and birding.

Haast offers a full range of hotel, lodge, motel, backpacker and holiday-park accommodation. Self-registration DoC camping grounds are located at Lakes Ianthe, Māpourika, Paringa and Gillespies Beach (near Fox Glacier).

Facilities Hokitika and Greymouth have supermarkets, banks, fuel, photography, pharmacies and clothing stores. At Franz Josef/Waiau and Fox Glacier there are small grocery stores, cafes, bars and restaurants, souvenir shops and craft galleries, ATM and fuel. Harihari and Whataroa each have cafe and hotel meals, fuel and an art gallery. There are cafes, restaurants, a tavern, fuel and grocery store at Haast. Ōkārito has public toilets and accommodation, but no shop or other services.

Information

West Coast Birding website: www.birdingwestcoast.co.nz.
Westland i-SITE Visitor Centre, Hokitika, 03 755 6166, hokitika@i-SITE.org.

Franz Josef Visitor Centre/Department of Conservation, 03 752 0796, vctemp@doc.govt.nz, www.glaciercountry.co.nz.

Haast Visitor Information Centre/Department of Conservation, 03 750 0809, haastvc@doc.govt.nz.

Licensed guiding operators

Ōkārito Nature Tours: guided or independent kayak hire, Ōkārito Lagoon, from $40 for a 2-hour rental to $75 for a 2-hour guided tour, 03 753 4014, kayaks@okarito.co.nz, www.okarito.co.nz.

Ōkārito Kiwi Tours: evening kiwi habitat tours, 2–3 hours, $60, bookings essential, 03 753 4330, okaritokiwitours@paradise.net.nz, www.okaritokiwitours.co.nz.

White Heron Sanctuary Tours: jetboat/walking tour through rainforest to white heron sanctuary, 2.5–3 hours, $110/adult, $45/child, 03 753 4120, info@whiteherontours.co.nz, www.whiteherontours.co.nz.

Glacier Valley Eco Tours: guided walks including Lake Matheson (forest birds) $70/adult and Ōkārito Lagoon ($400 half-day guided kayaking), 03 752 0699 or 0800 999 739, mike@glaciervalley.co.nz, www.glaciervalley.co.nz.

27

Oamaru penguin colonies

Where South Island east coast, near the town of Oamaru.

What's special Close-up viewing of blue penguin colony; more distant view of yellow-eyed penguins.

Birds to look for Blue penguin/kororā, yellow-eyed penguin/hoiho, Stewart Island shag/kōau, spotted shag/pārekareka, plus fantail/pīwakawaka and welcome swallow (mainly in winter).

Birdwatching options Night-time viewing as birds return to their colony; daytime tours of the blue penguin colony.

When to go Year-round, though penguin numbers vary throughout the year. November/December is when most birds come ashore (up to 200 each night) and chicks are present.

Background

Widespread and locally common around New Zealand, blue penguins generally nest in natural burrows or under rock piles, coastal shrubbery or driftwood. In the 1970s birds began moving into an old harbourside quarry on the edge of Oamaru township, finding spaces under timber stacks and rocks to nest. Initially they were viewed as pests by the quarry owners; however, when the quarry closed in the mid-1980s, locals rallied round their 'urban penguins' and embarked on a protection programme. The numbers have since flourished.

The programme, initially established by DoC, Forest and Bird, and the Waitaki District Council, involved predator control and placing wooden nest

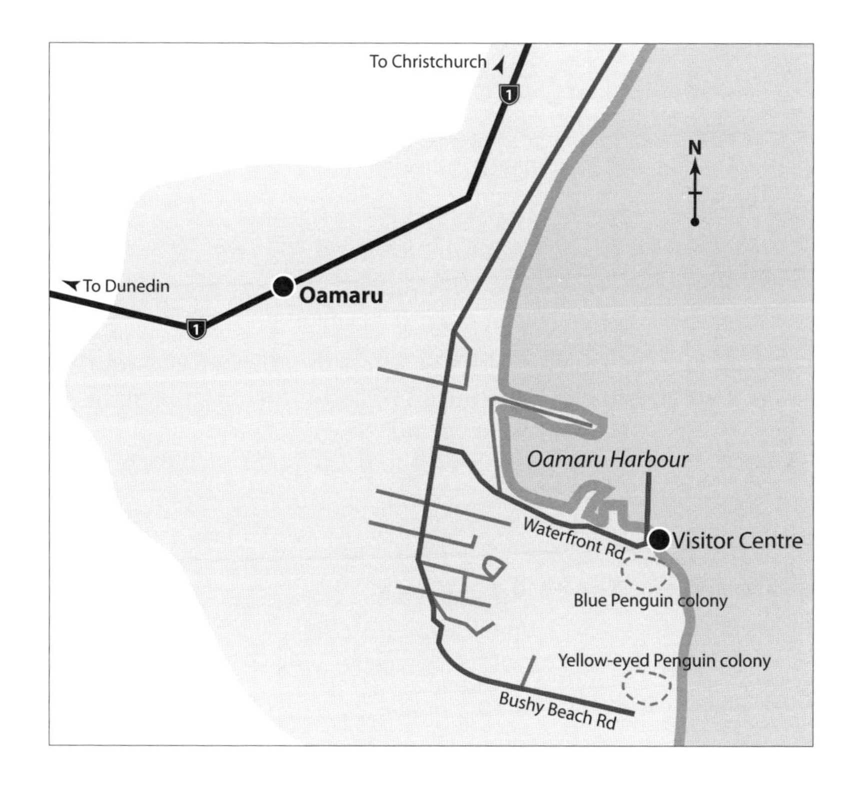

boxes in the quarry. These have been readily adopted by the penguins: within 18 years peak numbers arriving ashore each day rose from 42 to nearly 300 and the colony's breeding population increased from 14 to 158 pairs.

A visitor centre was established to manage the growing number of people arriving to see the penguins, and entry fees and other revenue are used to fund predator control and habitat improvement. More than 40,000 people a year now visit.

A public viewing grandstand enables visitors to watch the penguins come ashore and return to their burrows at night after fishing all day at sea. Nocturnal viewing is made possible by orange/yellow lighting that enables humans to see but is outside the range of light visible to penguins. Daytime 'behind the scenes' tours provide further information about the penguins and an opportunity to explore the colony.

The penguin protection programme is now completely self-funding and has had a significant impact on the local economy, as colony visitors usually stay overnight in Oamaru. The penguins are also thriving despite all the attention and their nightly public parade. Breeding success here has been among the highest recorded for the species.

A second colony nearby is closed to the public and used as a monitoring control site.

Visitors are likely to see more than blue penguins. Spotted and Stewart Island shags frequent the coast here and New Zealand fur seals haul ashore onto the rocks. During winter, the black form of the South Island subspecies of fantail is often seen around the colony.

Best birding areas

▷ Blue penguin colony and visitor centre

The visitor centre's viewing grandstand has seating capacity for 350 people and each evening's 'show' is accompanied by a commentary. Most birds come ashore within the first hour after dark. They can easily be seen as they raft up, then swim to shore and make their way up the stony beach. Generally they will pause for some preening and socialising before passing directly in front of and just metres away from the viewing stand.

Viewing times vary throughout the year, starting from 5 pm in mid-winter to 9.30 pm in mid-summer. Cameras and video cameras are not permitted in the evening.

On the 'behind the scenes' tours, visitors enter the breeding area where, if penguins or chicks are in residence, they can be viewed through unobtrusive tunnels and sitting at the entrance to their burrows. Tours run throughout the year, during the day and early evening. Cameras without flash and video cameras are allowed during day tours.

▷ Bushy Beach yellow-eyed penguin colony

While blue penguin are the stars at Oamaru, the northernmost colony of yellow-eyed penguin/hoiho is located just 4 km south of the town, at

Bushy Beach. The route is signposted from Oamaru town centre.

From the beach car park a cliff top path leads to a free (and at times crowded) viewing hide that looks down on the beach from about 200 m away. The birds generally come ashore in the late afternoon, but they are particularly shy and will not come out of the water if they see any potential threat. People are therefore urged to stay off the beach itself after 3 pm.

Coastline Tours runs the 'Penguin Express' daily from Oamaru to Bushy Beach, where passengers can join a Bushy Beach tour and watch the yellow-eyed penguins from the hide. The Penguin Express continues to the blue penguin colony. Because the yellow-eyed penguin comes ashore earlier each day than the blue penguin it is possible to see both species in one evening. Penguin Express Tours last around 2.5 hours and include a visit to the historic precinct. Cost (including entry to the Oamaru Blue Penguin Colony) is $25/adult, $10/child. Family and other discounts available. Email: penguinexpress@xtra.co.nz or visit www.coastline-tours.co.nz.

There are also free public viewing hides on the public conservation estate at two other yellow-eyed penguin colonies close to Oamaru. These are at Katiki Point, Moeraki (35 km south of Oamaru) and Shag Point (50 km south of Oamaru).

Getting there Oamaru is located on SH1, 1.5 hours' drive north of Dunedin and 3 hours' drive south of Christchurch. The town is on the national air network and daily coach services link with other South Island towns and cities. Local company Coastline Tours operates a daily service between Oamaru and Dunedin, as well as afternoon/evening tours of Oamaru and the Bushy Beach and Oamaru penguin colonies.

Getting around The colony and visitor centre are located beyond the southern end of the harbour on Waterfront Road, signposted 5 minutes' drive from the town centre. The viewing stand is alongside.

Accommodation Oamaru has motels, hotels, backpacker, holiday park, bed-and-breakfast, lodge, homestay and farmstay accommodation.

Facilities The visitor centre has a souvenir shop, toilets and an interpretation area with video presentation, a 'nestcam' filming penguin nests, and a static penguin display. Oamaru has numerous shops, supermarkets, banks, restaurants and fuel and a delightful restored Victorian-style precinct of shops made of the distinctive local limestone.

Information

Oamaru i-SITE Visitor Centre, 1 Thames Street, 03 434 1656, oamaru@i-SITE.org, www.tourismwaitaki.co.nz.

Licensed guiding company

Oamaru Blue Penguin Colony: evening viewing $22/adult, $10/child. 'Behind the scenes' tours $10/adult, $4/child. Family passes and special discounts available. Booking is advisable, especially during summer, and essential for the tour. 1 Thames Street, Oamaru, 03 433 1195, obpc@penguins.co.nz, www.penguins.co.nz.

Recommended reading

The Plight of the Penguin, Lloyd Spencer-Davis. Dunedin: Longacre Press, 2002.

Phillip the Penguin, John-Paul Fischbach. Serendipity Press, 2006 (for children under 10).

28

Otago Peninsula

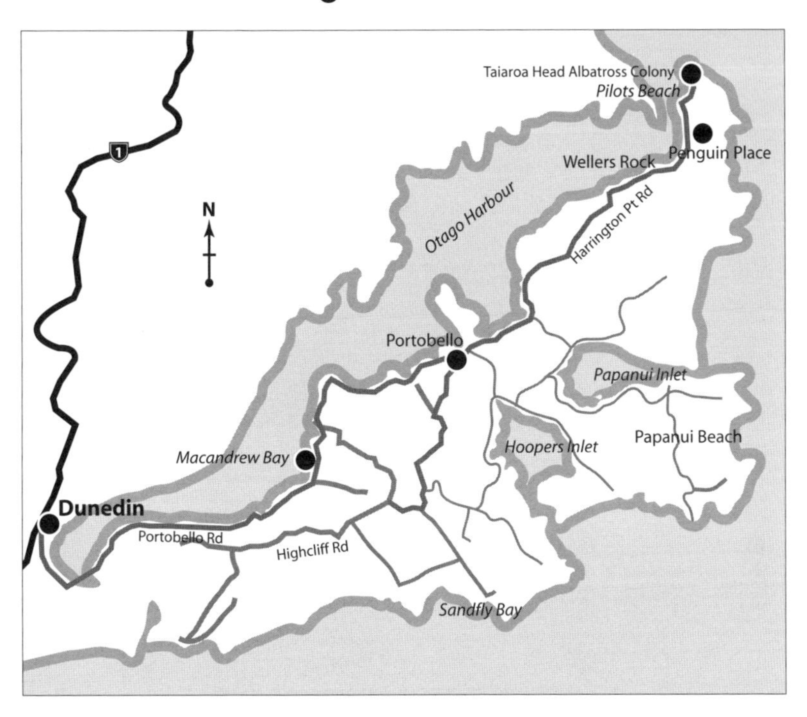

Where Dunedin, south-east coast of the South Island.

What's special A mainland colony of albatross, yellow-eyed penguin/hoiho colonies, plus more coastal birds and seabirds on headlands, ocean beaches and tidal inlets close to a major city.

Birds to look for Northern royal albatross/toroa and other albatross, yellow-eyed penguin/hoiho, Stewart Island shag/kōau, spotted shag/pārekareka as well as other shags, blue penguin/kororā, petrels, shearwaters, terns, gulls, waders, waterfowl and forest birds.

Birdwatching options Guided and self-guided walks and drives and harbour cruises. Tour guides work with each other, encompassing different operations into a single guided itinerary.

Top spots

- Taiaroa Head (half-day): northern royal albatross colony and Royal Albatross Centre, colonies of Stewart Island shag and spotted shag
- Monarch Wildlife Cruises (1 hour): Dunedin Harbour and Heads
- Penguin Place (1.5 hours): guided tour of yellow-eyed penguin conservation reserve
- Papanui Beach (half-day): yellow-eyed penguin, seals and sea lions, guided tour
- Sandfly Bay (2–3 hours): yellow-eyed penguin colony self-guided walk
- Hoopers and Papanui tidal inlets (1–2 hours): guided tour or self-drive
- Pilots Beach (1 hour): blue penguin colony.

When to go For royal albatross the best time is summer, especially February when all the chicks have hatched and the birds are most active. In late winter and early spring the adults are mostly at sea, returning only briefly to feed their young. During October and November the viewing hide is closed, but the birds can be seen on the Monarch Wildlife Cruise. Yellow-eyed penguin can be seen all year round: during winter they fish at sea all day and return to their nests in the late afternoon, while in summer they are nesting and raising chicks, with most activity during the day. February is a good time to see the large chicks. Mid-summer is best for blue penguin and migratory waders.

Background

Otago Peninsula extends some 30 km along the southern edge of volcanic Otago Harbour, across from downtown Dunedin. Windswept headlands and volcanic cliffs, long sandy beaches, small rocky bays and shallow tidal inlets create varied habitats close to a plentiful supply of food in the deep waters just offshore. These factors have attracted an abundance of wildlife, including species usually found further south.

Nowhere else do ocean-wandering royal albatross nest on a mainland so close to human settlement, as do the 20 or so northern royal pairs that nest on Otago Peninsula. (The number varies from season to season.) Other northern royals nest on the Chatham Islands, and southern royals on the subantarctic islands. Northern royal albatross began nesting at Taiaroa Head in the early 20th century. Since then, the colony has been carefully protected to safeguard the birds from threats that don't exist in more remote colonies. Such intensive management does create a somewhat modified environment in which to observe the birds; nevertheless, the Royal Albatross Centre provides a worthwhile experience. And while the nests and chicks are confined behind fences, the adult birds are not. For most of the year they can be seen from outside the colony, soaring around the headland.

Predator control at Taiaroa Head has also benefited other species, and the albatross now share their windswept environs with thousands of seabirds and shorebirds, many of which are otherwise found only on offshore islands. Nests of the largest mainland colony of Stewart Island shag cover the western slopes below the headland. Blue penguin burrow at the headland base. On the exposed ocean side, spotted shag roost and nest on steep cliffs. The largest mainland colony of sooty shearwater/tītī is established on the headland. Red-billed gull/tarāpunga and royal spoonbill/kōtuku-ngutupapa can also be seen.

Meanwhile, down on the beaches is a conservation success story: the endangered yellow-eyed penguin. The largest penguins living in a temperate region, they nest in coastal vegetation and are easily frightened by humans. At the end of the day's fishing, even if they have chicks to feed, they will stay at sea if they perceive any threat between sea and nest.

Yellow-eyed penguin numbers on the peninsula have fallen drastically because of habitat loss (through farm development), introduced predators and poor breeding seasons. Since 1987 a public campaign, spearheaded by the Yellow-eyed Penguin Trust, has made significant inroads to restoring and safeguarding penguin habitats. Some local landowners have installed nesting boxes and replanted vegetation to restore habitat, and built hides so the penguins can be observed without disturbance.

Best birding areas

⊳ Taiaroa Head

The Taiaroa Head northern royal albatross colony is a wildlife reserve managed by DoC. Public access is restricted to guided tours run from the Royal Albatross Centre. Tours involve a commentary, video and a 200-m walk to a tinted-glass observatory that overlooks most of the colony.

Admission to the centre is free and it provides a wealth of information about the albatross: their breeding habits, their amazing flying ability, endurance journeys across the southern ocean and the threat they face from long-line fishing boats. There is also a shop and cafe, along with tours pertaining to the military history of this strategically placed headland. Just being in the vicinity of Taiaroa Head, in the car park, on the beach below or on a wildlife cruise, can reward with splendid views of the albatross coming and going, including young birds learning to fly.

Late afternoon, when the breeze is usually strong, is a good time to watch. You may also see other birds, including Stewart Island shag, spotted shag, gulls, terns and shearwaters. The centre is open every day except Christmas Day. Tours to the viewing observatory operate daily except during the breeding season – from 17 October to 24 November. Bookings for colony tours are essential.

▷ Monarch Wildlife Cruise

The MV *Monarch* has been operating cruises around Taiaroa Head since the early 1980s. From the vessel there are excellent views of northern royal albatross, as well as other seabirds not generally seen from land. These include several other albatross – Buller's, wandering, shy, Salvin's and southern royals, plus Cape pigeon, sooty and other shearwaters, various petrels, Caspian tern/taranui and white-fronted tern/tara. The species seen will depend on the weather and wind direction.

The cruise also provides great viewing of the Stewart Island shag colony on the cliffs of Taiaroa Head. There's also the chance of spotting seals and occasionally sea lions and dolphins. Tours include commentaries, bird lists, fact sheets, species identification and the use of jackets and binoculars. There is open-deck viewing and a heated cabin. Cruises depart from Wellers Rock (near Taiaroa Head, 45 minutes' drive from the city) five times daily during summer and twice daily during winter.

▷ Penguin Place

Set on coastal farmland, this yellow-eyed penguin conservation reserve is a successful private restoration effort and tourism venture. Since 1985, when farmer Howard McGrouther began restoration work, penguin numbers have increased from eight breeding pairs to around 12 to 18 (depending on the season), making this one of the larger colonies in the South Island. A complex system of hides and tunnels making it possible to observe the birds without disturbing them. Tour groups are limited in number and carefully controlled, as guides liaise using radios to find the best viewing opportunities. It can seem contrived but does enable very close viewing and photographic opportunities.

Penguin Place is on Harrington Point Road, signposted from Harbourside Road about 3 km before Taiaroa Head. Tours last 90 minutes and involve a video and talk about the conservation of yellow-eyed penguins, a 10-minute coach ride to the colony, then an hour's easy walking around the colony itself.

During the summer breeding season, the penguins stay in the colony. From October to April, tours depart every 30 minutes from 10.15 am until 90 minutes before sunset. During winter, when the penguins are at sea during the day, tours depart every 30 minutes from 3.15 to 4.45 pm, timed to watch the penguins make landfall and make their way to their nests.

Visitors can drive direct to Penguin Place, or travel from Dunedin with Monarch Wildlife Cruises or Twilight Wildlife Conservation Experience.

▷ Papanui Beach

This delightful setting for viewing yellow-eyed penguin on a remote sandy beach is on private land and accessible only through Elm Wildlife Tours, which has exclusive visiting rights. Reasonable fitness is required to negotiate 2 km of hilly farmland to and from the beach, where there are two unobtrusive hides. An alternative tour offers vehicle access to the beach a small distance from where the penguins come ashore. Tours are restricted to groups of 10, so the experience is uncrowded and relaxed. Seabirds, including various albatross species, can often be seen offshore. New Zealand sea lions and seals are usually present.

Elm Wildlife Tours also looks at birds in Otago Harbour, Papanui and Hoopers tidal inlets and incorporates a visit to the Royal Albatross Centre. Daily tours last around 6 hours through the afternoon and early evening.

▷ Sandfly Bay

A yellow-eyed penguin colony at Sandfly Bay Wildlife Reserve, on the ocean side of the peninsula 18 km from Dunedin, is open to public access, though a visit to see penguins is best experienced with a guide. There is a viewing hide behind the eastern end of the beach, and good fitness is required to climb back up the steep sandhill. Sandfly Bay is a popular beach, so be aware that penguin viewing (and sadly the welfare of the penguins!) is likely to be compromised by other visitors. Volunteers on the beach offer information and monitor visitor behaviour at busy times.

The walking track to Sandfly Bay starts from the end of Seal Point Road, which turns off Highcliff Road along the hilly spine of the peninsula.

Give the penguins a chance

Recovery of yellow-eyed penguin populations depends particularly on habitat restoration, predator control – and *minimal disturbance by humans*. While watching the penguins, keep hidden and quiet, and do not use flash photography. They are very shy birds, and if they feel threatened will not come ashore to their nests. Stay well away from nesting or moulting birds.

The clearly signposted track descends through farmland for about 400 m and continues into the reserve down the giant sandhill, directly to the beach. Once on the beach, walk to the far end (about 1 km) where a sign indicates a short track to the viewing hide. Remember that yellow-eyed penguins are particularly shy and will not approach their nest if they see people or feel at all threatened.

Allow 30 minutes for the walk to the hide, and longer for the uphill return. Nature Guides Otago run personalised guided tours for small groups to this colony. For further information, contact DoC, 03 477 0677.

▷ Hoopers Inlet and Papanui Inlet

These shallow tidal inlets are on the eastern coastline. Species present here all year include South Island pied oystercatcher/tōrea, spur-winged plover, paradise shelduck/pūtangitangi, pūkeko, pied stilt/poaka, white-faced heron, kingfisher/kōtare, mallard and hundreds of black swan. During summer, bar-tailed godwit/kūaka and occasional other Arctic waders visit. During late summer and early winter New Zealand migrants may be present: black-billed gull/tarāpunga, black-fronted tern/tarapiroe and banded dotterel/tuturiwhatu.

The roads that follow the inlet margins provide easy access and good lookouts, in particular at low tide. Monarch Wildlife Cruises and Elm

Wildlife Tours include visits to these inlets in some itineraries.

You can continue beyond the eastern margin of Hoopers Inlet to the end of Allens Beach Road and walk along Allens Beach to the outlet of Hoopers Inlet. Here you can view seabirds, waders and possibly yellow-eyed penguin. Because of constantly shifting sand and tides, this can involve a walk of 300 m to 4 km. Sea lions are sometimes found on this beach.

Pilots Beach

This tiny beach at Taiaroa Head, on the harbour side below the Royal Albatross Centre car park, is home to a small blue penguin colony. During mid-summer the birds gather offshore until after dark, before coming ashore to their nests in coastal shrubbery. Their evening ritual has become a popular spectacle. To allow the birds safe passage, from October to March vehicle access to the beach is closed from late afternoon, and volunteers manage visitors. There is parking at the Royal Albatross Centre.

Getting there Dunedin is accessible by daily air and coach services. The peninsula is an easy drive from the city. First Portobello Road, then Harrington Point Road follows the harbour coastline to Taiaroa Head, about 1 hour's drive from the city centre.

City bus services only travel halfway along the peninsula, to Portobello Road, but wildlife tours leave from the city and can collect guests from their accommodation.

Getting around Self-driving or travelling with a wildlife tour operator are the best options. Alternatively, use accommodation on the peninsula and bikes to get around.

Accommodation Dunedin offers the full range of accommodation expected for a city of its size. On the peninsula there are motels, bed-and-breakfasts, farmstays, a holiday park and a backpackers.

Facilities On the peninsula, there is a cafe and pub at Portobello village, plus restaurants at Macandrew Bay. Several galleries reflect the

Beware of sea lions

Be very wary of the New Zealand sea lions and seals that frequent many of the ocean-side beaches of Otago Peninsula. Keep well away: they do not like being disturbed and can move surprisingly fast. Don't get between them and the sea, blocking off their escape route. They can also lie hidden among vegetation behind beaches, and can look like rocks when they lie still, so be vigilant.

peninsula's artist community. There are no supermarkets or gas stations. For birders, a visit to the Otago Museum bird gallery, in particular the displays on extinction and survival, is recommended. 419 Great King Street, 10 am to 5 pm, admission free, www.otagomuseum.govt.nz.

Information

Dunedin i-SITE Visitor Centre: 48 The Octagon, 03 474 3300, dunedin@i-SITE.org, www.dunedinNZ.com.

DoC Conservation House: 77 Lower Stuart Street, 03 477 0677, otago@doc.govt.nz.

Licensed guiding companies

Monarch Wildlife Cruises and Tours: wildlife cruise ($45/adult), peninsula wildlife tours and options to join other albatross and yellow-eyed penguin colony tours (costs vary accordingly), 03 477 4276, monarch@wildlife.co.nz, www.wildlife.co.nz.

Elm Wildlife Tours: half-day tour encompassing yellow-eyed penguins and other wildlife ($95/adult plus options to join Monarch Wildlife Cruise and Royal Albatross Centre colony tour), 0800 356 563, elmwildlifetours.co.nz, www.elmwildlifetours.co.nz.

Royal Albatross Centre: tours to the northern royal albatross colony ($40/adult, $20/child, family tickets and add-on historic features available), educational videos and displays, shop and cafe, 03 478 0499, reservations@albatross.org.nz, www.albatross.org.nz.

Penguin Place: private yellow-eyed penguin conservation reserve. Tours (1.5 hours), interpretive video and commentary, $40/adult (bookings essential), 03 478 0286, www.penguinplace.co.nz.

Nature Guides Otago: guided small-group tours. A good level of fitness is essential. Two tours are offered: Sunrise Penguin Walk (3 hours) $82, Peninsula Excursion and Albatross Encounter (6–7 hours with lunch) $290. A two-night package of accommodation in Nisbet Cottage B&B (4.5 stars) on the peninsula and both tours costs $600 per person.

Recommended reading

Wild Dunedin, Neville Peat and Brian Patrick, Dunedin: University of Otago Press, 2002.

Orokonui Ecosanctuary

Just 30 minutes' drive north of Dunedin is Orokonui, one of the largest community-managed, predator-proof sanctuaries in New Zealand. Endangered species reintroduced so far include South Island kākā, South Island saddleback (the only population on the South Island mainland) and South Island robin. Forest birds already resident here include South Island tomtit, brown creeper and rifleman. A visitor and education centre opened in 2009.

Orokonui Ecosanctuary: Blueskin Road, Waitati. Follow the signs from Dunedin's northern motorway or take the Orokonui Express, a half-day train excursion from Dunedin. Ecosanctuary entry $14.99/adult, $7.49/child. Guided tours (90 minutes) offered twice daily $37.99/adult, $18.99/child, 03 482 1755, info@orokonui.org.nz, www.orokonui.org.nz.

29
The Catlins

Where South-east corner of the South Island.

What's special A sparsely populated region with dramatic coastline and forest and farm landscapes. Habitats include beaches, estuaries, wetlands and rocky headlands, open farm and tussock land, magnificent dune podocarp forests and inland beech forests – possibly the best place to see the endemic and endangered mōhua/yellowhead. Many special features are easily accessible on good walking tracks.

Birds to look for Yellow-eyed penguin/hoiho, blue penguin/kororā, mōhua/yellowhead, South Island pied oystercatcher/tōrea, variable oystercatcher/tōrea, royal spoonbill/kōtuku-ngutupapa, pied stilt/poaka, fernbird/mātā, kingfisher/kōtare, New Zealand pipit/pīhoihoi, bellbird/korimako, common forest birds, shags/kōau, sooty shearwater/tītī (spring and summer), shining cuckoo/pīpīwharauroa (spring and summer).

Birdwatching options Self-guided walks and drives, guided walks and tours.

Top spots

- Nugget Point/Tokata (1–2 hours)
- Catlins Lake and Estuary (short walk and drive around margins, 2–3 hours)
- Catlins River Walk (4 hours return or 1-hour drive with guide)
- Papatōwai (multiple walks up to 2 hours)
- Tautuku (several short walks).

When to go Any time, as most birds are year-round residents. Winters are relatively mild and often more settled than in spring or early summer, but spring is when the birds are most active.

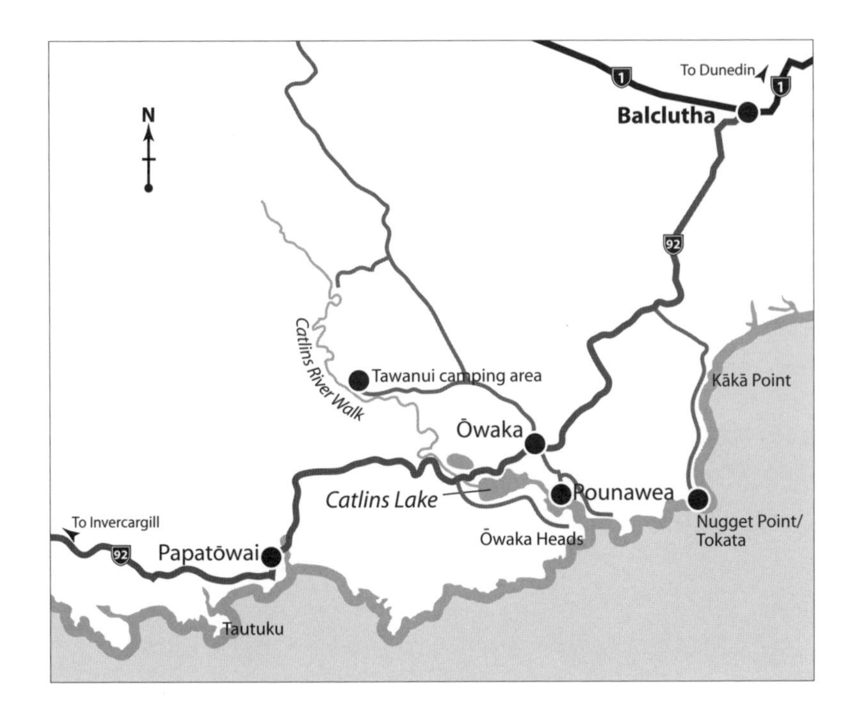

Background

The Catlins is one of New Zealand's lesser known yet most outstanding natural regions. It lies within an easy two-hour drive of both Dunedin and Invercargill but, being on the periphery of main transport routes, is less visited than other regions.

The coastline is a mixture of beaches, estuaries and headlands, the domain of sea lions, seals, penguins, shorebirds and seabirds. It is one of the few places in New Zealand where podocarp rainforest grows to the sea. Forest birds, including threatened mōhua, live in the inland beech forests.

The area was once heavily logged, but this has almost ceased and a few scattered farms, along with low-key tourism business, are the economic mainstay of this sparsely populated region.

Best birding areas

▷ Nugget Point/Tokata

This small, steep headland, a scientific reserve, is a dramatic spectacle and a favoured habitat for a diversity of marine life. Productive feeding grounds just offshore attract fur seals, sea lions and occasional elephant seals – the only place where these species co-exist – plus a host of sea and coastal birds.

From the car park a signposted walking track (1 hour return) leads to the lighthouse. Be wary of high winds! Throughout the year there is usually good viewing from here of several albatross species, plus the occasional Australasian gannet/tākapu, giant petrel, Arctic skua and Cape pigeon. On a very windy day there might be hundreds of birds, although they can be difficult to identify as they rarely come closer than about 100 m from land. Take binoculars.

Closer at hand, look for red-billed and black-backed gulls, spotted shag/pārekareka, Stewart Island shag (on the outer rocky islets) and the occasional white-faced heron. A few sooty shearwater nest on the point, and Australasian gannet sometimes nest on the offshore rocks, along with royal spoonbill that feed in the nearby Catlins Estuary. When the sea is calm, blue penguin can sometimes be seen in the water.

Several introduced birds are also present on Nugget Point: dunnock, goldfinch and chaffinch, yellowhammer, skylark and thrush. Remember to look for fur seals and occasional elephant seals on the rocks below.

There is a small yellow-eyed penguin colony at Roaring Bay, a shingle beach at the southern base of Nugget Point. A signposted track (20 minutes return) leads from the car park to a hide at the back of the beach, so the birds can be observed without being disturbed as they leave the water. (Note that they won't come ashore if people are visible.) Sea lions, which prefer sandy beaches to rocky shores, are also occasionally seen here.

Nugget Point is 30 km from Balclutha township and the road is clearly signposted. There are toilets at the car park.

▷ Catlins Lake and Estuary

The major estuary of the Catlins coast, this is a haven for wetland birds, migratory waders and waterfowl. Catlins Lake is essentially the upper end of the estuary, and is tidal. Short walks explore the margins, while several roadside parking spots provide excellent viewpoints.

Year-round residents include white-faced heron, pied stilt, South Island pied oystercatcher, variable oystercatcher, little shag, black shag, pūkeko, banded dotterel/tuturiwhatu, Caspian tern/taranui, paradise shelduck/pūtangitangi, grey duck/pārera, mallard, Australasian shoveler/kuruwhengi, kingfisher and black swan. During summer at least 50 bar-tailed godwit/kūaka stay over, occasionally accompanied by other Arctic waders. Small flocks of white-fronted tern/tara come and go to this and other estuaries along the Catlins coast. Good numbers of royal spoonbill also feed here.

Just east of Ōwaka a road leads to the tiny settlement of Pounawea, on the northern side of the estuary. An excellent bird-viewing spot is the Pounawea Nature Walk (90 minutes return), which leads from the Pounawea Motor Camp through tall podocarp forest to the salt marsh. Go at low tide to observe birds feeding on the mudflats. New Zealand pipit are usually on the salt marsh, while tūī, bellbird, fantail/pīwakawaka and New Zealand pigeon/kererū are likely to be seen and heard in the forest.

The main Catlins Highway (SH92) heads south from Ōwaka and after 7 km reaches Catlins Lake, where the road to Pūrakanui Falls turns left and leads to other roads that follow the southern estuary margins, almost to Ōwaka Heads. There are several obvious stopping points around the southern shore where wading birds can be observed at low tide. At high tide, keep an eye on paddocks around the margins for roosting birds. Little egret and spur-winged plover are also likely to be feeding on the paddocks and Australasian harrier/kāhu and introduced blackbird and starling are likely to be present. From late winter through to summer, welcome swallow nest on and under the road bridges.

Catlins River Walk

This walking track follows the Catlins River through a magnificent pure stand of silver beech forest. The forest supports an abundance of native birds, and is particularly significant as one of the last strongholds of the threatened mōhua.

More common bush birds here are bellbird, tūī, tomtit/miromiro, grey warbler/riroriro, fantail, brown creeper and New Zealand pigeon, with kingfisher, black shag, mallard and grey duck likely to be seen along the river. There's also a chance of spotting the tiny rifleman/tītīpounamu. Yellow-crowned parakeet/kākāriki and New Zealand falcon/kārearea are also present and becoming more common. In spring and early summer the distinctive call of the shining cuckoo and possibly the rarer long-tailed cuckoo/koekoeā will echo through the forest. Introduced species include chaffinch, dunnock, sparrow, blackbird, redpoll and, in open areas, yellowhammer (the latter not to be confused with the similarly coloured mōhua/yellowhead.)

Mōhua are quite conspicuous, as they gather in family groups and chatter constantly, often high in the canopy. They are present from the central gorge section of the walk at Franks Creek to the 'top end' at The Wisp. To reach mōhua territory from the southern (Tawanui) end involves a 2-hour walk each way. Alternatively it is possible, with local knowledge from a guide such as Catlins Wildlife Trackers, to drive direct to Franks Creek along 3 km of forestry roads. Independent travellers should not attempt this, as the access is not straightforward and closed at times.

The southern end of the walk starts from Tawanui Camping Ground, a DoC camping area with water supply and toilets. The turn-off to Tawanui from the main Catlins Highway is signposted 10 km west of Ōwaka township and from here it is 11.5 km to the camping ground on an unsealed road. The walk entrance is signposted on the forest edge at the camping ground.

From the northern end, it is 1 hour's walk to mōhua territory, although this section of track involves crossing two reasonably stable wire suspension bridges. Drive north from Ōwaka township along Ōwaka Valley Road, then turn left onto Wisp Road (signposted to Picnic Area). There is a picnic area (but no toilet) at the start of the track, almost 30 km from Ōwaka.

▷ Papatōwai

This small and picturesque estuary is fringed with majestic podocarp forest to the north and overlooked by a tiny holiday settlement. The same birds found in and around Catlins Estuary are present here, though in smaller numbers. Worthwhile for birders is Picnic Point Track, an easy 40-minute loop walk that starts at the Papatōwai picnic area, follows the estuary's sandy southern shoreline to the open coast, then heads south along the beach before returning back through forest. A good range of coastal, estuary and forest birds is likely to be encountered and possibly also sea lions or fur seals.

At times during summer both Fiordland and Snares crested penguins/pokotiwhā come onto the coast here to moult in caves and under coastal bushes. From the beach, watch for Australasian gannets diving offshore.

An extension of this walk, signposted at its southern end, climbs overland through forest then farmland for 30 minutes to Kings Rock and a possible sighting of two resident reef heron/matuku-moana.

Back in Papatōwai, New Zealand pigeon, tūī and bellbird can be abundant in fruiting and flowering seasons. If staying overnight, check for the morepork/ruru feeding on moths at the one street light in the settlement.

Papatōwai is located 28 km from Ōwaka on SH92.

▷ Tautuku

Just 5 minutes' drive south of Papatōwai, the long expanse of misty, sea-spray-covered Tautuku Beach, the dune forest, small estuary and forest-surrounded Lake Wilkie epitomise the primeval essence of the Catlins, despite a history of logging and farming.

Tautuku is notable as a fernbird stronghold, and the highlight of several delightful short walks in the area will be the Tautuku Estuary boardwalk (30 minutes return), where there is a good chance of spotting this bird.

This walk, signposted on the coastal side of the road 7 km from Papatowai, leads 300 m through regenerating forest to a boardwalk across an open expanse of jointed rush beside the estuary. Listen for the fernbird's distinctive double click; with luck the shy but curious bird will pop out to see who's passing by. Wading and wetland birds are also present on the estuary, though not in such numbers or variety as on the estuaries further north.

If no fernbird has revealed itself on the boardwalk, head to the 'Traill's Tractor' display. The 200-m track to this old bush tram, a restored relic from earlier sawmilling days, is found across the road and over the bridge from the entrance to the estuary boardwalk, on the driveway to the Forest and Bird Society's Tautuku Lodge. Chances of a fernbird encounter on this walk are high. During spring and summer, the spectacle of 50 or so New Zealand pigeon feeding on the flowering broom is a likely bonus.

Two other walks not to be missed at Tautuku, where both forest and wetland birds are present, are to Lake Wilkie, an old dune lake hidden in the forest (30 minutes return) and the Tautuku Nature Trail, an easy 15-minute wander through the dune forest to the beach. Both are clearly signposted.

▷ Other walks

Other Catlins walks worth exploring, for scenic appeal and the presence of forest birds, are to Matai Falls, Pūrakaunui Falls, McLean Falls, Cathedral Caves ($5 entrance fee; beach access only negotiable at low tide), Tahakopa Bay and Kākā Point. All are clearly signposted.

Getting there The Catlins Highway (SH92) runs from Balclutha, 80 km south of Dunedin, to Fortrose, 45 km from Invercargill. Daily coach services run to Balclutha from Dunedin and Invercargill and the Catlins Coaster (www.catlinscoaster.co.nz) provides a daily Dunedin–Invercargill service.

Getting around Self-driving or travelling with a guided tour operator are the only options. The main Catlins Highway is sealed but some other roads are unsealed. Day trips from Dunedin and Invercargill are manageable, though with so many good birding options it is worth spending longer.

Accommodation There are motels at Ōwaka (the main town), Kākā Point (north of Nugget Point) and Papatōwai. Motor camps are located at Pounawea and Kākā Point, and DoC camping areas are located at Tawanui, at the southern end of the Catlins River Walk, and Pūrakaunui. Several backpacker, bed-and-breakfast and self-catered accommodation options are located throughout the region.

Facilities Ōwaka has an information centre (open in summer), small supermarket, pharmacy, internet cafe, fuel, restaurants and a hotel. At Papatōwai there is a store selling basic groceries, takeaway food and fuel. Kākā Point also has a general store with a restaurant, cafe and fuel and there is a restaurant at Niagara Falls. There are no ATM machines in the Catlins: Balclutha has the nearest. Telecom cellphone reception is patchy and Vodaphone coverage is non-existent.

Information

Ōwaka Information Centre, Catlins Diner, 3 Main Road, Ōwaka, info@catlins.org.nz, www.catlins-nz.com.

Clutha i-SITE Visitor Centre, 4 Clyde Street, Balclutha. 03 418 0388, clutha.vin@cluthadc.govt.nz.

Invercargill i-SITE Visitor Centre, Queens Park, Victoria Ave, P.O. Box 1012, Invercargill. 03 214 6243, Invercargill.i-site@venturesouthland.co.nz.

Department of Conservation, www.doc.govt.nz.

Catlins Promotions website: www.catlins.org.nz/index.htm.

Licensed guiding company

Catlins Wildlife Trackers: nature tours, guided walks and accommodation, Papatōwai, ph/fax 03 4158 613, info@catlins-ecotours.co.nz, www.catlins-ecotours.co.nz.

Recommended reading

The Catlins and the Southern Scenic Route, Neville Peat. Dunedin: University of Otago Press, 1998.

Southern Scenic Route, a promotional brochure and website: www.southernscenicroute.co.nz.

30

Awarua Wetlands

Where Estuaries on the southern coast of the South Island, near Invercargill.

What's special Ramsar site, one of the top three wading-bird habitats in the South Island and internationally important grounds for summer migrants. Areas include, Awarua Bay and New River estuaries, Bushy Point fernbird habitat and Sandy Point estuarine, wetland and forest habitat.

Birds to look for Arctic waders (bar-tailed godwit/kūaka, turnstone, lesser knot/huahou), plus lesser numbers of Pacific golden plover, red-necked stint, sharp-tailed sandpiper and curlew sandpiper. Rarities include Siberian tattler, greenshank and sanderling (spring and summer). Southern New Zealand dotterel/tuturiwhatu (winter), Australasian bittern/matuku, marsh crake, fernbird/mātā, royal spoonbill/kōtuku-ngutupapa, Caspian tern/taranui and other terns, pied stilt/poaka, three shag species, ducks and herons.

Birdwatching options Self-guided walks, walks with local Ornithological Society members, guided walk (Bushy Point).

Top spots

- Awarua Bay (Muddy Creek, 2–3 hours over high tide; Cow Island, 2–3 hours over high tide)
- New River Estuary (from Stead Street wharf – 1 hour)
- Sandy Point (short walks up to 1 hour)
- Bushy Point (40 minutes' walk).

When to go October–late March for Arctic waders, April–August for southern New Zealand dotterel.

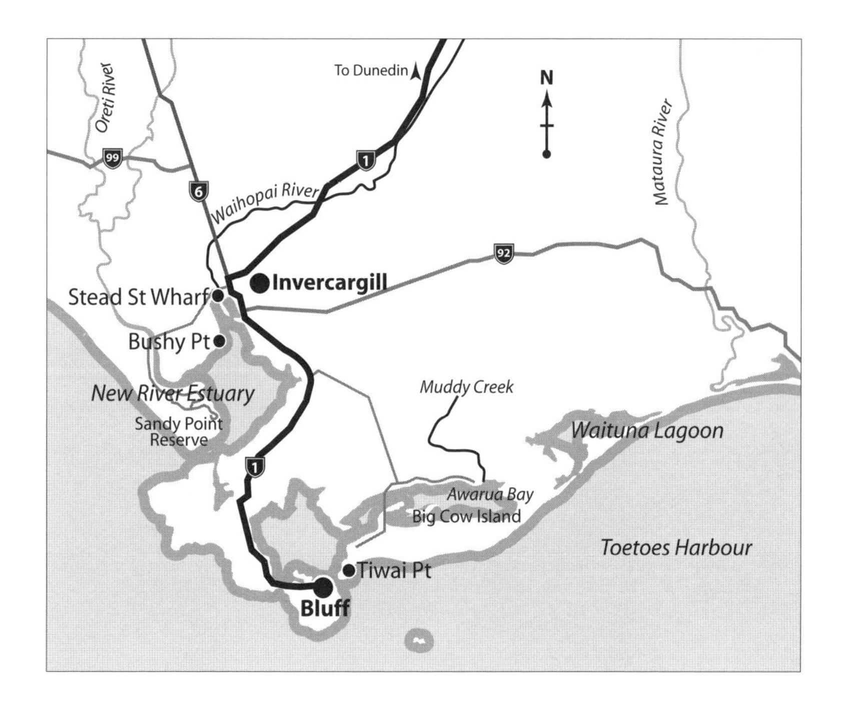

Background

Travellers tend to pass through Invercargill on their way to somewhere else, like Fiordland or Stewart Island/Rakiura, but for birders the estuaries and coastal lagoons near the town are particularly significant, accessible and well worth stopping over to see for a day or two.

Southland was first in the world to have a wetland recognised under the Ramsar Convention, when the Waituna Wetland Scientific Reserve, 3500 ha of peatland and lagoon, was registered in 1976. Waituna is just part of a much larger wetland complex that encompasses major estuaries, Awarua Bay and New River and Toetoes Harbour. In 2008, Waituna was included in these areas, which total 16,000 ha and are officially recognised as the Awarua Wetlands Ramsar site.

The habitats are very diverse: coastal wetlands, mudflats, peat bogs, salt marshes, tussock lands, flax swamps, manuka shrublands and totara-dominated coastal forest. Together, they rank among the top three wading-bird habitats in the South Island, alongside Farewell Spit and Lake Ellesmere/Te Waihora. More than 80 bird species have been sighted here, of which 65 depend on estuaries for part or all of their life.

From spring to late autumn the estuaries and lagoons of Southland are the feeding grounds for thousands of migratory waders from the northern hemisphere. Godwits are the most common migrant and turnstones rank second. The estuaries support a diversity of fish, shellfish and invertebrates, while insect life is also remarkably diverse, including over 80 species of moth alone. Special plant life includes moor-like cushion bogs that are more usually found in sub-alpine regions than at sea level.

Awarua Bay is also a neighbour to the huge Tiwai Point aluminium smelter. Pylons carrying power to the smelter from Fiordland form a somewhat incongruous presence on these otherwise largely unmodified estuary flats.

Best birding areas

▷ Awarua Bay

Awarua is the least modified harbour in Southland. Its main waterway, Muddy Creek, passes through a large conservation area before entering the bay, so the water quality is high. Most years the bay has the greatest diversity of bird species in Southland, and the second greatest numbers of birds. Migratory waders, southern New Zealand dotterel and fernbird are the special species to look for. There are two key birding areas at Awarua: the head of the bay and Cow Island.

To get there from Invercargill, drive towards Bluff and about 8 km from the town turn left onto the road signposted to Tiwai. To reach the head of the bay, turn left just before the causeway and follow the road for 7 km to a parking area by the only bridge, at Muddy Creek. Park here: the road continues a further 200 m beyond the bridge but the mud and tides here are a hazardous combination.

At low tide the birds will be feeding out on the flats, several hundred metres away, so the best time to see them is at high tide. The nearest roosting area is the secondary roost but it is here that most of the rarer migratory species are usually recorded. To reach it, walk from the bridge around the shore line for about 20 minutes. Be prepared for some wading, up to knee deep. Follow the estuary margin (listen for fernbird calls on a still day) then walk along a gravel ridge across the tidal flat. As the tide comes in, this ridge is vaguely discernable beneath the water.

Leave the car park 2–2.5 hours before high tide and watch over the top of the tide. Be prepared to walk back at least knee deep – obviously the closer to high tide, the deeper the water, but it is always walkable.

Most migratory waders are present from October to late March but some of the more common species regularly overwinter here. Usually at least two Siberian tattlers are seen here each year; in fact, over a 10-year survey period a third of all Siberian tattlers recorded in New Zealand were seen in Awarua Bay. Other uncommon New Zealand visitors recorded here are greenshank, marsh sandpiper, sanderling, Mongolian dotterel and terek sandpiper.

It is possible to continue another 20–30 minutes around the bay to the primary roost, but the first roost is likely to be more rewarding.

Note that the tide at Awarua is 1–1.5 hours after the Bluff tide, the time for which is given in the local paper. Evening viewing is directly into the setting sun, so morning is a better time. This is an exposed location, so even on a warm summer day take a parka and woolly hat; conversely, be prepared for sunburn even on an overcast day.

To reach Cow Island, drive back from Muddy Creek and cross the causeway towards the aluminium smelter. It is worth walking along the little spit by the causeway to look for white-fronted tern, banded dotterel and the occasional Caspian tern, although black-backed gulls tend to dominate this spot.

Southern New Zealand dotterels gather, mostly from April to July, on the southern shore of Awarua Bay. About a third of the total population (estimated at just over 300 in 2006) fly here from their mountain breeding grounds on Stewart Island/Rakiura. They feed regularly in the little bay where an old fenceline runs through the mudflats, and roost near the small point at the western end of the next bay east. Park beside the second pair of pylons on the south-west side of the causeway and walk around the estuary margin to the bay. Set out 1–1.5 hours before high tide. Birds are likely to be close to the shore line anywhere beyond 20 minutes' walk from the road, and it is possible to keep your feet dry. During summer, rarer visiting waders such as Asiatic whimbrel, eastern curlew and Mongolian dotterel are sometimes seen here.

Note the tide here, too, is 1.5 hours after the Bluff tide. Do not attempt to cross to Cow Island as there is a deep channel.

To walk inland, written permission is required from the smelter owners Comalco (write to General Manager, Private Bag 90110, Invercargill 9515) but it is probably simpler just to follow the margins.

An easily accessed spot to observe fernbird is beside Tiwai Road. Pull off the road by the last pair of pylons, then walk a few metres into the shrubbery to where the terrain opens up a little. There are also a few ponds hidden in here, and the shy but curious fernbird will possibly announce its presence with its characteristic double-click call.

▷ New River Estuary

From the Invercargill/Bluff highway there are glimpses of the estuary margins and shell banks, but you should resist the temptation to cross the railway line and walk directly to them, as the going is very difficult. Access and visibility are better along the Invercargill Estuary Walkway.

This walkway starts from the old Stead Street wharf, on the eastern bank of the estuary beside the Waihopai River outlet, close to the city centre. This is a good spot for royal spoonbill, pied stilt, the very occasional black stilt/kakī, Australasian shoveler/kuruwhengi, grey teal/tētē and other waterfowl and the southernmost population of Caspian tern. Compared with Awarua Bay there are usually more migratory waders here, but fewer species. Lots of tūī live in the coastal shrubbery. Allow an hour for the walk.

Across the road from Stead Street Wharf another walkway leads about 10 km along the Waihopai River. The first 1–2 km is noticeably tidal and a good spot for royal spoonbill, bar-tailed godwit, and usually about one visiting white heron/kōtuku each autumn and winter.

▷ Bushy Point

Even if briefly stopping at Invercargill Airport on the way to somewhere else, there is likely to be time to see fernbird in Bushy Point Reserve, just 10 minutes' drive from the airport and 6 km from Invercargill, at the end of Grant Road. A 600-metre track and boardwalk provides easy walking through the otherwise impenetrable vegetation. This is a small but significant remnant of coastal podocarp forest, swampy shrub lands and salt marsh. It supports a significant fernbird population as well as wetland, shore and forest birds.

The reserve is privately owned and protected by a Queen Elizabeth II National Trust open-space covenant. Access is by courtesy of the owners, ardent conservationists Jenny and Ian Gamble, who also offer homestay B&B accommodation, should you wish to wake with the dawn chorus.

▷ Sandy Point Reserve

Ancient and relatively rare sand-dune forests, of mainly tōtara and mataī, grow beside estuarine mudflats, salt marshes and freshwater lagoons, and provide diverse bird habitats on this reserve and recreational area by the Ōreti River mouth.

Drive 7 km west of Invercargill on Stead Street, which becomes Dunns Road, cross the Ōreti River bridge and turn left into the signposted entrance. On the left is an information centre (open summer weekends and by arrangement for groups), and a road continues through the reserve to Sandy Point.

To see a good mixture of the forest and estuarine habitats, and thus a cross-section of the bird life, take the track that leads from Daffodil Bay around the estuary edge along Rovers Track then Petries Track (1.5 hours return). Also from Daffodil Bay a 40-minute walk leads in the opposite direction around the estuary edge then climbs to Hatch's Hill Lookout. From the lookout a loop walk returns to Daffodil Bay through the forest (1.5 hours total), but returning the same way, via the estuary, is better for seeing birds.

In the forest look for brown creeper/pipipi, tomtit/miromiro, grey warbler/riroriro, tūī, bellbird/korimako and possibly the normally nocturnal morepork/ruru, known to venture out during the day in this area. Present along the estuarine margins are royal spoonbill, paradise shelduck/pūtangitangi, pūkeko, pied stilt and in spring, Pacific golden plover. Fernbird also frequent the shrubby margins.

Waituna Lagoon

A 250-m boardwalk off the Waituna Loop Track, accessed via Waghorn Road off the Southern Scenic Route, overlooks the lagoon. Birding is feasible with binoculars; however, access to the lagoon's best viewing areas is difficult, involving at least a muddy 1.5-hour walk around the western end and a number of channel crossings. The lagoon is also accessible via a 2-hour walk from Awarua Bay with several deep and dangerous channel crossings to reach the main wader roosts. A visit to either of these sites should be undertaken only when the lagoon is open to the sea, and with a local guide. Awarua Bay and New River Estuary are preferable options.

Forest Hill Scenic Reserve

The largest forest reserve on the Southland Plains, 30 km north of Invercargill, is renowned for its large population of brown creeper. There are also good numbers of grey warbler, bellbird, tūī, fantail/pīwakawaka, tomtit, rifleman/tītīpounamu, silvereye/tauhou and New Zealand pigeon/kererū. The reserve is on Forest Hill Road, 6.5 km east of SH6 and 8 km south of Winton.

Ōtatara Scenic Reserve

Also good for forest birds, and closer to town (Dunns Road, 3 km west of the airport turn-off).

Getting there Several daily flights to Invercargill connect with all major domestic centres. The airport is 3 km from the city centre. By road, Invercargill is 217 km (3 hours' drive) south-west of Dunedin and 187 km (less than 3 hours' drive) south of Queenstown. Regular coach services link with Dunedin, Queenstown and Te Anau.

Getting around Good roads lead from Invercargill to the estuaries. Self-drive is the best option, but most of the good spots are only a short taxi ride from town. New River Estuary is right beside the city.

Accommodation A range of hotel, self-catering motel, bed-and-breakfast and backpacker options is available.

Facilities Invercargill has cafes, restaurants, bars, banks, shops, supermarkets, fuel, plus golf courses, parks and gardens and an excellent museum that contains an outstanding subantarctic gallery and is one of the few places where one can see live tuatara.

Information

Invercargill i-SITE Visitor Centre, Queens Park, 03 214 6243, Invercargill.i-site@venturesouthland.co.nz.

Guides

Jenny and Ian Gamble offer guided tours and B&B accommodation at Bushy Point. Best to phone ahead; tour $20 includes coffee in their home, 03 213 1302, enquiries@fernbirds.co.nz, www.fernbirds.co.nz.

Local OSNZ members are happy to make themselves available to guide genuinely interested birders and can provide more detailed information or maps. Contact Lloyd Esler (03 213 0404) or Wynston Cooper (03 217 5281).

Caution: The game bird hunting season runs from the first Saturday in May until 30 July. Be aware that numerous hunting shelters are located in the estuaries. Most hunting takes place at dawn and dusk. For further advice contact Southland Fish & Game, 03 215 9117.

31

Stewart Island/Rakiura

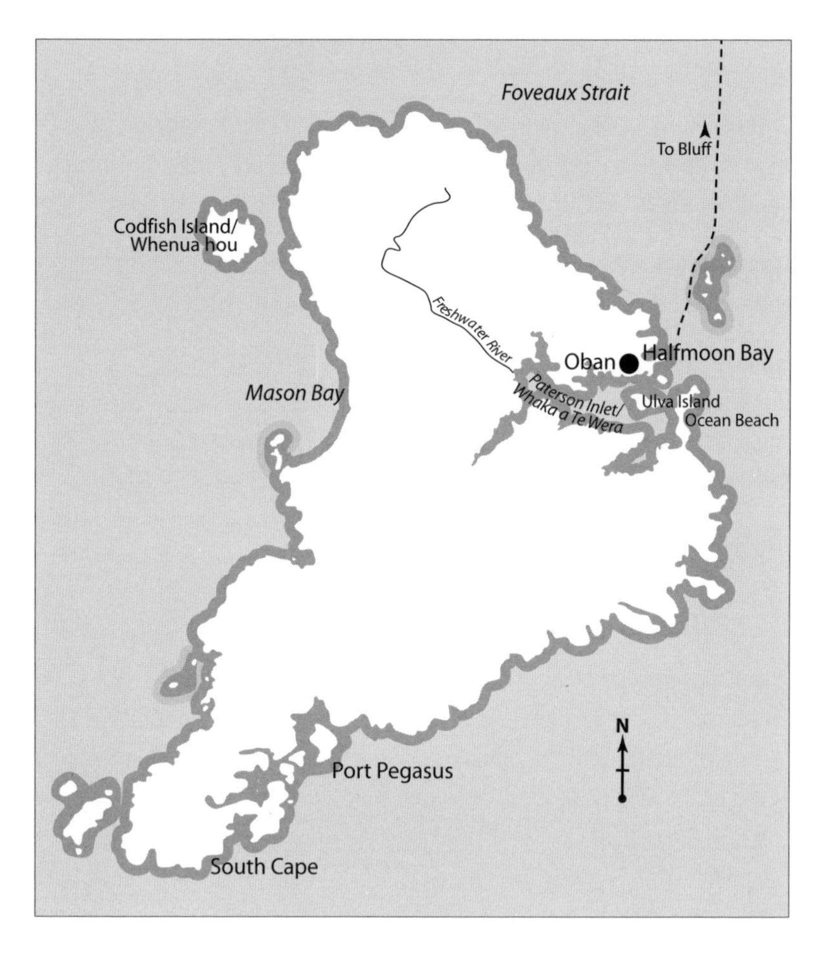

Where New Zealand's third largest island, 35 km south of the South Island.

What's special One of the top birdwatching spots in New Zealand and one of the best chances of seeing kiwi in the wild. Pristine rainforests, wetlands, island sanctuary, harbours and southern oceanic waters. Includes Rakiura National Park and Ulva Island Open Sanctuary.

Birds to look for Southern tokoeka (Stewart Island brown kiwi), fernbird/mātā, forest birds including kākā, saddleback/tīeke, mōhua/yellowhead, Stewart Island robin/toutouwai, red-crowned and yellow-crowned parakeet/kākāriki, weka, New Zealand pigeon/kererū, seabirds including albatross/toroa, petrels, shearwaters, prions, terns, Stewart Island shag and other shags, penguins including yellow-eyed/hoiho, Fiordland crested/tawaki (August–November) and blue/kororā, waders and shorebirds including variable oystercatcher/tōrea and white-faced heron.

Birdwatching options Guided walks, self-guided walks and multi-day hikes, pelagic cruises, sea kayaking (guided or not), guided night-time kiwi tours.

Top spots

- Ulva Island Open Sanctuary (half-day)
- Halfmoon Bay township (short walks)
- Ocean Beach (evening cruise/walk)
- Foveaux Strait and Paterson Inlet/Whaka a Te Wera (day and half-day cruises)
- Mason Bay (overnight or one-day fly/walk and water taxi combo, tide dependent).

How long Two days will allow time for the essential activities - an Ulva Island visit, kiwi-spotting trip and a seabird cruise. There are also longer options, such as longer cruises and overnight guided walks or multi-day hiking trips in Rakiura National Park.

When to go Year-round for most birds. Summer has very long twilights, while winter weather is generally more settled - cold but sunny.

Background

Stewart Island/Rakiura is one of the largest naturally forested islands remaining anywhere – a primeval wilderness of podocarp rainforests, freshwater wetlands, dune lands and granite mountains, surrounded by 170 smaller islands and rocky islets.

Set across the hostile Roaring Forties, there has been minimal human occupation since Māori first settled here several hundred years ago. Today barely 400 people live on the island, in and around Oban township in Halfmoon Bay. Just over 80 per cent of the island is protected as Rakiura National Park. Nature tourism, conservation, marine farming and commercial fishing are the main activities.

Southern tokoeka, the island's own species of kiwi, has survived in greater numbers compared with some mainland species, and differs from others in that it feeds during the day as well as the night. Hence this is the best place for sighting kiwi in the wild.

The island has remained free of many introduced animal pests such as stoats, ferrets, mice and goats. Predation by possums, rats and cats has nevertheless affected birdlife. In recent years pest control in areas of the national park, on islands and around Halfmoon Bay has resulted in habitat recovery, increased bird numbers and enabled the reintroduction of several species, in particular on offshore islands such as Ulva Island.

Foveaux Strait and the surrounding waters provide a breeding ground for some 20 seabird species and support a host of ocean-travelling species, many from subantarctic island breeding grounds. These include at least six species of albatross, plus petrels and shearwaters, in particular sooty shearwater/tītī that breed on tribally owned offshore islands. Fortunately the traditional harvesting of young birds, also known as muttonbirds, which still occurs each year on the islands does not seem to have a detrimental impact on their numbers.

Best birding areas

▷ Halfmoon Bay

Some of the best birding can be enjoyed simply by walking around Oban township and along the short walking tracks of Halfmoon Bay. Ironically, birdlife is more prolific here than in the remote forests of the national park, owing to the close proximity of the Ulva Island sanctuary and the habitat restoration undertaken since 2003 by local residents.

Most obvious are the forest birds, the honey eaters tūī and bellbird/korimako, plus fantail/pīwakawaka, tomtit/miromiro and grey warbler/riroriro. Flocks of loud and boisterous kākā and colourful New Zealand pigeon are usually prominent around town. Red-crowned and yellow-crowned parakeet may be heard and seen in the canopy. Weka, reintroduced from an offshore island in 2005, are thriving, sometimes nesting in residents' gardens. Stewart Island robin have also been reintroduced.

There are several marked trails through forest areas around Halfmoon Bay (see DoC's Day Walks brochure). Recommended is an evening walk to Ackers Point Lighthouse (2–3 hours return), to watch blue penguin and, in late summer, sooty shearwater returning after a day's fishing. Forest, shore and seabirds are all likely to be seen on this walk, which follows the coastal road for a kilometre around Halfmoon Bay, then a marked walking track to Ackers Point, a great viewpoint looking out to several offshore islands.

Occasional early evening kiwi sightings have been reported in the vicinity of Traill Park, between Oban and Golden Bay. Access is via the Golden Bay Road or Fuchsia Walk. Other coastal walks, for example to Thule Bay and Ryans Creek (3–4 hours return), and the road past Mill Creek, Bathing Beach and Horseshoe Bay to Lee Bay (4 km), can reward with sightings of kingfisher/kōtare, several species of shag including the endemic Stewart Island shag, and waders such as white-faced heron, reef heron/matuku-moana, cattle egret, occasional white heron/kōtuku and both variable and South Island pied oystercatchers.

▷ Ulva Island Open Sanctuary

Prolific bird life, including several endangered forest species, thrives on this predator-free island sanctuary, one of the few of its kind open to public visitation. Located in Paterson Inlet/Whaka a Te Wera, the 250-ha island is covered with mature podocarp forest. Rare and endangered species, including Stewart Island robin, South Island saddleback, yellowhead and rifleman/tītīpounamu have been returned and are now breeding here.

Water taxis make the 10-minute trip to Ulva Island from Golden Bay, two minutes' drive from Oban, and direct from Halfmoon Bay wharf. There are excellent walking tracks and visitors can walk independently (a self-guiding brochure is available) or take a guided tour (around 3 hours, allowing unhurried time to observe the birds). For those wishing to see as many species as possible, a guided tour is definitely recommended.

As well as the reintroduced species, other birds likely to be seen are tūī, bellbird, brown creeper (flocks of up to 100), fantail, grey warbler, New Zealand pigeon/kererū, kākā, red-crowned and yellow-crowned parakeet and, foraging the island's beaches, weka and variable oystercatcher. A few southern tokoeka/kiwi remain, and very occasionally are spotted feeding during the day.

On the boat trip to Ulva Island you may see seabirds and shorebirds, including herons, shags and penguins – four species of shags and colonies of little blue and yellow-eyed penguins live and feed in the inlet.

Note: Special care must be taken to avoid reintroducing unwanted plant seeds and animal pests such as rats and mice to Ulva Island.

▷ Ocean Beach

One of the best chances to see kiwi is with a guided evening tour in the vicinity of Ocean Beach, near the southern end of Paterson Inlet/Whaka a Te Wera. This involves a twilight 35-minute boat cruise from Halfmoon Bay, then around two hours' easy walking. Tours leave half an hour before dusk and, though weather-dependent, are available most evenings. Numbers are limited to 15 so booking is essential. Reasonable agility is required (it is sometimes necessary to climb a ladder from the boat to the wharf) and parts of the track can be muddy and slippery. Nevertheless there's a high probability of seeing kiwi, and the scenery is pretty special too.

Mason Bay

The island's largest concentration of kiwi live among extensive tussock lands and dune lands around Mason Bay, on the west coast. Other birds there include banded dotterel/tuturiwhatu, various shearwater and petrel species, occasional Snares crested penguin and storm-wrecked albatrosses, and in late summer, southern New Zealand dotterel/tuturiwhatau.

There are several options for visiting Mason Bay, where the 20-bunk DoC hut has become a very popular base for kiwi-watchers. Expect crowds, especially during summer.

One guided option is an overnight trip from Halfmoon Bay, combining water taxi and a 4-hour walk each way, and staying in a hut or tent. The second is a 4-day trip, first by plane or boat from Riverton, near Invercargill, then a combination of walking, sea kayaking and water-taxi transport.

For independent travellers, Mason Bay can be reached from Halfmoon Bay by small plane, which lands on the beach at low tide. Otherwise it's a 2-day walk (with a hut to stay overnight en route), or a 40-minute water-taxi trip and a 4-hour walk. The track is notoriously muddy but flat and there is a good chance of seeing kiwi along the way. Robin and bellbird are likely companions as the track passes through regenerating mānuka forest. Fernbird will call and possibly pop out from cover to check who is passing through the open wetland and tussock areas.

It's possible to observe kiwi for some time if they are not disturbed. When watching kiwi, don't shine torches directly at them (they are sensitive to bright light) or use a flash. Keep at least 5 m away and don't follow them when they run away.

Foveaux Strait and Paterson Inlet/Whaka a Te Wera

Specialist seabird cruises leave from Halfmoon Bay and explore Paterson Inlet/Whaka a Te Wera Inlet, the island's eastern coast and Foveaux Strait.

Occasionally they venture further to South Cape, circumnavigate the entire island or even travel as far as Solander Island or the Snares Islands. Some cruises combine fishing and seabird watching.

About 6 species of albatross frequent these waters. White-capped, northern royal, southern royal, Gibson's and Salvin's are present year-round and Buller's albatross from February to November. Other seabirds include the petrels, in particular diving petrel but also endemic Cook's and mottled petrels, plus fairy prion (winter), Cape pigeon and Arctic skua. Shearwaters are prolific, in particular sooty as well as Hutton's and Buller's. White-fronted tern/tara are relatively common, while Antarctic tern sightings are possible.

In summer, blue penguin/kororā, Fiordland crested and yellow-eyed penguins are likely to be seen on seabird cruises, especially in Paterson Inlet/Whaka a Te Wera and Port Pegasus.

Saving species

Species recovery work by New Zealand conservation scientists had its early beginnings on Big South Cape Island, off the south-western corner of Stewart Island/Rakiura.

During the early 1960s an ecological calamity occurred when rats, accidentally introduced to the island, destroyed the last of two endemic species, Stead's bush wren and Stewart Island snipe, and almost killed the only remaining South Island saddleback. In the first-ever translocation of a bird species, the saddleback were transferred to smaller, rat-free islands nearby, thus saving them from extinction. Saddleback have subsequently been translocated to Ulva Island and Orokonui Ecosanctuary, in Otago, making these the only places to see the South Island species.

A second major species recovery occurred on Stewart Island/Rakiura

The cruises get particularly close to shag rookeries on Whero and Ulva Islands, for excellent viewing of the endemic Stewart Island shag, plus black, pied and spotted shags.

Bonus sightings possible on seabird cruises include bottlenose dolphin, New Zealand fur seal/kekeno, New Zealand sea lion/kakerangi, sea elephants and whales.

Getting there There are 3 flights daily from Invercargill (20 minutes), which include transfers from the airstrip to Oban (a 5-minute drive). Direct flights can also be chartered from Invercargill to Mason Bay (tide-dependent). Stewart Island Flights www.stewartislandflights.com.

A catamaran ferry sails from Bluff (1 hour), with two sailings daily in winter, four in summer, and possible sightings of seabirds, mollymawks,

in the mid-1970s, with the rediscovery of the only remaining viable population of New Zealand's unique nocturnal ground parrot, kākāpō. Over the next 15 years, several kākāpō were found in the island's remote mountains. During the 1980s, as feral cats were destroying this remnant population, conservation staff captured the last 40 birds and relocated them to Codfish Island/Whenuahou and other predator-free islands.

The third species-recovery story relates to the southern New Zealand dotterel. Intriguingly, alpine shrublands are home to a colony of this coastal wading bird which, unlike its northern subspecies – which breeds and feeds on coastal sands – travels from mountaintop to coast to feed. After a decade of intensive feral cat control on the mountaintops the dotterel population has risen from 62 birds to over 300.

petrels and shearwaters, dolphins and seals en route. Stewart Island Ferry Services www.stewartislandexperience.co.nz. Helicopter charters are available from Stewart Island, Invercargill and Bluff. Rakiura Helicopters, 03 219 1155, rakiheli@xtra.co.nz.

Getting around Just 28 km of roads, mostly sealed, extend from Oban township. Vehicles, motorbikes and bikes are available for hire. Walking tracks, water taxis and chartered cruises provide access throughout the national park and to islands. Small planes can be chartered to land on some remote beaches.

Accommodation A great range including stylish bed-and-breakfasts and lodges, one modern motel, a few basic backpackers, the historic South Seas Hotel and a variety of self-contained accommodation. Pre-booking is essential.

Facilities General store, restaurants, cafes and bars (fresh Foveaux Strait blue cod and locally farmed mussels and salmon recommended), museum, national park and i-SITE visitor centres, craft shops. Note there is no bank or ATM machine on the island, though most businesses accept credit cards. There is limited cellphone coverage for Telecom 027 numbers only.

Information

Invercargill i-SITE, 03 211 0895, info@southlandnz.com.
Stewart Island i-SITE Visitor Centre, 03 2191 400, stewartisland@i-SITE.org.

Rakiura National Park Visitor Centre, 03 219 0009, stewartislandfc@doc.govt.nz.

Licensed guiding companies

Costs for birding tours vary depending on group numbers, where they go and mode of transport. As a rule, guided trips to Ulva Island cost $95–120/adult; independent trips to Ulva Island cost $25 for water taxi hire and $2 for a self-guiding brochure. The overnight guided walk to

Mason Bay is $425/adult. The twilight Ocean Beach kiwi spotting cruise costs $120/adult and seabird cruises start at $65. The companies listed here specialise in birding.

Aurora Charters: seabird cruises, Ulva Island tours, www.auroracharters.co.nz.

Bravo Adventure Cruises: evening kiwi cruises and seabird charters, philldismith@xtra.co.nz.

Kiwi Wilderness Walks: Mason Bay and Ulva Island, www.nzwalk.com.

Pterodroma Pelagics: seabird cruises run in association with Kiwi Wildlife Tours, www.nzseabirds.com.

Ruggedy Range Wilderness Experience: Ulva Island and Mason Bay, www.ruggedyrange.com.

Stewart Island Water Taxi and Eco Guiding: Ulva Island and customised trips, www.portofcall.co.nz.

Talisker Charters: Ulva Island and yacht charters, www.taliskercharter.co.nz.

Te Manu Adventures: Rakiura Wildlife Experience (Rakiura Maori Land Trust), www.seethebirds.co.nz.

Ulva's Guided Walks: Ulva Island specialist, www.ulva.co.nz.

Recommended reading

Day Walks brochure, DoC. (Walks around Halfmoon Bay and environs.)

Ulva Island self-guiding booklet, DoC and Ulva Island Trust.

Parkmap: Rakiura National Park 336-10, Department of Conservation.

Stewart Island: a Rakiura Ramble, Neville Peat. Dunedin: University of Otago Press, 2004.

The Wilderness of Stewart Island, Rob Brown. Nelson: Craig Potton Publishing, 2006.

32

The subantarctic islands

Where Southern Ocean, between New Zealand and Antarctica.

What's special World Heritage-listed islands in the vast southern oceans, among the world's most outstanding natural conservation areas – home to the greatest diversity of seabird populations, breeding grounds for millions of birds and thousands of marine mammals.

Very restricted access, limited to licensed and heavily regulated tour operators.

Birds to look for Great numbers of global albatross, petrel, prion and shearwater species, including several endemics; four penguin species including two endemics; many other endemics including shags, red-crowned parakeet/kākāriki, Campbell Island teal, Campbell Island snipe, Auckland Island teal, Snares tomtit, Snares Island fernbird/mātā, Auckland Island pipit, Campbell Island pipit and Auckland Island snipe. Many more endemics are found on Macquarie Island, which is regarded as an integral part of the subantarctic group even though it is Australian territory.

Birdwatching options Expedition cruises provide viewing from both the cruise ship and small inflatable boats ('zodiacs') which take groups close to the islands. Guided island walks are restricted to a few specially-permitted operators at specific sites on Campbell and Auckland Islands.

Top spots

- Enderby Island (Auckland Islands)
- South West Cape/Puhiwaero (Auckland Islands)
- Campbell Island/Motu Ihupuka
- Macquarie Island (Australian territory)
- From offshore: Bounty Islands, Snares Islands/Tini Heke, Antipodes Islands.

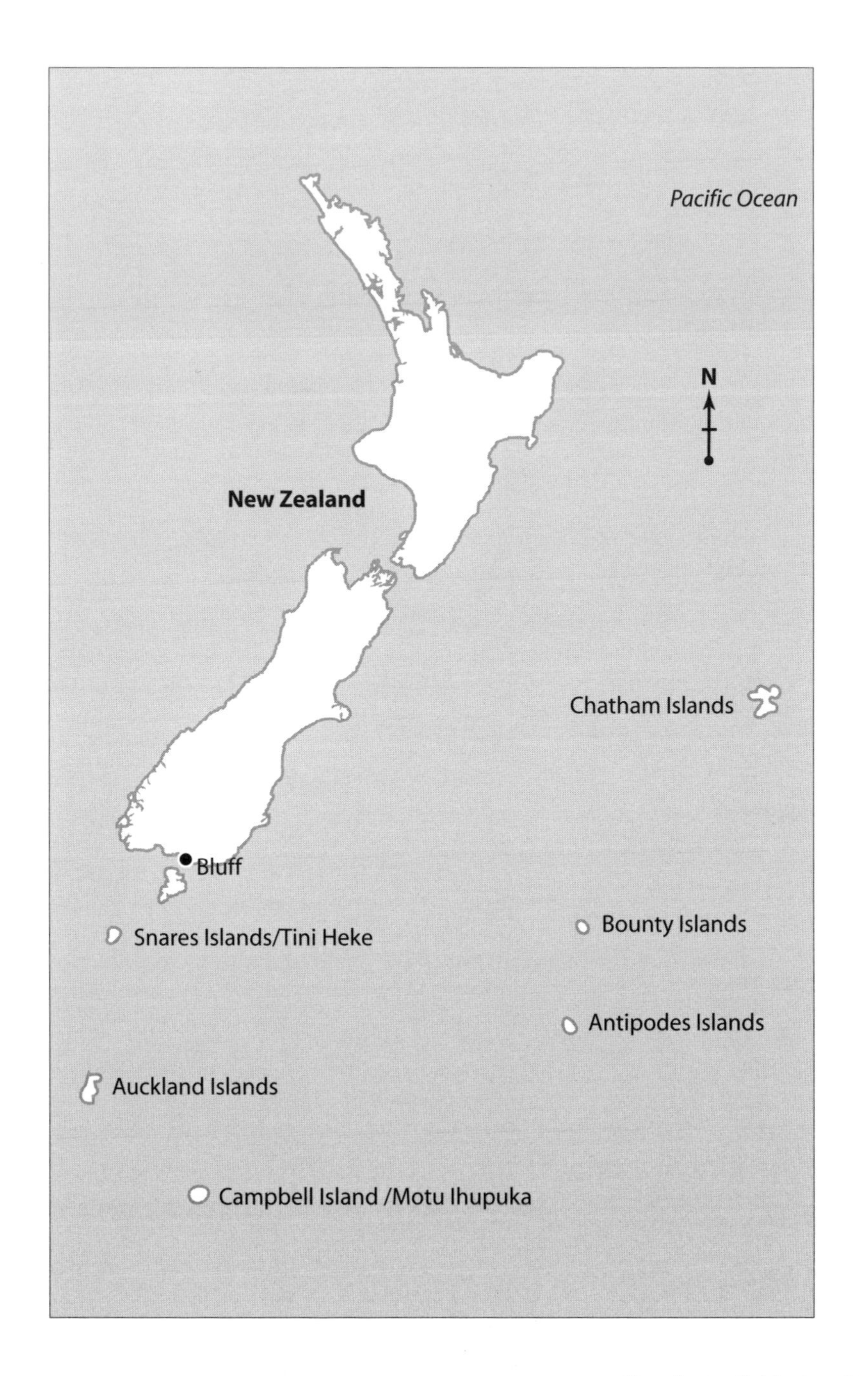
Pacific Ocean
N
New Zealand
Chatham Islands
Bluff
Snares Islands/Tini Heke
Bounty Islands
Antipodes Islands
Auckland Islands
Campbell Island /Motu Ihupuka

When to go Cruises operate during summer; most birds are present from November to February. Cruises are generally 2–4 weeks ex-New Zealand; some combine the subantarctic islands with the Chatham Islands and Antarctica.

Background

If anywhere is the seabird capital of the world, then it must be the subantarctic islands. Because landmasses are so few and far between in the southern ocean, these remote, windswept islands are crowded breeding grounds for seabirds. More than 40 species live there, and over 80 species of land birds breed there or regularly visit. The diversity of seabirds and the high number of endemic land species are notable features.

While their isolation has protected most birds from the large-scale effects of human settlement, there has been considerable detrimental interference by people and the animals they have introduced, in particular on the larger Campbell and Auckland Islands.

Recent conservation efforts have contributed significantly to environmental restoration. In 2001 rats were eradicated from Campbell Island – a major achievement in such challenging, remote conditions. This was the largest-ever island rat eradication at that time, and has resulted in a resurgence of the birdlife and megaherb flora.

Some unique relationships exist between the land and seabirds, for example parakeets, a tropical or subtropical species, live here in close association with penguins. Endemic land birds, such as tomtits, fernbird and teal, have evolved in complete isolation from the mainland species.

Best birding areas

▷ Enderby Island (Auckland Island group)

Enderby Island is one of the few places where landings are allowed, and then only by government-approved operators with a permit.

Going ashore on Enderby is an outstanding opportunity to see some of the greatest diversity and highest number of endemic land birds in the subantarctic islands. Both birdlife and vegetation have recovered remarkably since cattle and rabbits were taken off in 1993. Highlights include Auckland Island snipe, Auckland Island teal, Auckland Island dotterel/tuturiwhatu (larger than the mainland New Zealand species), red-crowned parakeet, bellbird/korimako, tūī, Auckland Island tomtit, Auckland Island pipit and New Zealand falcon/kārearea. Seabirds include southern royal albatross/torea, northern giant petrel, Auckland Island shag, yellow-eyed penguin/hoiho, brown skua and Antarctic tern.

Enderby is also home to the second-largest colony of New Zealand sea lion, one of three colonies on the Auckland Islands.

▷ South West Cape/Puhiwaero (Auckland Island)

This is another permitted landing site. The most notable birds here are the white-capped albatross, with a colony perched high above the sea cliffs.

▷ Campbell Island/Motu Ihupuka

Perseverance Harbour, which cuts deep into the eastern coast of Campbell Island, is one of the permitted landing sites used by expedition companies.

Since rats were eradicated, pipit populations have exploded and New Zealand's rarest duck, the endemic Campbell Island teal, might be seen at the head of the harbour. The teal were thought to be extinct until about 40 were discovered on a little islet called Dent Island. A captive-breeding programme on mainland New Zealand, combined with the rat eradication, cleared the way for the birds to be reintroduced to Campbell Island in 2004. As their numbers build up, sightings should become more frequent.

The island is the main breeding ground for southern royal albatross and they make a grand sight nesting on the tussock-covered hills among early-summer-flowering megaherbs. Five other albatross species breed on Campbell, a level of diversity exceeded only on the Crozet Islands in the southern Indian Ocean.

Continued habitat recovery following the removal of rats is expected to benefit the Campbell Island snipe, which was first discovered as recently as 1997. Snipe numbers are low but recovering and birds have been sighted by tourist expeditions in recent years. Conservation scientists expect their population will build up significantly within 5–10 years.

▷ Bounty Islands

A collection of tiny islets and rock stacks, the Bounty Islands are regarded as the most visually dramatic of the subantarctic islands. They have no significant vegetation, but are virtually covered by hundreds of shags and thousands of penguins, albatrosses, Cape pigeon and around 20,000 seals, all competing for space.

Landing is not permitted but cruising close to the shore in small boats affords good views of Bounty Island shag, which, with a population of fewer than 600, is considered one of the world's rarest shags. Erect-crested penguin (declining in number and now confined to the Bounty and Antipodes Islands) and Salvin's albatross can also be seen.

▷ Snares Islands/Tini Heke

For sheer numbers of birds, the Snares Islands are the most outstanding, with a million or more seabirds breeding on just over 300 ha of scattered islands, islets and rock stacks.

No pests or predators have ever been introduced to the Snares, and no landing is permitted. Nevertheless, small boats can get close to the steep cliffs and afford great views of the masses of birds, including likely sightings of Buller's albatross, plus three endemics – Snares crested penguin and the land birds Snares Island tomtit and Snares Island fernbird. Watching penguins climb a perilously steep rock slope to the top of the island is an impressive spectacle. Most spectacular, however, are the early-morning displays of millions of sooty shearwaters taking off, like a massive black cloud. In the evening they congregate in their thousands offshore well before dark, then descend on their nests.

▷ Antipodes Islands

Landings are also not permitted on this most remote subantarctic island group; however, if sea conditions are suitable boats can get close enough for sightings of the endemic Antipodes parakeet and the smaller Reischek's parakeet. Small-boat trips off the Antipodes also provide some of the best viewing of erect-crested and rockhopper penguins.

▷ Macquarie Island

Most expedition cruises also visit Macquarie Island, an Australian territory that one operator describes as 'a sliver of land covered in teeming wildlife'. Visitors can land at the research base at Buckles Bay. Highlights of Macquarie are the endemic royal penguin and Macquarie Island shag, along with king, rockhopper and gentoo penguin and imperial shag.

Getting there Licensed companies offer expedition cruises, often calling on the subantarctic islands en route to the Antarctic. The islands are approximately 2 days' sailing from Bluff, at the southern tip of the South Island. Not all cruise operators have permits for their passengers to land. Cruise vessels can also be chartered, but the same permit and landing conditions apply.

Getting around Travel between the island groups on the cruise vessel provides opportunities to observe great numbers of seabirds. Small boat trips take passengers close to coastal rookeries and colonies on islands where landings are not permitted.

Landings are restricted to a few sites on Auckland and Campbell Islands. Permits are highly restricted and visitors must adhere to a strict code. All visits are accompanied by a government representative, to ensure compliance with the quarantine and wildlife conditions of entry permits.

Accommodation Only on board ship: no overnight stays are permitted on the islands.

Facilities There are boardwalks on Campbell Island and Enderby Island, and a protected historic site at Hardwicke on the main Auckland Island.

Information

Department of Conservation, Southern Islands Area. For general information and details of charter operators, contact invercargill@doc.govt.nz.

Subantarctic islands, an educational web-based resource: www.subantarcticislands.com.

Licensed guiding companies

The following are New Zealand-based companies. Other international expedition cruise companies travel to the subantarctic islands and Antarctica. Costs fluctuate depending on fuel prices.

Heritage Expeditions (NZ) Ltd: This company offers specialist birding cruises to the subantarctic (licensed for landings) every November, plus other nature heritage cruises, on the 72-m ice-strengthened *Spirit of Enderby*. Cost inclusive of food, US$8588 (shared cabin) to US$12,996 (suite) plus US$50 landing fees. www.heritage-expeditions.com.

Tiama: offers up to five passenger berths joining government-chartered research trips or purpose-designed trips on the 15.15-m sailing vessel *Tiama*. Shared cabins, cost $4380 plus $870 landing fees. www.tiama.com.

Recommended reading

Complete Guide to Antarctic Wildlife, Hadoram Shirihai, Princeton University Press, 2002.
Subantarctic New Zealand – A Rare Heritage, Neville Peat. Wellington: Department of Conservation, 2006.

Galapagos of the Antarctic: Wild Islands to the South of New Zealand, Christchurch: Heritage Expeditions, 2009.

The Chatham Islands

The Chathams are a remote island group 800 km east of the mainland and home to an exceptionally high number of endemic species. Some 52 native bird species breed on the Chathams, 18 of them endemic. Many evolved in isolation from the New Zealand species after colonising the islands.

The Chathams are renowned for two remarkable stories: returning the black robin from the brink of extinction (from five birds including just one breeding pair in 1980, to 237 birds in 2010) and, in 1978, the rediscovery of the Chatham Islands taiko or magenta petrel, long considered extinct. Both species are still critically endangered, and their habitats remain off-limits to the public.

The main islands are Chatham (90,000 ha) and Pitt (6000 ha). These are the only two islands permanently inhabited by people, for whom fishing and farming are the main occupations. Many other tiny, remote and predator-free islands are bastions for birds and plants, and as such are restricted or closed to public access.

There are island-based tour operators, plus a few specialist birding groups lead guided tours to the Chatham Islands and some nature cruises include the group in their tours to the subantarctic islands.

Highlights include the endemic forest birds Chatham Island pigeon/parea, one of the world's largest pigeons, Chatham Island warbler, Chatham Island red-crowned parakeet/kākāriki, Chatham Island fantail and Chatham Island tūī (reintroduced by the Taiko Trust from Pitt Island in 2009). Chatham Island tomtit and Chatham Island tūī are present on Pitt Island. Weka, introduced to the Chathams, are considered a pest for their predation on ground-nesting birds and can be legally harvested.

Coastal birds readily seen are the endemic Chatham Island shag, Pitt Island shag and Chatham Island oystercatcher. Nature cruises generally pick up good sightings of seabirds, for example Chatham Island albatross, northern royal albatross/toroa, northern giant petrel, Buller's albatross and sooty shearwater/tītī.

While most birders travel to the Chatham Islands with organised groups, it is possible to make arrangements to travel independently. Air Chathams flies regularly from Christchurch, Wellington and Auckland. There is a range of accommodation on the main island, rental vehicles are available and if you're fit the main island is comparatively easy to travel around by mountain bike, though roads are unsealed.

However, note that there is not the same ease of access to the coast as is often the case on mainland New Zealand, and while there are a number of publicly accessible forest and coastal reserves, many of the best birding spots are on or accessed via private land. There are no official island-based tour operators, though some residents might oblige on a private basis. Anyone intending to travel unguided is strongly advised to discuss their plans in advance with DoC staff.

Chatham Island DoC office: P.O. Box 114, Waitangi, Chatham Islands, 03 305 0098.

Chatham Islands Visitor Centre: 03 305 0443, www.chathams.com.

Companies which lead guided tours to the Chatham Islands include Heritage Expeditions, www.heritage-expeditions.com and Wrybill Birding Tours, www.wrybill-tours.com.

On the island, Hotel Chathams offers guided walking tours, taking in natural and cultural highlights (year round) and a specialist birding tour in December, www.hotelchatham.co.nz.

Recommended reading

Birds of the Chatham Islands, Hilary Aikman and Colin Miskelly. Wellington: Department of Conservation, 2004.

The Chatham Islands: Heritage & Conservation. Christchurch: Canterbury University Press in association with DoC, 1996, reprinted 2008.

The Black Robin. Saving the World's Most Endangered Bird. David Butler and Don Merton. Auckland: Oxford University Press, 1994.

Appendix: Full list of bird species

This list includes all bird species mentioned in this book. It is not a definitive list of all species resident in or visiting New Zealand. For the definitive list consult the OSNZ's NZRBN List on www.bird.org.nz/nzrbn or *The Field Guide to the Birds of New Zealand* (Barrie Heather and Hugh Robertson, Auckland: Viking, revised edition 2005). Listed here are the common name, Māori name (if not the common name) including all regional variances, and taxonomic name.

APTERYGIFORMES: Kiwi

Brown kiwi/kiwi *Apteryx mantelli*
Little Spotted Kiwi/pukupuku *Apteryx owenii*
Great Spotted Kiwi/roroa *Apteryx haastii*
Ōkārito Brown Kiwi/rowi *Apteryx rowi*
Haast Tokoeka/tokoeka *Apteryx australis 'Haast'*
Southern Tokoeka/tokoeka *Apteryx australis 'Fiordland'*
Southern Tokoeka/tokoeka *Apteryx australis 'Rakiura-Stewart Island'*

PODICIPEDIFORMES: Grebes

Australasian Crested Grebe/kāmana *Podiceps cristatus australis*
Australasian Little Grebe *Tachybaptus novaehollandiae*
New Zealand Dabchick/weweia *Poliocephalus rufopectus*

PROCELLARIIFORMES: Tube-nosed birds

DIOMEDEIDAE: ALBATROSSES/TOROA
Wandering Albatross *Diomedia antipodensis*
Northern Royal Albatross *Diomedea sanfordi*
Southern Royal Albatross *Diomedea epomophora*
White-capped (formerly Shy) Albatross *Thalassarche steadi*
Campbell Island Albatross *Thalassarche melanophrys*
Campbell Island Albatross *Thalassarche eremita*
Grey-headed Albatross *Thalassarche chrysostoma*
Salvin's Albatross *Thalassarche salvini*
Buller's Albatross *Thalassarche bulleri*
PROCELLARIIDAE: SHEARWATERS, DIVING PETRELS, FULMARS, PRIONS, GADFLY PETRELS
Flesh-footed Shearwater/toanui *Puffinus carneipes*
Buller's Shearwater *Puffinus bulleri*
Sooty Shearwater/tītī *Puffinus griseus*
Hutton's Shearwater/tītī *Puffinus huttoni*
Fluttering Shearwater/pakahā *Puffinus gavia*
Black Petrel/tāiko *Procellaria parkinsoni*
Westland Petrel/ tāiko/tītī *Procellaria westlandica*
Cape Pigeon *Daption capense*
Antarctic Fulmar *Fulmarus glacialoides*
Giant Petrel *Macronectes giganteus/ halli*
Fairy Prion/tītī wainui *Pachyptila turtur*
Pycroft's Petrel *Pterodroma pycrofti*

Cook's Petrel/tītī *Pterodroma cookii*
Black-winged Petrel *Pterodroma nigripennis*
Kermadec Petrel *Pterodroma neglecta*
Grey-faced Petrel/oi *Pterodroma macroptera*
Chatham Island Taiko/taiko *Pterodroma magentae*
HYDROBATIDAE: STORM PETRELS
Grey-backed Storm Petrel *Oceanites nereis*
New Zealand White-faced Storm Petrel/takahikare-moana *Pelagodroma marina maoriana*
New Zealand Storm Petrel *Pealeornis maoriana* (rediscovered 2003, morphologically confirmed by the OSNZ Rare Birds Committee 2007, at the time of printing awaiting taxonomic confirmation, when all data including DNA comparisons with three recognised museum species are published and peer reviewed)

SPHENISCIFORMES: Penguins
King Penguin *Aptenodytes patagonicus*
Yellow-eyed Penguin/hoiho *Megadyptes antipodes*
Gentoo Penguin *Pygoscelis papua*
Blue Penguin/kororā *Eudyptula minor*
White-flippered Blue Penguin/kororā *Eudyptula minor albosignata*
Rockhopper Penguin *Eudyptes chrysocome*
Fiordland Crested Penguin/tawaki *Eudyptes pachyrhynchus*
Snares Crested Penguin/pokotiwha *Eudyptes robustus*
Erect-crested Penguin *Eudyptes sclateri*

PELECANIFORMES: Pelicans, Gannets, Shags
SULIDAE: GANNETS, BOOBIES
Australasian Gannet/tākapu *Morus serrator*
PHALACROCORACIDAE: CORMORANTS, SHAGS
Black Shag/kōau/kawau *Phalacrocorax carbo novaehollandiae*
Pied Shag/kōau/kāruhiruhi *Phalacrocorax varius varius*
Little Black Shag/kawau *Phalacrocorax sulcirostris*
Little Shag/kōau/kawaupaka *Phalacrocorax melanoleucos*
New Zealand King Shag//kawau *Leucocarbo carunculatus*
Stewart Island Shag/kawau *Leucocarbo chalconotus*
Chatham Island Shag *Leucocarbo onslowi*
Bounty Island Shag *Leucocarbo ranfurlyi*
Auckland Island Shag *Leucocarbo colensoi*
Spotted Shag/pārekareka *Stictocarbo punctatus*

CICONIIFORMES: Herons, Ibises, Storks and Allies
ARDEIDAE: HERONS, EGRETS, BITTERNS
White-faced Heron *Ardea novaehollandiae*
White Heron/kōtuku *Egretta alba modesta*
Little Egret *Egretta garzetta*
Reef Heron/matuku-moana *Egretta sacra sacra*
Cattle Egret *Bubulcus ibis*
Australasian Bittern/matuku *Botaurus poiciloptilus*
THRESKIORNITHIDAE: IBISES, SPOONBILLS
Glossy Ibis *Plegadis falcinellus*
Royal Spoonbill/kōtuku-ngutupapa *Platalea regia*

ANSERIFORMES: Duck-like Birds

ANATIDAE: SWANS, GEESE, DUCKS

Black Swan *Cygnus atratus*

Canada Goose *Branta canadensis*

Paradise Shelduck/pūtangitangi/pūtakitaki *Tadorna variegata*

Blue Duck/whio/kōwhiowhio *Hymenolaimus malacorhynchos*

Mallard *Anas platyrhynchos*

Grey Duck/pārera *Anas superciliosa superciliosa*

Grey Teal/tētē *Anas gracilis*

Brown Teal/pāteke *Anas chlorotis*

Campbell Island teal/pāteke *Anas nesiotis*

Auckland Island teal/pāteke *Anas aucklandica*

Australasian Shoveler/kuruwhengi *Anas rhynchotis*

New Zealand Scaup *Aythya novaeseelandiae*

FALCONIFORMES: Diurnal Birds of Prey

ACCIPITRIDAE AND FALCONIDAE

Australasian Harrier/kāhu *Circus approximans*

New Zealand Falcon/kārearea *Falco novaeseelandiae*

GALLIFORMES: Game Birds

Californian Quail *Callipepla californica*

Pheasant *Phasianus colchicus*

GRUIFORMES: Rails, Cranes and Allies

RALLIDAE: RAILS, GALLINULES, COOTS

Banded Rail/moho-pererū *Rallus philippensis assimilis*

Weka *Gallirallus australis*

Spotless Crake/pūweto *Porzana tabuensis plumbea*

Marsh Crake *Porzana pusilla affinis*

Pūkeko *Porphyrio porphyrio*

Takahē *Porphyrio hochstetteri*

Australasian Coot *Fulica atra*

CHARADRIIFORMES: Waders, Gulls, Terns, Auks

HAEMATOPODIDAE

South Island Pied Oystercatcher/tōrea *Haematopus finschi*

Variable Oystercatcher/tōrea *Haematopus unicolor*

Chatham Island Oystercatcher *Haematopus chathamensis*

RECURVIROSTRIDAE: STILTS, AVOCETS

Pied Stilt/poaka *Himantopus himantopus*

Black Stilt/kakī *Himantopus novaezelandiae*

CHARADRIIDAE: PLOVERS, DOTTERELS, LAPWINGS

Southern New Zealand Dotterel/tuturiwhatu *Charadrius obscurus obscurus*

Northern New Zealand Dotterel/tuturiwhatu *Charadrius obscurus aquilonius*

Banded Dotterel/tuturiwhatu *Charadrius bicinctus bicinctus*

Auckland Island Dotterel/tuturiwhatu *Charadrius bicinctus exilis*

Black-fronted Dotterel *Charadrius melanops*

Mongolian Dotterel *Charadrius mongolus*

Shore Plover *Thinornis novaeseelandiae*

Wrybill/ngutuparore *Anarhynchus frontalis*

Pacific Golden Plover *Pluvialis fulva*

Spur-winged Plover *Vanellus miles*

Turnstone *Arenaria interpres*

SCOLOPACIDAE: SNIPE, SANDPIPERS, GODWITS, CURLEWS

Campbell Island Snipe *Coenocorypha new sp.*

Auckland Island Snipe *Coenocorypha aucklandica aucklandica*
Lesser Knot/huahou *Calidris canutus*
Great Knot *Calidris tenuirostris*
Sanderling *Calidris alba*
Curlew Sandpiper *Calidris ferruginea*
Sharp-tailed Sandpiper *Calidris acuminata*
Pectoral Sandpiper *Calidris melanotos*
Red-necked Stint *Calidris ruficollis*
Ruff *Philomachus pugnax*
Eastern Curlew *Numenius madagascariensis*
Asiatic Whimbrel *Numenius phaeopus variegata*
Bar-tailed Godwit/kūaka *Limosa lapponica*
Siberian Tattler *Tringa brevipes*
Greenshank *Tringa nebularia*
Terek Sandpiper *Tringa terek*
PHALAROPES
Red-necked Phalarope *Phalaropus lobatus*
STERCORARIIDAE: SKUAS
Brown Skua *Catharacta skua*
Arctic Skua *Stercorarius parasiticus*
LARIDAE: GULLS, TERNS, NODDIES
Black-backed Gull/karoro *Larus dominicanus*
Red-billed Gull/tarāpunga *Larus novaehollandiae*
Black-billed Gull/tarāpunga *Larus bulleri*
White-winged Black Tern *Chlidonias leucopterus*
Black-fronted Tern/tarapirohe/tarapiroe *Sterna albostriata*
Caspian Tern/taranui *Sterna caspia*
White-fronted Tern/tara *Sterna striata striata*
Antarctic Tern *Sterna vittata*
New Zealand Fairy Tern/tara-iti *Sterna nereis davisae*
Grey Ternlet *Procelsterna cerulea*

COLUMBIFORMES: Pigeons, Doves
New Zealand Pigeon/kererū/kūkupa/kūku *Hemiphaga novaeseelandiae*
Chatham Island Pigeon/parea *Hemiphaga chathamensis*

PSITTACIFORMES: Cockatoos, Parrots
PSITTACIDAE: PARROTS
Kākāpō *Strigops habroptilus*
Kākā *Nestor meridionalis*
Kea *Nestor notabilis*
Antipodes Island Parakeet *Cyanoramphus unicolor*
Red-crowned Parakeet/kākāriki *Cyanoramphus novaezelandiae*
Reischek's Parakeet/kākāriki *Cyanoramphus hochstetteri*
Chatham Island Red-crowned Parakeet/kākāriki *Cyanoramphus novaezelandiae chathamensis*
Yellow-crowned Parakeet/kākāriki *Cyanoramphus auriceps*

CUCULIFORMES: Cuckoos, turacos
CUCULIDAE: CUCKOOS
Shining Cuckoo/pīpīwharauroa *Chrysococcyx lucidus lucidus*
Long-tailed Cuckoo/koekoeā *Eudynamys taitensis*

STRIGIFORMES: Owls
STRIGIDAE: TYPICAL OWLS
Morepork/ruru *Ninox novaeseelandiae*

CORACIIFORMES: Kingfishers, Bee-eaters, Rollers and Allies

ALCEDINIDAE: KINGFISHERS

Kingfisher/kōtare *Todiramphus sanctus*

PASSERIFORMES: Passerine Birds

ACANTHISITTIDAE: NEW ZEALAND WRENS

Rifleman/tītīpounamu *Acanthisitta chloris*

Rock Wren/pīwauwau *Xenicus gilviventris*

ALAUDIDAE: LARKS

Skylark *Alauda arvensis*

HIRUNDINIDAE: SWALLOWS, MARTINS

Welcome Swallow *Hirundo tahitica*

MOTACILLIDAE: PIPITS

New Zealand Pipit/pīhoihoi *Anthus novaeseelandiae*

PRUNELLIDAE: ACCENTORS

Dunnock *Prunella modularis*

MUSCICAPIDAE: THRUSHES

Blackbird *Turdus merula*

Thrush *Turdus philomelos*

SYLVIIDAE: OLD WORLD WARBLERS

Fernbird/mātā/mātātā *Bowdleria punctata*

Snares Island Fernbird *Bowdleria caudata*

PACHYCEPHALIDAE: WHISTLERS AND ALLIES

Whitehead/pōpokatea *Mohoua albicilla*

Mōhua/Yellowhead *Mohoua ochrocephala*

Brown Creeper/pīpipi *Mohoua novaeseelandiae*

ACANTHIZIDAE: AUSTRALASIAN WARBLERS

Grey Warbler/ riroriro *Gerygone igata*

Chatham Island Warbler *Gerygone albofrontata*

MONARCHIDAE: MONARCH FLYCATCHERS

Fantail/pīwakawaka *Rhipidura fuliginosa*

EOPSALTRIIDAE: AUSTRALASIAN ROBINS

Tomtit/miromiro *Petroica macrocephala*

Snares Island Tomtit *Petroica dannefaerdi*

North Island Robin/toutouwai *Petroica australis longipes*

South Island Robin/kakaruai/toutouwai *Petroica australis australis*

Stewart Island Robin/kakaruai/ toutouwai *Petroica australis rakiura*

Black Robin *Petroica traversi*

ZOSTEROPIDAE: WHITE-EYES

Silvereye/tauhou *Zosterops lateralis*

MELIPHAGIDAE: HONEYEATERS

Bellbird/korimako *Anthornis melanura*

Tūī *Prosthemadera novaeseelandiae*

EMBERIZIDAE: BUNTINGS, CARDINALS, TANAGERS

Yellowhammer *Emberiza citrinella*

FRINGILLIDAE: FINCHES

Chaffich *Fringilla coelebs*

Greenfinch *Carduelis chloris*

Redpoll *Carduelis flammea*

PLOCEIDAE: SPARROWS, WEAVERS

Sparrow *Passer domesticus*

STURNIDAE: STARLINGS, MYNAS

Starling *Sturnus vulgaris*

CALLAEIDAE: WATTLEBIRDS

North Island Kōkako/Kōkako *Callaeas cinerea wilsoni*

Saddleback/tīeke *Philesturnus carunculatus*

South Island Saddleback *Philesturnus carunculatus*

Stitchbird/hihi *Notiomystis cincta* (Recent DNA analysis shows this is a member of a family whose closest relatives might be wattlebirds.)

Recommended reading

Ballance, Alison and Morris, Rod, *Beautiful New Zealand Birds.* Auckland: Random House, 2006. (One hundred species, including stunning Rod Morris photographs.)

Braunias, Steve, *How to Watch a Bird.* Wellington: Awa Press, 2007. (A somewhat quirky, at times random yet nonetheless informative look at birds and birders in New Zealand.)

Butler, David, *Quest for the Kakapo.* Auckland: Heinemann Reed, 1989.

Butler, David; Gaze, Peter; Hawkins, Jenny, *Birds of the Nelson Region and Where to Find Them.* Pukerua Bay: David Butler Associates Ltd, 1990.

Chambers, Stuart, *Birds of New Zealand: Locality Guide.* Hamilton: Arun Books, revised edition 2000. (Descriptions of most birds and where to find them.)

Crowe, Andrew, *Which New Zealand Bird?* Auckland: Penguin, 2001. (Well laid out, with charts and keys for bird and habitat identification.)

De Roy, Tui and Jones, Mark, *New Zealand, A Natural World Revealed.* Auckland: David Bateman, 2006. (Packed with images, of interest to anyone with a passing interest in New Zealand and its wildlife.)

Gibbs, George, *Ghosts of Gondwanaland.* Nelson: Craig Potton Publishing, 2006. (Heavily illustrated with photographs and diagrams, contemporary science writing exploring New Zealand's natural history.)

Handbook of Australian, New Zealand and Antarctic Birds (seven volumes), Birds Australia, Oxford University Press, 2004. (The definitive reference to all birds occurring in this region.)

Hayman, Peter; Marchant, John; Prater, Tony, *Shorebirds: An identification guide to the waders of the world.* London: Croom Helm, 1986. (Essential international wader watcher's guide. Currently out of print.)

Heather, Barrie and Robertson, Hugh, *The Field Guide to the Birds of New Zealand.* Auckland: Viking, revised edition 2010. (The indispensable volume for anyone interested in New Zealand birds, and the only field guide endorsed by the Ornithological Society of New Zealand.)

Heather, Barrie and Robertson, Hugh, *Hand Guide to the Birds of New Zealand.* Auckland: Penguin, 1999. (Companion to the field guide, ideal for those travelling light.)

Hunt, Janet, *Wetlands of New Zealand.* Auckland: Random House, 2007.

Hutching, Gerard, *Back from the Brink: The fight to save our endangered birds.* Auckland: Penguin, 2004.

Hutching, Gerard, *The Natural World of New Zealand.* Auckland: Penguin, 2004.

Lindsey, Terrence and Morris, Rod, *Field Guide to New Zealand Wildlife.* Auckland: Collins, 2000. (Beautifully designed volume including all mammals, freshwater

fish and reptiles as well as birds.)
Medway, David, *Common New Zealand Shorebirds.* Auckland: Reed, 2000. (Useful text on the more common waders, gulls and terns, with photographs.)
Medway, David, *Sea and Shore Birds of New Zealand.* Auckland: Reed, 2002. (More compact, pocket companion.)
Moon, Geoff, *Birds of New Zealand: A photographic guide.* Auckland: New Holland, 2002. (Compact, with images of most New Zealand birds.)
Moon, Geoff, *Reed Field Guide to New Zealand Birds.* Auckland: Reed, revised edition 1996. (Contains photos and text for virtually all species occurring on mainland New Zealand and the most common seabirds, by one of New Zealand's most eminent bird photographers.)
O'Connor, Tom, *New Zealand's Subantarctic Islands.* Auckland: Reed, 1999.
Ombler, Kathy, *National Parks and Other Wild Places of New Zealand.* Cape Town: New Holland, 2001.
Ombler, Kathy, *A Visitor's Guide to New Zealand National Parks.* Auckland: New Holland, 2005.
Ongley, Derek and Bartle, Sandy, *Identification of Seabirds of the Southern Ocean.* Wellington: Te Papa Press, revised 2006. (A guide for scientific advisers on board fishing vessels.)
Orbell, Margaret, *Birds of Aotearoa: A Natural and Cultural History.* Auckland: Reed, 2003. (Examines individual species with particular emphasis on Māori culture and folklore in relation to each.)
Parkinson, Brian, *Field Guide to New Zealand Seabirds.* Auckland: New Holland, 2000. (Photographs, identification and best viewing spots of many of New Zealand's seabirds.)
Peat, Neville, *Kiwi, The People's Bird.* Dunedin: Otago University Press, 2006.
Power, Elaine, *Sea and Shore Birds of New Zealand.* Auckland: David Bateman, 1990. (Beautiful illustrations by one of New Zealand's best-known illustrators of birds.)
Robertson, C.J.R., *Reader's Digest Complete Book of New Zealand Birds.* Sydney: Reader's Digest, 1985. (Descriptions of every bird that lives in or visits the New Zealand region.)
Tennyson, Alan, *Extinct Birds of New Zealand.* Wellington: Te Papa Press, 2006. (Picturesque and thoughtful view into the world of New Zealand's lost birds.)
Wilson, Kerry-Jayne, *Flight of the Huia.* Christchurch: Canterbury University Press, 2004. (Excellent overview of New Zealand ecology, what the country was like, what it has become and how it all happened.)
Young, David, *Whio, Saving New Zealand's Blue Duck.* Nelson: Craig Potton Publishing, 2006.

Bibliography

Arthur's Pass National Park, *The Story of Arthur's Pass National Park.* Arthur's Pass National Park (Department of Lands and Survey), 1986.

Bercusson, Linda, *The Hauraki Gulf: From Bream Head to Cape Colville.* Christchurch: Shoal Bay Press, 1999.

Brownell, Bill, *Muddy Feet: Firth of Thames Ramsar Site Update 2004.* Kaiaua: EcoQuest Education Foundation, 2004.

Butler, David; Gaze, Peter; Hawkins, Jenny, *Birds of the Nelson Region and Where to Find Them.* Pukerua Bay: David Butler Associates Ltd, 1990.

Heather, Barrie and Robertson, Hugh, *The Field Guide to the Birds of New Zealand.* Auckland: Viking, revised edition 2005.

Hutching, Gerard, *The Natural World of New Zealand.* Auckland: Penguin, 2004.

Ngāi Tahu Claims Settlement Act 1998; Section 287, Schedule 97 [list of 'taonga species', i.e. species of special significance to Ngāi Tahu] and Schedule 96 [list of place names of special significance to Ngāi Tahu].

Ombler, Kathy, *National Parks and Other Wild Places of New Zealand.* London: New Holland, 2001.

Ombler, Kathy, *A Visitor's Guide to New Zealand National Parks.* Auckland: New Holland, 2005.

Reed, A.W., *The Reed Dictionary of Māori Placenames.* Auckland: Reed, 2004 reprint.

Taylor, Graeme, *Action Plan for Seabird Conservation in New Zealand.* Wellington: Biodiversity Recovery Unit, Department of Conservation, 2000.

Williams, H.W., *Dictionary of the Maori Language.* Wellington: Legislation Direct, 7th edition, revised 2005.

Websites

www.nzbirds.com
Narena Oliver's delightful site covers all sorts of news, history, verse and artwork pertaining to New Zealand birds and is updated weekly.

www.groups.yahoo.com/group/birding-nz/
A New Zealand birding newsgroup. Its primary purpose is to enable birders to immediately broadcast rare or unusual bird sightings. It also provides relevant information on birding, birding events and birding locations.

www.kererudiscovery.org.nz
The New Zealand Pigeon–Kereru Discovery Project

www.yellow-eyedpenguin.org.nz
Yellow-eyed Penguin Trust

www.penguin.net.nz
General information about New Zealand penguins.

www.brownteal.com
Addresses the conservation management of brown teal/pāteke.

www.members.tripod.com/larus/bbgull
Black-billed gull information

www.kakaporecovery.org.nz
The Kākāpō Recovery Programme website, with history and information, video and sound recordings.

www.taiko.org.nz
Chatham Island Taiko Trust

Glossary

beech forest – *Nothofagus* (southern beech) covers over half the area of New Zealand's native forests. There are four native species: red (*N. fusca*), hard (*N. truncata*), black (*N. solandri*) and silver (*N. menziesii*), and a subspecies, mountain beech (*N. solandri* var. *cliffortioides*).

DoC – Department of Conservation, the government organisation that manages Crown-owned conservation land.

endangered – refers to a species in very low or declining numbers that requires careful management to avoid extinction. The terms 'endangered' and 'threatened' are used more or less interchangeably.

endemic – said of plants or animals unique to a particular region, or country.

iwi – Māori tribal group.

metal road – unsealed road, common in more remote areas of New Zealand.

bush – common term for native forest.

fellfield – an area of low-growing plants found in open alpine areas, above the forest line.

Backpackers – budget accommodation, traditionally with shared dormitories, bathrooms and kitchen, increasingly offering a wider selection of single, double and ensuite rooms (and as such referred to as 'flashpackers').

migrant – a bird that travels seasonally between breeding and non-breeding areas, both within New Zealand and internationally.

mustelid – introduced mammalian predators, such as stoats, ferrets and weasels, which have caused major harm to native birdlife.

pākihi – boggy wetland, consisting of tussocks, rushes, low shrubs, mosses and ferns.

pelagic – refers to ocean-travelling birds.

podocarp – one of the major types of New Zealand forest, including rimu *Dacrydium cupressinum*, tōtara *Podocarpus totara* and kahikatea *Dacrycarpus dacrydioides*. Podocarps are conifer; the name means 'seed with a foot' and refers to the fleshy stalk on the end of the seed.

possum – the brush-tailed possum, a small native Australian marsupial originally introduced to New Zealand with the aim of establishing a fur trade. In fact, possums eat native vegetation and the eggs of some native birds, and have been an ecological disaster.

Southern Alps/Kā Tiritiri o te Moana – mountainous backbone, or main divide, of the South Island.

track – common New Zealand term for trail.

threatened – *see* endangered.

Index of bird names

Index of place names